# Lecture Notes in Computer Science 14524

The series Lecture Notes in Computer Science (LNCS), including its subseries Lecture Notes in Artificial Intelligence (LNAI) and Lecture Notes in Bioinformatics (LNBI), has established itself as a medium for the publication of new developments in computer science and information technology research, teaching, and education.

LNCS enjoys close cooperation with the computer science R & D community, the series counts many renowned academics among its volume editors and paper authors, and collaborates with prestigious societies. Its mission is to serve this international community by providing an invaluable service, mainly focused on the publication of conference and workshop proceedings and postproceedings. LNCS commenced publication in 1973.

Asbjørn Følstad · Theo Araujo ·
Symeon Papadopoulos · Effie L.-C. Law ·
Ewa Luger · Morten Goodwin ·
Sebastian Hobert · Petter Bae Brandtzaeg
Editors

# Chatbot Research and Design

7th International Workshop, CONVERSATIONS 2023
Oslo, Norway, November 22–23, 2023
Revised Selected Papers

 Springer

*Editors*
Asbjørn Følstad (iD)
SINTEF
Oslo, Norway

Theo Araujo (iD)
University of Amsterdam
Amsterdam, The Netherlands

Symeon Papadopoulos (iD)
CERTH-ITI
Thessaloniki, Greece

Effie L.-C. Law (iD)
Department of Computer Science
Durham University
Durham, UK

Ewa Luger (iD)
Design Informatics
University of Edinburgh
Edinburgh, UK

Morten Goodwin (iD)
Centre for AI Research
University of Agder
Grimstad, Norway

Sebastian Hobert (iD)
TH Lübeck – University of Applied Sciences
Lübeck, Germany

Petter Bae Brandtzaeg (iD)
SINTEF and University of Oslo
Oslo, Norway

ISSN 0302-9743        ISSN 1611-3349 (electronic)
Lecture Notes in Computer Science
ISBN 978-3-031-54974-8        ISBN 978-3-031-54975-5 (eBook)
https://doi.org/10.1007/978-3-031-54975-5

This Springer imprint is published by the registered company Springer Nature Switzerland AG
The registered company address is: Gewerbestrasse 11, 6330 Cham, Switzerland

Paper in this product is recyclable.

# Preface

## Introduction

The last year has been a period of substantial advancement within chatbot research, applications, and design. While large language models have been a topic of substantial research interest in recent years, the public launch of ChatGPT by Open AI in November 2022 held important implications for the field: new research challenges, changing user expectations, and new opportunities for improved conversational interactions.

In consequence of the rapid changes to the field, it is highly important to have active meeting places for researchers and practitioners with a professional interest in chatbots and conversational AI. The CONVERSATIONS international workshop series is intended as such a meeting place, specifically addressing chatbot research, applications, and design. This year, we extended the scope of the workshop to explicitly encourage contributions on large language models in the context of chatbots and conversational AI.

CONVERSATIONS is an open and inclusive arena for sharing and discussing chatbot research, applications, and design. The workshop is conducted as a two-day event. It is free of charge and since 2021 has been conducted as a hybrid event.

CONVERSATIONS 2023 was the seventh workshop in the series. The workshop took place on November 22–23, 2023, hosted by the University of Oslo and its Centre for Research on Media Innovations (CRMI), in collaboration with SINTEF, University of Amsterdam, Centre for Research and Technology Hellas, Durham University, University of Edinburgh, Lübeck University of Technology, and the University of Agder.

In total, 147 participants from 23 countries registered for the workshop – 39 on-site, the remainder online.

## Paper Invitation, Review, and Revision

The workshop call for papers addressed seven areas of key interest to chatbot research, applications, and design – concerning user insight, user experience, chatbot frameworks and platforms, human-chatbot collaboration, chatbots for all, ethical implications, and ways to leverage recent advances in AI. The call for papers accentuated a particular interest in contributions addressing large language models.

We distributed the call for papers through the network of researchers and practitioners associated with the CONVERSATIONS workshop series, as well as through relevant mailing lists. Authors could make four types of contributions: Full papers, position papers, project presentations, and groupwork proposals.

We received 35 submissions, 25 full papers, six position papers, two project presentations, and two groupwork proposals. The full papers, position papers, and project presentations were assessed through a double-blind review process. For each paper, three program committee members provided independent reviews, and one of the eight workshop organizers was assigned responsibility as review lead. The review leads summarized reviewer comments and provided meta-reviews. The program committee members reviewed between two and three submissions each. The organizers led the review process for four or five submissions. Acceptance decisions were made in a dedicated organizers' meeting after all reviews had been provided. The two groupwork proposals were assessed by a jury, consisting of the organizers.

Twelve full papers were accepted, seven after minor revision and five after major revision. Revisions were accepted following a compliance check by the respective lead reviewer. If necessary, one or two rounds of additional revisions were requested. The acceptance rate for full papers was 48%.

## Workshop Program and Outcomes

The workshop program included six paper sessions with a total of 21 paper presentations, in addition to two keynote speakers.

The keynote speakers were Nena van As (boost.ai) and Finn Myrstad (Norwegian Consumer Council). In her talk, Nena van As addressed the future of conversational AI in customer service. Finn Myrstad discussed generative AI from a consumer perspective and how this may represent threats to consumer rights.

These post-event proceedings present the full papers, structured into four overarching themes.

The first theme, *understanding and enhancing conversational interactions*, includes works investigating user perspectives on three specific chatbot applications. Nina Van Zanten and Roel Boumans present a study of conversational voting assistants and how these may impact voters in local elections. Anouck Braggaar, Jasmin Verhagen, Gabriëlla Martijn, and Christine Liebrecht explore conversational interactions in the context of customer service, with particular concern for conversational repair. Rafael Del Hoyo, Vega Rodrigálvarez, and Iñigo Zubizarreta reflect on experiences from implementing a chatbot as a guide to open government data.

The second theme, *LLM-driven conversational design and analysis*, covers three papers leveraging large language models to support understanding and development of conversational interactions. Leon Hanschmann, Ulrich Gnewuch, and Alexander Mädche present their work on utilizing the Furhat social robot for human-like sales conversations. Jan de Wit reflects on his experiences with using large language models to simulate users for early phase feedback in conversational design. Boxuan Wang, Mariet Theune, and Sumit Srivastava present their study of lexical alignment in two different large language models with implications for understanding their application in conversational interactions.

The third theme concerns *ethical perspectives and bias*. Here, Verena Traubinger, Sebastian Heil, Julián Grigera, Alejandra Garrido, and Martin Gaedke investigate the prevalence and implications of dark patterns in the design of chatbots. Sviatlana Höhn, Bettina Migge, Britta Schneider, Doris Dippold, and Sjouke Mauw explore whether and how language ideology might introduce bias in conversational interactions. In the final paper of this section, Arturo Cocchi, Tibor Bosse, and Michelle van Pinxteren discuss gender in conversational interactions – specifically whether a chatbot should relate to the gender identity of the user.

The fourth and final section of these proceedings includes a set of papers providing *complementary perspectives*. Samuel Rhys Cox and Wei Tsang Ooi present a study of user perspectives on non-playable game characters powered by large language models. Roberta De Cicco provides an overview of the existing literature on user abuse of conversational agents and its potential implications. Finally, Jacob Penney, João Felipe Pimentel, Igor Steinmacher, and Marco Gerosa present their work on using design fiction to understand and anticipate future needs of chatbot users.

The CONVERSATIONS Best Paper Award is given to the highest scoring paper following a juried process. Among the accepted full papers, three papers are identified as best paper nominees based on their average scores from the review process. The best paper award is then given to one of these, following a juried process involving the workshop organizers. The best paper nominees for CONVERSATIONS 2023 were Roberta De Cicco with *Exploring the Dark Corners of Human-Chatbot Interactions: a Literature Review on Conversational Agent Abuse*, Anouck Braggaar, Jasmin Verhagen, Gabriëlla Martijn, and Christine Liebrecht with *Conversational Repair Strategies to Cope with Errors and Breakdowns in Customer Service Chatbot Conversations*, and Jacob Penney, João Felipe Pimentel, Igor Steinmacher, and Marco Gerosa with *Anticipating User Needs: Insights from Design Fiction on Conversational Agents for Computational Thinking*. The winners of the Best Paper Award were Jacob Penney, João Felipe Pimentel, Igor Steinmacher, and Marco Gerosa.

This year's edition of the CONVERSATIONS workshop series was a success in terms of the quality of the submitted papers, the engaging presentations of accepted papers, and the good discussions between the workshop participants. We thank all authors, program committee members, presenters, participants, and supporters who contributed to this success. The workshop series is intended to strengthen the community of chatbot researchers. We look forward to the continuation and have already started planning CONVERSATIONS 2024.

November 2023

Asbjørn Følstad
Theo Araujo
Symeon Papadopoulos
Effie L.-C. Law
Ewa Luger
Morten Goodwin
Sebastian Hobert
Petter Bae Brandtzaeg

# Organization

## General Chairs/Workshop Organizers

Asbjørn Følstad · SINTEF, Norway
Theo Araujo · University of Amsterdam, The Netherlands
Symeon Papadopoulos · Centre for Research and Technology Hellas, Greece
Effie L.-C. Law · Durham University, UK
Ewa Luger · University of Edinburgh, UK
Morten Goodwin · University of Agder, Norway
Sebastian Hobert · Technische Hochschule Lübeck, Germany
Petter Bae Brandtzaeg · University of Oslo & SINTEF, Norway

## Program Committee

Alexander Mädche · Karlsruhe Institute of Technology KIT, Germany
Ana Paula Chaves · Northern Arizona University, USA
Anna Grøndahl Larsen · SINTEF, Norway
Carolin Ischen · University of Amsterdam, The Netherlands
Charlotte van Hooijdonk · Utrecht University, The Netherlands
Christine Liebrecht · Tilburg University, The Netherlands
Despoina Chatzakou · Centre for Research and Technology Hellas, Greece
Elayne Ruane · University College Dublin, Ireland
Eren Yildiz · University of Umeå, Sweden
Fabio Catania · MIT, USA
Frode Guribye · University of Bergen, Norway
Guy Laban · University of Glasgow, UK
Jo Dugstad Wake · NORCE and University of Bergen, Norway
Jo Herstad · University of Oslo, Norway
Kevin Matthe Caramancion · University of Wisconsin-Stout, USA
Konstantinos Boletsis · SINTEF, Norway
Marcos Baez · Bielefeld University of Applied Sciences, Germany
Marita Skjuve · SINTEF, Norway
Matthias Kraus · University of Augsburg, Germany
Roberta De Cicco · University of Urbino "Carlo Bo", Italy

Sara Pidò                        Politecnico di Milano, Italy
Stefan Schaffer                  DFKI – German Research Center for Artificial
                                 Intelligence, Germany
Sviatlana Höhn                   University of Luxembourg, Luxembourg
Yi-Chieh Lee                     National University of Singapore, Singapore
Yvon Ruitenburg                  TU/e Eindhoven University of Technology,
                                 The Netherlands
Zia Uddin                        SINTEF, Norway

# Contents

**Complementing Perspectives**

# Understanding and Enhancing Conversational Interactions

# Voting Assistant Chatbot for Increasing Voter Turnout at Local Elections: An Exploratory Study

Nina van Zanten and Roel Boumans[✉]

Faculty of Social Sciences, Radboud University, Nijmegen, Netherlands
roel.boumans@ru.nl

**Abstract.** Local Dutch elections suffer from a voter turnout decrease with 23% between 1986 and 2022. This raises general quality concerns about the local democracy. A Conversational Agent Voting Advice Application (CAVAA) chatbot was developed to aid in solving this problem. The objective of the study was to analyze the effect of the CAVAA chatbot on the perceived political knowledge and intention to vote in municipal elections.

An experimental within-subject study (N = 95) in the run-up to the Dutch municipal elections of March 16, 2022 among a typical Dutch municipality of 27,000 inhabitants was conducted. The CAVAA chatbot asked the participant's opinion on 20 local issues, provided further background information if desired in a dialogue, and concluded the interaction with a voting advice.

Participants reported a greater understanding of local political issues after CAVAA use. However, no effect was found on the intention to vote.

The study therefore suggests that a voting assistant chatbot may contribute to a higher voter turnout, but the results should be interpreted with caution and further research is desirable.

**Keywords:** Voting assistant chatbot · local elections · voter turnout

## 1 Introduction

On Wednesday, March 19, 1986, the quadrennial municipal elections took place in the Netherlands [1]. In retrospect, this election day would be a highlight in Dutch history in terms of democracy and politics, because that day, 72.7% of the electorate cast their vote, the highest turnout in municipal elections ever. Looking at the turnout figures since 1986, people have voted less over the years [2]. In the most recent municipal elections in March 2022, only about half (50%) of the eligible voters cast their vote. An analysis by Van Ostaaijen, Epskamp and Dols shows that the local elections of 2006, 2010 and 2014 are characterized by a slight increase, followed by decrease and stabilization [2]. Research by Hendriks, Van Ostaaijen, Krieken & Keijzers shows that the Netherlands score low in turnout for local elections when compared to other European countries [3]. This raises the question, to what extent this decreasing voter turnout poses a threat to Dutch democracy? How does this differ from the national elections [4]? And how can municipalities motivate potential voters to cast their vote in the elections?

A. Følstad et al. (Eds.): CONVERSATIONS 2023, LNCS 14524, pp. 3–22, 2024.
https://doi.org/10.1007/978-3-031-54975-5_1

Political knowledge influences the motivation to vote, according to Riemersma, Stroop and Tieleman in their research on young people and their voting intentions [5]. The less someone understands politics, the less likely they will vote in the elections. Digital voting aids, also called Voting Advice Applications (VAA), can offer a solution. VAAs are applications that help voters with finding a political party that stands closest to their preferences. Voters fill a form consisting of a set of political statements, and the app calculates the political party that fits best to the given answers. Research by Van Ostaaijen et al. shows that digital voting aids increase turnout in local elections [2]. Ruusuvirta and Rosema also show that digital voting aids were responsible for a 3% increase in turnout in municipal elections [6]. Furthermore, voting aids contribute to increasing political knowledge for and interest in the participating parties [7, 8]. In addition, scientists argue that voting aids improve the turnout among young people [9, 10]. This group of young adults scores traditionally low in turnout figures and is also described by Jansen and Boogers as 'local dropouts'.

Other research on Voting Advice Applications (VAA) shows that users feel that their political knowledge had improved after completing a VAA [11]. Also, inhabitants in other European countries evaluated VAAs positively [6, 12, 13].

Nevertheless, Kamoen and Holleman raised a fundamental problem with VAA forms in 2017 because of their research on the municipal elections in 2014. Their research showed that 1 in 5 questions in the VAA caused comprehension problems among users. In combination with the low motivation of users to look up additional information, the chance of incorrect voting advice was high. For that reason, in 2020, Van Limpt introduced the Conversational Agent Voting Advice Application, abbreviated as CAVAA [14]. As with a VAA, users give their opinion on political propositions, but now a chatbot presents these propositions. This should make it easier for users to request additional political information and increase their political knowledge [12]. At the same time, political knowledge can be divided into perceived knowledge, i.e. the knowledge people believe they hold, and their actual knowledge, and for example Park has shown that these do not necessarily correlate [14, 43]. For feasibility reasons, this study evaluates the voter's perceived knowledge, from which it has been shown to have a positive correlation with the intention to vote [10].

Previous research into the use of CAVAAs focused on its application in national elections, on the differences between CAVAA, VAA and VAA+ (VAA supplemented with additional information) and on the differences between CAVAA-designs [12, 15]. Research into the effect of CAVAA on the political knowledge of voters in local elections and their voting intentions is scarce. It is therefore important to conduct more in-depth research into these factors, and to include demographic characteristics like voter age and education level.

By means of a quantitative research design, this research aimed at gaining more insight into the effects of a voting assistant chatbot on its users for future municipal elections. It intended to provide more insight into the ways in which voting assistant chatbots influence the degree of political knowledge and intention to vote of the user. The research question is therefore: *"What is the effect of a voting assistant chatbot on the perceived political knowledge and voting intention of residents for municipal elections, and are these effects different for people with different ages and education levels?"*

## 2  Theory and Hypotheses

### 2.1  The Use of Communication Means in Municipal Elections

Considering the ways in which municipal means of communication can persuade potential voters to vote, their means of communication exert a minimal influence on voting behavior [2]. Political knowledge, on the other hand, does have an effect: Riemersma, Stroop & Tieleman point out that the more knowledge someone has of local political issues, the greater the chance will be that they will cast their vote [5]. Steenvoorden and Van der Waal found that people who were able to answer questions correctly in the research by were more likely to cast their votes [16]. Steenvoorden and Van der Waal also indicate that people have a greater chance of voting when they receive more information about political developments [16]. On the other hand, data from the Dutch statistics organization 'Sociaal en Cultureel Planbureau' show that the willingness to vote in national elections among people, who find politics complicated, is lower than among people who find politics less complicated [17]. The question is if this also applies to local politics? The media do not report on national television of an average town council debate. It is therefore not surprising that 68% of the Dutch population indicates that they are only poorly informed about what is happening in the town council [17]. This also explains why the turnout percentages are relatively low in the municipal elections.

### 2.2  The Role of Cognitive Processes in the Use of Voting Aids

Considering the cognitive processes that take place in the mind of a Voting Advice Application user, it is important to know how people process questionnaires. A commonly used theoretical model for this is the 'Tourangeau model', which shows that the user goes through four phases [19]. The first step deals with the user's ability to understand a question or proposition. Secondly, the users must determine what kind of attitude or opinion is asked of them. Where one user needs little time to retrieve additional information related to the subject from long-term memory, the effort of another user during phase two may take more time [20]. In the third phase, in which users review their individual beliefs, a well-considered judgment should result. Finally, in the fourth phase, the user focuses his answer on the most appropriate answer option.

However, this model ignores the fact that the first stage may be more complex than just understanding the question. For example, research by Zwaan and Radvansky shows that users initially construct a semantic representation of the literal meaning of the question. In other words: does the user understand what is being meant [21]? Next, users create a second representation of the question, called the pragmatic representation. This refers to the general knowledge that one has and that applies to the question.

Previous research by Van Camp et al. has alluded to comprehension problems among users of voting aids, and therefore Van de Ven et al. put this problem to the test in 2017 [11, 22, 23]. Van Camp et al. had shown that one in five questions in voting aids is ambiguously formulated, and about the same number of questions contain vaguely quantified terms. Van de Ven also underlined earlier that questions or propositions in voting aids often contain denials or political jargon. This while most methodological manuals on questionnaires recommend against the use of denials and ambiguous questions.

Moreover, using simple words is recommended above the use of technical or political jargon.

Enough reasons for Kamoen and Holleman to conduct further research in 2017 with the aim of gaining insight into the comprehension problems of VAA users. A total of two studies were conducted, starting with an interview study among sixty voting aid users around the municipal elections for Utrecht [11]. This study concluded that on average, one in five questions or propositions resulted in a comprehension problem among users. This study was followed by a statistical analysis of some 350,000 voting assistant users [11]. It turned out that semantic problems more often result in an average answer. According to Kamoen and Holleman, this is caused by incomprehensible tax names, political jargon, unclear geographical locations, or pragmatic problems of understanding the issue [11]. Difficult concepts, such as welfare committee, and the pros and cons of property tax or dog tax, also caused difficulties. It turned out that in the case of semantic problems, the user checked the answer option 'no opinion' more often. In the case of a pragmatic problem, the user chose the 'neutral' option more often. This raises the question: How can these kinds of comprehension problems be countered?

Kamoen and Holleman evaluated to what extent people were looking for additional information to get a better understanding of what they were being asked to do [11]. It turned out that only 1.4% (26 out of 1800 respondents) of the respondents were looking for additional information. The other respondents based their answers on self-fabricated assumptions. This result is in line with the idea of Krosnick, namely that respondents make just enough effort when answering questionnaires to construct a plausible answer that satisfies the researcher [24]. Krosnick also describes this behavior as satisficing behavior. According to Kamoen and Holleman, this is a sign that respondents view voting aids as a tool to quickly get an idea about the issues at stake.

A potential solution is to offer extra information within the VAA. Galesic et al. concluded in their research on respondents' effort to view additional information in online surveys that information should best be offered in an accessible way [25]. Users are then more likely to look at this extra information.

In summary, a voting assistant user goes through four cognitive phases while filling in a voting aid. Especially in the first phase, certain comprehension problems may arise, such as semantic or pragmatic problems. Additionally, few people make an effort to solve these problems by looking up additional information. Supplementary information to help a voter is desirable and should be offered as accessible as possible.

### 2.3  Conversational Agent Voting Advice Application

The results of the study by Kamoen and Holleman formed the starting point for Van Limpt's research into a new way to provide voting assistant users with additional information [11, 14]. According to the reasoning of Van Limpt, regular voting assistants are not able to meet the need for additional semantic and pragmatic information from voting assistant users. Looking up information via external tools, such as Google, also takes too much effort [12, 14, 24]. For that reason, Van Limpt launched a different type of voting aid with extra information in 2020, namely the voting aid chatbot, referred to as a Conversational Agent Voting Advice Application, abbreviated as CAVAA [14].

A chatbot is defined herein as a computer program designed to simulate conversations with human users, specifically over the internet. Since the launch of the first chatbot in 1966 by the MIT Artificial Intelligence lab, the chatbot has been on the rise in the twenty-first century. The use of the Siri and Google Search mobile app applications in 2012 ensured that chatbots became accessible to the public for the first time. However, the main reason chatbots have become increasingly popular lies in their commercial use. About 80% of these companies start to use chatbots at some level of the business, for example for frequently asked questions on their products. In addition to the commercial field, chatbots are increasingly applied in social areas, such as education and medical health care. This raises the question, what could be the added value of a voting assistant chatbot within the political domain?

First, chatbots are characterized by immediacy. In other words, the fact that users immediately get the answer they need. For example, Lasek and Jessa write that chatbots help customers navigate websites, reduce clicks, and reduce the time it takes to look up information [26]. Following on from this, Brandtzaeg & Følstad concluded that the dynamic characteristics of chatbots mean that users must make less effort to collect information [27]. Additionally, chatbots enjoy a form of neutrality. This means that chatbots cannot judge their users. All users are treated equally. This could lower the threshold for voting assistant users to ask questions about things they don't understand.

## 2.4 The Effect of CAVAA on Political Knowledge and Voting Intention

So far, little research has been done on CAVAAs and was mainly focused on national elections [12, 14, 28–30]. Van Limpt investigated the effects of a voting assistant chatbot and the tone of the message in the chatbot on political knowledge, voting intention and the evaluation of the chatbot, when compared to a traditional voting assistant, for the national parliamentary elections [14]. In addition, it was investigated whether political sophistication mediated these relationships. Political sophistication is a theoretical construct that encompasses various aspects, including education level, political knowledge, and political interest [14, 31, 32]. The results showed that compared to traditional voting aids, the voting assistant chatbot resulted in both higher actual and higher perceived political knowledge. In addition, users were more positive about the voting assistant chatbot than about the traditional voting assistant.

However, it remained unclear whether the effects were due to the presentation of the voting assistant in a static versus dynamic form, or precisely because of the additional information. For this reason, following Van Limpt, Daane investigated whether the effects of voting aids still differed significantly from each other for political knowledge, voting intention and entertainment value when an extra, traditional voting aid with additional information (VAA+) was added [12, 14]. However, this only showed that the effect of the voting assistant chatbot on actual political knowledge differed significantly between CAVAA and VAA and between VAA+ and CAVAA. Finally, McCartan made a comparison between three types of voting assistant chatbots and evaluated the bots for user-friendliness, entertainment value, perceived political knowledge and voting intention [15]. She concluded that the respondents as best evaluated a structured design. In this design, the chatbot included only buttons and no text bar. The three designs did not differ significantly from each other on the other dependent variables.

The current research elaborates on what is already known from these studies, namely by examining to what extent a voting assistant chatbot influences the perceived political knowledge of potential voters. This study extends that research to municipal elections, where voter turnout is often much worse than in national parliamentary elections. Reasons for this lower local voter turnout are lower voter knowledge about local issues, less media coverage, less campaign funds spend by parties on local elections, and less affiliation of voters with local politicians [41, 42]. Therefore, within that local context, we pose the following hypothesis H1: *After using a voting assistant chatbot, potential voters have more perceived political knowledge.*

Even though voting assistants may improve the voter's political knowledge, this does not necessarily mean that their intention to vote will increase too. Therefore, we pose the following additional hypothesis H2: *After using a voting assistant chatbot, potential voters will have higher voting intentions.*

### 2.5   The Impact of CAVAA on Young People

Young people between 18 and 24 years old make up about 10.6% of the electorate [33]. However, Jansen and Boogers describe young people as 'local dropouts' since they vote relatively less often in municipal elections [34]. Daane briefly discussed the difference in perceived political knowledge between young people and older adults as potential cause for low turnout [12]. According to Den Ridder and Dekker, this low turnout has three causes: young people are less connected to local politics, have less interest in it, and therefore participate less [17]. At the same time, Van der Meer et al. write that political opinions are formed during the period between the twelfth and twenty-fifth year of life [33]. After this, one holds on to fundamental beliefs. The views of young people are therefore important for the future political climate.

Furthermore, young people contribute to electoral shifts [33]. Möller therefore emphasizes the importance of creating an upward spiral among young people [35]. When young people have more perceived political knowledge, the chance of political participation is greater. Compared to the elderly, most young people still have little political knowledge. On the other hand, young people are often 'early adopters', i.e., that they pick up new trends first. This may ensure that they can deal better with the voting assistant chatbot compared to older people [36]. Therefore, our third hypothesis H3 is: *Young adults show a greater increase in perceived political knowledge than older adults after using a voting assistant chatbot.*

In addition to the fact that age strongly determines voting behavior, education level also plays a key role [2]. For example, higher educated people have more knowledge about politics, have more interest in it, and therefore have a higher voting intention. Kamoen et al. thus recommended in a follow-up study on voting assistant chatbots to take a closer look at the differences between higher and lower educated people [28]. They found that lower educated voters considered the CAVAA more playful and providing more political knowledge. Based on this, our last hypothesis H4 has been formulated as follows: *Lower and intermediary educated voters have gained more perceived political knowledge than higher educated voters after using a voting assistant chatbot.*

To test these hypotheses, a web-based voting assistant chatbot has been developed that presents the voter with 20 political propositions on local issues, and if desired, voters could gain additional knowledge by asking for additional background information on these propositions. At the end of the interaction participants received a voting advice.

# 3  Method

## 3.1  Research Design

For this study a within subjects' design was chosen, which means that all users would use the same voting assistant chatbot. Political knowledge and intention to vote were measured before and after the use of the voting assistant chatbot. Previous studies, as described in the previous chapter, have compared multiple voting aids with each other, and they drew conclusions about the differences between voting aids in general.

This study aimed to study the direct effect of the voting assistant chatbot on voting behavior within a local community, and no comparison between different voting aids was necessary for that purpose. In addition, the pre-measurement in this study was equivalent to the control condition, in which participants had not yet been exposed to an experimental condition. As a result, differences within the group of potential local voters could be exposed.

## 3.2  Participants

The survey population is formed by all eligible voters in a typical Dutch municipality. This municipality is a representative Dutch town with 27,225 inhabitants and is centrally located in the Netherlands, about 70 km south-east of Amsterdam. Regarding the selection of the participants, an opportunistic sampling was used [37]. The authors asked adults from social environment to participate in this study. In addition, information about the voting assistant was emailed to the participating local parties, and the municipality was asked to promote the research. Furthermore, flyers were distributed in various villages in the municipality and the link to the research was shared via social media channels, including Facebook, Instagram, and LinkedIn. Although there were no incentives, the voting advice that participants received could be seen as a kind of reward. For example, the messages on social media and the flyers contained the text: "Do you live in the municipality? And are you 18 years or older? Then fill out my research and find out for which local party you should vote!"

In total, 265 participants participated in the experiment. However, thirty-eight people only opened the survey and filled in nothing. One person did not give permission to participate, and 131 people only completed the pre-measurement, therefore they were excluded.

Ninety-five participants have completed the entire study and were therefore included. This sample involved fifty-three females, forty-one males and one person with a different sex type. Participants had an average age of $M = 34.4$ years ($SD = 16.58$, range 18–72 years). A Chi-square test comparing the gender distributions in the sample and the municipality population did not suggest that these differed significantly ($\chi2 = 1.68$; p $= 0.195$).

The study also used age groups, including "young adults" and "older people". The group of young adults was formed by the participants from 18 to 35 years old (n = 56).

The category of older people consisted of people aged 55 and older (n = 17). The middle group was not explicitly analysed, as the study aimed to analyse groups that would be reasonably different, as in younger than 35, and older than 55.

In addition, two groups were created based on the level of education of the participants. The group of highly educated voters was formed by participants with university level education (CBS, no date) (n = 56). The other group of voters consisted of participants with a lower or intermediate level of education (n = 37). Incidentally, two respondents filled in that they had received a different education. These respondents were therefore not included in the analysis for educational level.

All participants have given informed consent. This research meets the requirements set for research by the Ethical Committee of the Radboud University, faculty of Social Sciences, with reference number ECSW-LT-2022-3-21-57381.

### 3.3 Procedure

The data collection took place online by means of a questionnaire in Qualtrics. The respondents could access the experiment via an online link, or via a QR code on the flyer.

During the survey, respondents first answered a number of general questions about their age, gender, education level, and living in the municipality. After this, three items related to perceived political knowledge were presented to the respondents and three items on voting intention. The respondent was then redirected to the chatbot by means of a link. After completing the interaction with the chatbot, the respondent was returned to the questionnaire. Finally, the respondent answered again three items on perceived political knowledge and also three items related to voting intention. After everything was filled in, the participants were thanked.

### 3.4 The Conversational Agent Voting Advice Application Design

The voting assistant chatbot was developed with the software of Flow.ai (https://flow.ai/nl/), a visual platform for designing AI chatbots [12]. Flow.ai was specifically chosen, because previous studies also made use of this chatbot development environment [12, 14, 15]. In addition, at the moment of the experiment (December 2021/January 2022) Flow.ai was a freely accessible platform, in which both manual commands and JavaScript could be added for the dialogue flow and for calculating voting advice. Both actions are combined in the design of the chatbot. The chatbot has been pilot tested, which resulted amongst others in a more condensed formulation of the information about propositions.

The chatbot included 20 propositions, which are shown in Table 1. All propositions with answer options as well as selectable semantic and pragmatic information are provided in Appendix A.

All propositions were defined in consultation with the political parties in the municipality. The experiment was conducted over two months (Dec 2021/Jan 2022). At the time, all parties were actively preparing for the upcoming municipality elections of March 16th, 2022, and had just published their election programs, or were in the process of publishing. This means that the propositions were checked against these programs and all related to very actual political discussions in the municipality.

**Table 1.** Propositions relevant to the local political issues in the municipality, 2022

1. Entrepreneurs have to decide for themselves whether or not they are open on Sundays.
2. In the cores of the municipality, a maximum speed of 30 km/h is allowed.
3. Local associations are important and should be encouraged, e.g. in the form of a subsidy or remission of the property tax.
4. There must be an active policy against discrimination and racism.
5. Agricultural companies should be given as much room as possible for expanding their workspace.
6. Extra strict measures against organized crime must be taken.
7. More resources are needed for youth care.
8. No new construction or expansion of livestock sheds in the municipality.
9. The municipality supports schools in offering children a healthy lunch.
10. Historical monuments must remain in the possession of the municipality at all costs.
11. The current cemeteries policy (2019-2029) must remain unchanged.
12. The municipality should provide public transport itself.
13. Placing wind turbines along the A15 East is one of the solutions for the energy transition.
14. Sustainability in one's own home is a citizen's own responsibility.
15. Possibilities for splitting homes must be increased in order to have more living space available without building.
16. Every primary and secondary school child should have access to a laptop.
17. The municipality must prevent homes from being bought up and rented out by investors.
18. A circular economy must be strived for in all municipal cores.
19. Logistics companies in the municipality have to move to industrial estates.
20. Primary schools are housed in multifunctional buildings, e.g. with childcare, library and activities (sports, relaxation, culture).

Each proposition was preceded by an information message, in which respondents could click two or three different buttons (Fig. 1) (Figs. 2, 3 and 4).

Based on previous research into designs for the chatbots [15], a semi-structured design was chosen. This means that participants could enter text into the chatbot as well as click buttons. With regard to the layout of the chatbot, the neutral colours grey and white have been chosen. The background of the chatbot also has a neutral pattern. In this way it was prevented that participants might unconsciously make an association between the chatbot and a political party. Furthermore, every message that the chatbot sent contained a round ball with eyes. The eyes of the chatbot in combination with the three dots, which respondents saw when the chatbot was busy sending a message, were intended as a form of anthropomorphism, and enabling participants to attribute human characteristics to the chatbot. This could make participants feel closer to the chatbot and feel more overlap with the chatbot [38]. The twenty relevant propositions could be answered with four answer options, namely 'agree', 'neutral', 'disagree' and 'don't know'.

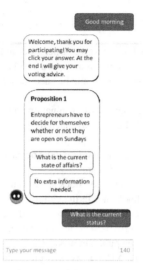

**Fig. 1.** Welcome, first proposition and information message

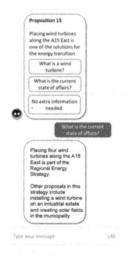

**Fig. 2.** User asks for explanation

## 3.5 Measuring Instrument

In this study, four hypotheses were tested. The independent variable was formed by the interaction with the voting assistant chatbot. The dependent variables consisted of the perception of political knowledge and voting intention. In addition, the third and fourth hypotheses contained a moderation. This means that the relationship between the independent and dependent variable could differ considering the age or the education level of participants. In this case, the authors expected that young adults would have a greater increase in perceived political knowledge after completing the voting assistant

**Fig. 3.** User selects his agreement with the proposition

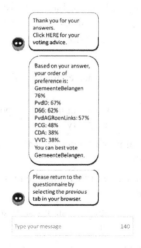

**Fig. 4.** Voting advice

chatbot than older people. Next, it was expected that lower and mid-level educated people would have gained more perceived political knowledge after filling in the chatbot than higher educated people.

The perception of political knowledge, following previous research by Ladner et al., Van Limpt and Daane, was measured with three items were drawn up with regard to the municipal elections in the municipality (Table 2). Daane and Van Limpt measured perception only measured after interaction with the voting assistant, and its direct effect was not measured. For that reason, this study uses a pre- and post-assessment.

Despite the fact that no existing scales have been found for the perception of political knowledge in pre- and post-measurements, the authors looked at various pre-measurements of perceptions, namely the preliminary measurements from the voice assistance studies and the preliminary measurements from the research of Driscoll and Salwen [12, 14, 39]. In their latest study, the focus was on self-perceived knowledge of participants. Although no knowledge of politics was measured specifically, the scales were still considered useful. The knowledge of respondents in the Driscoll and Salwen survey was measured on a five-point scale using three items. However, instead of a five-point scale, in this study a seven-point scale was used, in agreement with Daane and Van Limpt. This scale included the values totally disagree, disagree, slightly disagree, neutral, slightly agree, agree, totally agree. The resulting scale items are given in Table 2. Pre and post test items differ slightly in wording, such that they fit more naturally in the moment in the procedure and refer directly to the use of the chatbot, but the intentions were the same. The overall perceived political knowledge was calculated by averaging the scores on the three items.

The internal consistency of the scale for perceived political knowledge from the pre-measurement is questionable (three items; Cronbach's $\alpha = .638$). An analysis showed that the internal consistency increased to good after the removal of the last proposition (two items; Cronbach's $\alpha = .822$). The scale construction in the post-measurement, on the other hand, proved acceptable (three items; Cronbach's $\alpha = .768$).

**Table 2.** Items measuring perception of political knowledge

| | |
|---|---|
| Before chatbot use | I feel well informed about the current positions of the local political parties in the municipality |
| | I feel well informed about the local political landscape in the municipality |
| | I feel motivated to further immerse myself in the politics of the municipality |
| After chatbot use | After using the voting assistant I understand the positions of the local political parties better |
| | After using the voting assistant I obtained more knowledge about the political landscape |
| | After using the voting assistant I am motivated to further immerse myself in politics |

Based on Glynn, Huge and Lunney, two items were identified to measure voting intention [40]. As in the studies by Van Limpt and Daane, a third item on actual voting intent was added [12, 14]. These items were also measured on a seven-point scale, namely from 1 (strongly disagree) to 7 (totally agree). Although voting intention would initially only be measured after the interaction with the chatbot, during the research the authors was given access to a manuscript that had just been accepted at the time for publication about voting assistant chatbots. In this manuscript, Kamoen, McCartan and Liebrecht shared the recommendation to include voting intention in future studies as a pre- and post-measurement [28]. The items in the pre- and post-measurement are given in Table 3. The overall intent to vote was calculated by averaging the scores on the three items.

**Table 3.** Items measuring voting intention before and after voting assistant use

| Before chatbot use | I intend to vote in the municipal elections in the municipality on 16 March 2022 |
| --- | --- |
| | I feel insufficiently informed to vote |
| | If there are elections now, I would not vote |
| After chatbot use | I plan to vote in the municipal elections in the municipality on March 16, 2022 |
| | After using the voting assistant chatbot, I feel sufficiently informed to vote |
| | If there are elections now, I would vote. The voting assistant chatbot has contributed to this |

As for the internal consistency between the items in the pre-measurement, it turned out that this internal consistency is questionable (three items; Cronbach's $\alpha$ = .626). Removing item 2 yielded an acceptable scale (two items; Cronbach's $\alpha$ = .777). The voting intention scale in the post-measurement proved unacceptable to measure the construct of voting intention (three items; Cronbach's $\alpha$ = .492). After removing the first item, there was a coherence between items 2 and 3 (two items; Cronbach's $\alpha$ = .619). With that, the internal consistency of the scale still remained questionable.

Finally, three control variables were measured, namely age, gender and education level, and a check was conducted if the participant lived in the municipality.

### 3.6  Data Analysis

IBM SPSS Statistics 26 was used to process the collected data. For the first hypothesis on political knowledge, averaged data from pre- and post-measurement were compared using a paired-samples t-test.

For the second hypothesis on voting intention, each item was analyzed and tested separately. The second and third items in the pre-measurement were formulated negatively in the questionnaire to prevent response set, and were recoded before comparison.

For the third hypothesis participants were stratified by age into young adults, middle-aged adults and older adults. Subsequently, in line with the hypothesis, an independent t-test was used to determine to what extent the perception of political knowledge had increased for the two groups young adults and older adults.

For the fourth hypothesis, participants were grouped by education level, and the difference scores of perceived political knowledge before and after the interaction with the chatbot was determined.

# 4   Results

## 4.1   The Effect of the Voting Assistant Chatbot on Perceived Political Knowledge

The expectation (H1) that potential voters will have more perceived political knowledge after using the voting aid chatbot is supported by the results. The analysis showed that the average value for perceived political knowledge in the post-measurement ($M = 4.95$; $SD = 1.14$) was higher than in the pre-measurement ($M = 3.93$; $SD = 1.21$), t(94) = -5.615, $p < .001$, and the effect was strong, namely $d = 0.868$.

## 4.2   The Effect of the Voting Assistant Chatbot on the Voting Intention of Potential Voters

The results showed that after use of the chatbot, the average intention to vote after chatbot use on the scale ($M = 5.18, SD = 1.01$) has not changed compared to the intention to vote before chatbot use ($M = 5.36, SD = 1.23$), t(94) = $-1.36$, $p = .089$, 95% CI [$-0.45$, 0.08].

From the individual scale constructing items, first the prediction and naming of the proposition: "I will vote in the municipal elections in the municipality on 16 March 2022" was examined. The analysis showed that the averages of the pre-measurement ($M = 6.17$; $SD = 1.27$) and the post-measurement ($M = 6.14$; $SD = 1.20$) (t(94) = 0.359, $p = 0.72$) do not differ significantly.

We then looked at the extent to which people felt sufficiently informed to vote and whether this has changed after using the chatbot. The analysis shows that no significant differences were found between the pre-measurement ($M = 4.34$; $SD = 1.77$) and the post-measurement ($M = 4.71$; $SD = 1.47$), t(94) = $-1.691$, $p = 0.09$.

Finally, it was examined whether the voting aid specifically contributed to the intention to vote. This comparison showed significant differences between the pre-measurement ($M = 5.58$; $SD = 1.79$) and the post-measurement ($M = 4.69$; $SD = 1.62$), t(94) = 3.57, $p = .001$. The effect is significant, but also the opposite of what the authors expected, because the results indicate that the voting intention has decreased after interacting with the chatbot. In summary, the hypothesis about the increase in voting intention after interaction with the voting assistant is not supported.

## 4.3   The Effect of the Voting Assistant Chatbot on Young Adults and the Elderly

The authors expected that young adults between the ages of 18 and 35 (n = 56) would have experienced a greater increase in perceived political knowledge after interacting with the chatbot than people aged 55 or older (n = 17). The analysis showed however that there was no significant difference in increase between young adults ($M = -1.13$; $SD = 1.81$) and older adults ($M = -0.82$; $SD = 2.03$) in terms of their perceived political knowledge after the interaction with the chatbot t(71) = $-0.596$, $p = .553$.

### 4.4 The Effect of the Voting Assistant Chatbot on Lower, Secondary and Higher Educated Voters

The last hypothesis presumed that lower and intermediary educated voters (n = 37) after using the voting assistant chatbot could have a greater increase in perceived political knowledge than higher university level educated people (n = 56). The differences in increase between lower and intermediary educated participants ($M = -1.21; SD = 1.47$) and higher university level educated participants ($M = -0.90; SD = 1.97$) was not significant t(91) = $-0.719$, $p = .474$. Based on these results, this hypothesis was rejected.

## 5  Discussion

This research has shown that participants have gained a better understanding of the political issues in the municipality after using the chatbot. This result is in agreement with previous research by Van Limpt [14]. Daane, on the other hand, showed no effect, but did show a significant difference in political perception between young and old participants [12]. These different results were previously explained based on the idea that perception of political knowledge is established by self-reports. Nevertheless, the results in this research are an indication that a voting assistant chatbot could increase perceived knowledge.

With regard to the effect of the voting assistant chatbot on voting intentions of potential voters, also interesting results were found. The authors expected that participants would have a higher intention to vote after using the chatbot [2, 6]. However, the results show that no effect was found. Participants did not gain a higher intention to vote. These findings are in agreement with previous research by Daane and Van Limpt [12, 14], where no effects were found as well, although the voting intention in these studies was measured only afterwards. The reason for not finding an increase may be due to the operationalization of the concept. The items in the questionnaire could have been interpreted differently by the participants than intended by the authors. The third item read: "If there are elections now, then I would vote. The voting assistant chatbot has contributed to this". Perhaps a respondent intended to vote, but the chatbot did not contribute to this. The score of the respondent would then therefore be lower in the measurement. This while the respondent may have achieved a higher score on the almost identical item in the pre-measurement about his or her willingness to vote, if his willingness to vote was already at a certain level. This could explain why the voting intention in the pre-measurement was higher than in the post-measurement for the third item. A future researcher could also ask to what extent the chatbot has contributed to the voting intention of respondents. For example, Daane checked this after the parliamentary elections in 2021 [12].

In the context of differences between age groups, it was found that there were no major differences in the perception of political knowledge. This contradicts the findings in the study by Daane [12]. She showed that voting applications were found more user-friendly by older people than younger people and that younger people, after using voting applications, thought that they better understood the several political viewpoints in comparison to older people. The lack of the difference in this research can be caused by various reasons. For example, the elderly and young adults possibly experienced the same increase in knowledge. In any case, it remains interesting to investigate for which target group the chatbot means the most.

With regard to the differences for lower and higher educated people, no clear differences were found for these groups either. As a result, the suggestion of Kamoen et al. about a greater increase in perceived knowledge among lower and secondary educated people compared to higher educated people cannot be confirmed [28].

Regarding the four phases of the Tourangeau model within the voting assistant chatbot, the authors have tried to guide the respondent as good as possible during the first and second phases. For each proposition, the respondent had the opportunity to request additional information. Regarding the content, several respondents reported that adding positions of the political parties would help them even more to choose the right answer option. It is therefore a good recommendation for follow-up studies to build in a button about the positions of parties in addition to the buttons with pragmatic and semantic information. In relation to the third and fourth phases, more attention could have been paid to the difference in meaning between the answer options 'neutral' and 'I don't know'. Kamoen and Holleman also showed that respondents cannot always distinguish these meanings from each other. In the current survey, this has not been explained to respondents because of the explanation instructions already given to respondents. The authors noticed in the test phase of the chatbot that respondents hardly took the time to read all the instructions and chose to delete additional instructions about answer options. Also, the connection between the Tourangeau model and VAAs could be elaborated more extensively.

This research has a number of limitations. Firstly, limited consideration has been given to other factors that may affect voting intentions, such as age, municipality size and political sophistication. It is therefore interesting to involve these confounds in follow-up research.

Secondly, the digital roll-out of the experiment also deserves a critical note, also in view of potential practical implementations. The experiment was carried out completely digitally due to COVID-19. The advantage of this was that the experiment was conducted in a natural setting, namely at the participants' homes. However, this also brought disadvantages. For example, many participants were filtered out of the analysis, because after completing the pre-measurement, they did not understand how they were sent to the chatbot. Perhaps others have filled in the chatbot, but not the post-measurement.

Thirdly, the study did not evaluate the increase in actual political knowledge through use of the CAVAA. Such evaluation would have required a significant number of additional test questions and would have increased the participant's burden and the risk for drop-outs. Comparing the increase in perceived and actual knowledge could be a topic for future research.

Fourthly, the chatbot icon was created as a symbolic face with eyes, to induce a form of anthropomorphism among participants. This could be a confounding variable but this effect was not explicitly tested.

Finally, as another practical implication, several respondents filled in the chatbot on their phone, such that the type bar was not visible at first. The participant had to scroll down for this, this may not have been clear to everyone. To prevent this in the future, a different screen design could be used in the future. In addition, the experiment could probably be physically taken in the future. For example, by having participants fill in a questionnaire before and after. In the meantime, they could fill in the chatbot in a computer room. A controlled environment would be good for the experiment. However, in this research, the author has created an environment that is more natural than a lab, making it more ecologically responsible. This makes the results more relevant to practice and also more realistic.

In line with this recommendation, the findings from this study provide inspiration for a qualitative follow-up study in the future. For example, the author received various signals from participants about the propositions, voting advice and information in the chatbot. It is interesting to use a focus group study to further investigate how participants experience the interaction with the voting assistant chatbot. Perhaps a comparison could also be made between other voting aids, such as the CAVAA and the CAA+. In addition, one could investigate how potential voters give meaning to their voting advice.

Despite these critical notes and the fact that many improvements can still be made to the voting assistant chatbot, the increase in perceived political knowledge is a valuable result. After all, political knowledge influences the motivation to vote [5]. By means of the chatbot, participants have the feeling that they understand politics better and this increases the chance that they will go to the polls. For a small municipality, this is very valuable, given the low turnout in 2018 and 2022. The municipality therefore strives to encourage citizens to vote. Through this research the authors intended to contribute to a higher voter turnout in municipal elections and thereby strengthening the local democracy.

# References

1. Koeneman, L., Lucardie, P., Noomen, I.: Chronicle 1986: Overzicht van de partijpolitieke gebeurtenissen van het jaar 1986 [Dutch]. Jaarboek 1986 Documentatiecentrum Nederlandse Politieke Partijen, Groningen: University of Groningen, 1987, pp. 15–61 (1987). (Improvement on the way: An exploration into effective municipal use of communication tools for turnout in local elections)
2. Van Ostaaijen, J., Epskamp, M., Dols, M.: Verbetering op komst: Een verkenning naar een effectieve gemeentelijke inzet van communicatiemiddelen voor de opkomst bij lokale verkiezingen [Dutch]. Tilburg University (2016). (Improvement on the way: An exploration into effective municipal use of communication tools for turnout in local elections)
3. Hendriks, F., Van Ostaaijen, J., Van der Krieken, K.: Een metamonitor van de legitimiteit van het democratisch bestuur in Nederland [Dutch] (2013). http://www.anostaaijen.nl. (A metamonitor of the legitimacy of democratic governance in the Netherlands)
4. Jansen, G., Denters, B.: Democratie dichterbij: Lokaal Kiezersonderzoek 2018 [Dutch] Universiteit Twente (2018). (Democracy closer: Local Voter Survey 2018)
5. Riemersma, R., Stroop, J., Tieleman, S.: Aged Dutch Democracy: why young people vote less. Universiteit Utrecht, Utrecht (2017)
6. Ruusuvirta, O., Rosema, M.: Do online vote selectors influence electoral participation and the direction of the vote. In: 2009 ECPR General Conference, pp. 13–12 (2009)
7. Kruikemeier, S., Van Noort, G., Vliegenthart, R., De Vreese, C.H.: Nederlandse politici op Twitter: wie, waarover, wanneer en met welk effect? [Dutch] Tijdschrift voor Communicatiewetenschap, vol. 43, no. 1 (2015). (Dutch politicians on Twitter: who, what, when and with what effect)

8.  Neijens, P., Vreese, C.: Hulp voor kiezers in referendums: is de Informatie en Keuze Enquête een steun voor niet-geïnformeerde of juist voor geïnformeerde kiezers [Dutch]. Res Publica, vol. 52, no. 1, pp. 130–132 (2010). (Help for voters in referendums: is the Information and Choice Survey a support for uninformed or informed voters)
9.  Gemenis, K., Rosema, M.: Voting advice applications and electoral turnout. Elect. Stud. **36**, 281–289 (2014). https://doi.org/10.1016/j.electstud.2014.06.010
10. Ladner, A., Pianzola, J.: Do voting advice applications have an effect on electoral participation and voter turnout? Evidence from the 2007 Swiss Federal Elections. In: Tambouris, E., Macintosh, A., Glassey, O. (eds.) ePart 2010. LNCS, vol. 6229, pp. 211–224. Springer, Heidelberg (2010). https://doi.org/10.1007/978-3-642-15158-3_18
11. Kamoen, N., Holleman, B.: I don't get it: response difficulties in answering political attitude statements in Voting Advice Applications. In: 7th International European Survey Research Association Conference, vol. 11, no. 2, pp. 125–140 (2017)
12. Daane, R.J.: Online stemhulpen in verkiezingstijd (2021). http://arno.uvt.nl/show.cgi?fid=155276. Accessed 1 Apr 2021
13. Marschall, S., Schultze, M.: Voting Advice Applications and their effect on voter turnout: the case of the German Wahl–O–Mat. Int. J. Electron. Gov. **5**(3–4), 349–366 (2012). https://doi.org/10.1504/IJEG.2012.051314
14. Van Limpt, S.: Conversational agent voting advice applications: the effect of tone of voice in (CA) VAAs and political sophistication on political knowledge, voting intention, and (CA) VAA evaluation. Master thesis, Tilburg University (2020)
15. McCartan, T.: Conversational Agent Voting Advice Applications (CAVAAs). What are the effects of three CAVAA-designs: structured, semi-structured and non-structured, on the user-friendliness, entertainment value, perceived political knowledge and voting intention of both higher and lower educated adults? Master thesis Business Communication and Digital Media, School of Humanities and Digital Sciences, Tilburg University (2021)
16. Steenvoorden, E., Van der Waal, J.: Stemgedrag bij gemeenteraadsverkiezingen [Dutch] (2016). (Voting behavior in municipal elections). http://repub.eur.nl
17. Den Ridder, J., Den Draak, M., Van Houwelingen, P., Dekker, P.: Burgerperspectieven 2014 | 4 [Dutch]. Sociaal en Cultureel Planbureau (2014). (Citizen perspectives)
18. Kamoen, N., Holleman, B., Krouwel, A., Van de Pol, J., De Vreese, C.: The effect of voting advice applications on political knowledge and vote choice. Ir. Polit. Stud. **30**(4), 595–618 (2015)
19. Tourangeau, R., Rasinski, K.A.: Cognitive processes underlying context effects in attitude measurement. Psychol. Bull. **103**(3), 299 (1988). https://doi.org/10.1037/0033-2909.103.3.299
20. Tourangeau, R., Rips, L.J., Rasinski, K.: The Psychology of Survey Response. Cambridge University Press (2000). https://doi.org/10.1037/0033-2909.123.2.162
21. Zwaan, R.A., Radvansky, G.A.: Situation models in language comprehension and memory. Psychol. Bull. **123**(2), 162 (1998)
22. Van Camp, K., Lefevere, J., Walgrave, S.: The content and formulation of statements in voting advice applications: matching voters with parties and candidates. Voting advice applications in comparative perspective, pp. 11–32 (2014)
23. Van de Ven, D.: Formuleringseffecten in stemhulpen: aanwezig of niet afwezig? Experimenteel onderzoek naar de effecten van valence framing en attitudesterkte op de antwoorden die mensen geven op stellingen in stemhulpen [Dutch]. Ph.D. Thesis, Tilburg University (2014). (Wording effects in VAAs: present or absent? Experimental research into the effects of valence framing and attitude strength on the answers in VAAs)
24. Krosnick, J.A.: Response strategies for coping with the cognitive demands of attitude measures in surveys. Appl. Cogn. Psychol. **5**(3), 213–236 (1991). https://doi.org/10.1002/acp.2350050305

25. Galesic, M., Tourangeau, R., Couper, M.P., Conrad, F.G.: Eye-tracking data: new insights on response order effects and other cognitive shortcuts in survey responding. Public Opin. Q. **72**(5), 892–913 (2008). https://doi.org/10.1093/poq/nfn059

26. Lasek, M., Jessa, S.: Chatbots for customer service on hotels' websites. Inf. Syst. Manage. **2**, 146–158 (2013)

27. Brandtzaeg, P.B., Følstad, A.: Why people use chatbots. In: 2017 International Conference on Internet Science, pp. 377–392 (2017)

28. Kamoen, N., McCartan, T., Liebrecht, C.: Conversational agent voting advice applications: a comparison between a structured, semi-structured, and non-structured chatbot design for communicating with voters about political issues. In: Conversations: 5th International Workshop on Chatbot Research (2021)

29. Liebrecht, C., Kamoen, N.: Hey Siri, wat is de hondenbelasting? Voicebots en tekstbots in een politieke context [Dutch]. Tekst [blad], vol. 27, no. 1, pp. 22–24 (2022). (Hey Siri, what is the dog tax? Voicebots and textbots in a political context)

30. Mekel, P.: Conversational Agent Voting Advice Applications (CAVAA's). Het effect van het CAVAA-design en politieke sofisticatie op het politiek begrip van de gebruiker, en de gebruiksvriendelijkheid en amusementswaarde van het design [Dutch]. Ph.D. Thesis, Tilburg University (2020). (Conversational Agent Voting Advice Applications (CAVAAs). The effect of CAVAA design and political sophistication on the user's political understanding, and the usability and entertainment value of the design)

31. Luskin, R.C.: Explaining political sophistication. Polit. Behav. **12**(4), 331–361 (1990). https://doi.org/10.1007/BF00992793

32. Rapeli, L.: The Conception of Citizen Knowledge in Democratic Theory. The Theories, Concepts and Practices of Democracy (PSTCD). Springer, London (2013). https://doi.org/10.1057/9781137322869

33. Van der Meer, T., Van der Kolk, H., Rekker, R.: Aanhoudend wisselvallig: Nationaal Kiezersonderzoek 2017 [Dutch]. Stichting Kiezers Onderzoek Nederland (2017). (Continued change: National Voter Survey)

34. Jansen, G., Boogers, M.: Opkomst en stemgedrag [Dutch]. Democratie dichterbij: Lokaal Kiezersonderzoek 2018, SKON, Stichting Kiezers Onderzoek Nederland, pp. 7–17 (2019). (Turnout and voting behavior)

35. Möller, J.: Growing into citizenship: The differential role of the media in the political socialization of adolescents. Ph.D. Thesis, University of Amsterdam (2013)

36. Hartmann, M.: Young people='young' uses? Questioning the "key generation". In: Carpentier, N., Pauwels, C., Van Oost, O. (red.), Het On(be)grijpbare Publiek. Een Communicatiewetenschappelijke verkenning van het Publiek [Dutch]. VUBPress, Brussel, pp. 355–376 (2004). (The Elusive Public. A Communication Science Exploration of the Public)

37. Boeije, H.: Analyseren in kwalitatief onderzoek [Dutch]. Denken en doen (2005). (Analysis in qualitative research)

38. Epley, N., Waytz, A., Cacioppo, A.J.: On seeing human: a three-factor theory of anthropomorphism. Psychol. Rev. **114**(4), 864 (2007). https://doi.org/10.1037/0033-295X.114.4.864

39. Driscoll, P.D., Salwen, M.B.: Self-perceived knowledge of the OJ Simpson trial: third-person perception and perceptions of guilt. J. Mass Commun. Q. **74**(3), 541–556 (1997). https://doi.org/10.1177/107769909707400308

40. Glynn, C.J., Huge, M.E., Lunney, C.A.: The influence of perceived social norms on college students' intention to vote. Polit. Commun. **26**(1), 48–64 (2009). https://doi.org/10.1080/10584600802622860

41. Cancela, J., Geys, B.: Explaining voter turnout: a meta-analysis of national and subnational elections. Elect. Stud. **42**, 264–275 (2016). https://doi.org/10.1016/j.electstud.2016.03.005

42. Kouba, K., Novák, J., Strnad, M.: Explaining voter turnout in local elections: a global comparative perspective. Contemp. Polit. **27**(1), 58–78 (2020). https://doi.org/10.1080/13569775.2020.1831764

43. Park, C.-Y.: News media exposure and self-perceived knowledge: the illusion of knowing. Int. J. Public Opin. Res. **13**(4), 419–425 (2001). https://doi.org/10.1093/ijpor/13.4.419

# Conversational Repair Strategies to Cope with Errors and Breakdowns in Customer Service Chatbot Conversations

Anouck Braggaar[1]([⊠])[iD], Jasmin Verhagen[1][iD], Gabriëlla Martijn[2][iD],
and Christine Liebrecht[1][iD]

[1] Tilburg University, PO Box 90153, 5000 LE Tilburg, The Netherlands
A.R.Y.Braggaar@tilburguniversity.edu
[2] Utrecht University, Trans 10, 3512 JK, Utrecht, The Netherlands

**Abstract.** This study aimed to investigate (1) what errors and conversational repair strategies appear during conversations with a real-life customer service chatbot and (2) how people perceive these errors and repair strategies in terms of user satisfaction, brand attitude, and trust. This study involved a corpus study of real-life conversations ($N=100$) with a customer service chatbot to investigate which errors and repairs occurred to inform a follow-up online experiment ($N=150$) on the perception of these errors and repairs. The experiment employed a 3 (error; excess of information, unsolvable question, lack of information) by 3 (repair strategy; repeat, options, defer) mixed subject design with the type of error as between-subjects factor and repair strategy as within-subjects factor. The results revealed that the repair strategy *defer* most positively impacted perceptions of trust and brand attitude, followed by the strategy *options*, and lastly *repeat*. In contrast, no significant main effects of error type nor interaction effects were found on user satisfaction, trust, and brand attitude. However, the open-ended questions revealed that there might be a connection between the nature of the customer request and the repair strategy.

**Keywords:** Customer service chatbots · Errors · Conversational breakdowns · Repair strategies

## 1 Introduction

Since 2020, the use of AI in customer service has increased by 88%, indicating a growing reliance on chatbots and other automated solutions in the service industry [33]. Implementing chatbots for customer service purposes allows organizations to reduce costs and enable faster, more efficient, 24/7 service provision [10,12,23]. Additionally, when customers perceive the chatbot as helpful and useful, they also tend to have a positive attitude toward the brand behind the chatbot [38]. Despite the evolution of chatbots, (customer service) chatbots still need to learn to operate error-free [1,37]. Errors can be defined as 'any event that might have a negative impact on the flow of the interaction, and more in general on its quality, potentially resulting in conversation breakdowns'

A. Følstad et al. (Eds.): CONVERSATIONS 2023, LNCS 14524, pp. 23–41, 2024.
https://doi.org/10.1007/978-3-031-54975-5_2

[34, p.151]. Users frequently experience conversational breakdowns during interactions with chatbots, as the chatbot often struggles to accurately interpret (complex) requests or understand the intended meaning [9,23,24,29,36]. Conversational breakdowns may frustrate users, diminishing their trust in chatbots [2,11,37] while also reducing user satisfaction and willingness to continue using a chatbot [1]. To diminish the negative effects of conversational breakdowns, organizations can implement conversational repair strategies in a chatbot [1]. Contrary to repair in human-human conversations, repair strategies in human-chatbot conversations require more explicit communication and guidance as the chatbot depends on algorithms to process the users' input, which is considered a 'black box' for the users [1].

Although users' preferences for conversational repair strategies are investigated in various studies [1,2,32], few to no studies investigate context-dependent repair strategies (e.g., if specific errors require specific repairs). Additionally, Ashktorab et al. [1] investigated context-dependent repair strategies by exploring participants' favored repair strategies. Nevertheless, their research was solely guided by communication theory and not by practice. Furthermore, little research has been done on which repair strategies are effective in mitigating users' loss of trust and dissatisfaction [35], but knowledge is lacking on which repair strategies are most suitable for specific errors.

The aim of the current study is therefore twofold. First, we aim to discover which errors and conversational repair strategies occur in conversations with a real chatbot in customer service. A corpus study will address the following research question (**RQ1**): What errors and conversational repair strategies occur during conversations with a customer service chatbot? Second, we aim to investigate the effectiveness of the repair strategy in relation to the error types that can occur in a chatbot conversation on both perceptions of the chatbot and perceptions of the organization behind the chatbot. An experimental study will answer the second research question (**RQ2**): To what extent do the type of error and conversational repair strategy used by a customer service chatbot affect user satisfaction, trust in the chatbot, and brand attitude?

## 2   Theoretical Framework

*Errors & breakdowns.* Customer service chatbots still face challenges in achieving error-free interactions with customers. It is quite common to encounter these errors as chatbots experience difficulties in understanding natural human language [32], potentially leading to conversational breakdowns [34]. When a conversational breakdown occurs, the user's input is either misinterpreted or not interpreted at all [3]. Conversely, customers face challenges in coping with the chatbot's responses [6], resulting in customer frustration [13] and a decrease in overall customer satisfaction [23]. Therefore, it is crucial to prevent errors and possible subsequent breakdowns. Consequently, due to the chatbots' limited understanding, deploying them with the right repair strategies becomes imperative to ensure effective communication and user satisfaction.

Previous research has attempted to categorize different kinds of errors occurring in both human-human and human-chatbot interaction. For example, Sanguinetti et al. [34] developed an annotation scheme to detect the presence of errors during conversations with the chatbot of an Italian telecommunication service provider. Their annotation scheme was inspired by the Gricean maxims [14], dividing error classes in *quantity* (insufficient or excess of information), *relation* (irrelevant response), *manner* (ill-formed messages), and *generic* (non-cooperative stance customer) [34].

Similarly, the work of Reinkemeier and Gnewuch [32] focused on text-based dialogue systems in a specific domain (in their case insurance). Their primary aim was to identify the causes of breakdowns by clustering messages before a breakdown occurs. Their cluster analysis led to the identification of four distinct breakdown types. First, *elaborated messages* encompass messages characterized by excessive verbiage or those that extend beyond a single sentence (i.e., 'I received my monthly invoice but it is higher than usual. I don't understand why? Do you know why? And, also can you send my the specific details because I don't understand'). Next, *specific messages* consist of highly detailed queries that often fall outside the chatbot's operational scope (i.e., 'Which route can I take to Amsterdam to secure the most economical train ticket?'). Subsequently, *brief messages* comprise words familiar to the chatbot (i.e., greetings, insults), yet they lack the necessary context for a comprehensive response (i.e., 'Hello. Train card'). Lastly, *cryptic messages* involve the use of unknown words or concise queries riddled with grammatical errors or typos (i.e., 'I want to end my subscription'), presenting challenges for the chatbot's comprehension. The latter two breakdown types can be classified as the Gricean maxim Manner, whereas the former two can be related to Quantity and Relation.

There have also been attempts to create taxonomies of errors for open-domain conversational systems [16,17] but little is known about which errors appear in other service contexts. Study 1 therefore aims to investigate which error types occur in Dutch human-chatbot conversations between travellers and the customer service chatbot of a public transportation organization. Furthermore, since research shows that conversational errors occur in no less than 38 percent of chatbot conversations [22], the study will also examine which strategies the chatbot uses to repair the conversation.

*Repair Strategies.* Similar to the categorization of errors, previous research has made efforts to categorize repair strategies. Both Benner et al. [2] and Asktorab et al. [1] examined previous research and formulated a comprehensive set of categories for repair strategies applicable in chatbot communication (Table 1).

Additionally, Ashktorab et al. [1] conducted an experiment by using simulated customer service interactions. The findings of their study revealed a preference among participants for the *options* and *defer* strategies. The *options* strategy was deemed efficient, as it necessitated less effort in terms of question reformulation or typing. Participants viewed this strategy positively due to the chatbot's proactive display of initiative, leading them to perceive the chatbot as more intelligent. On the other hand, the *defer* strategy was only preferred

**Table 1.** Chatbot repair strategy categorization

| Strategy | Source | Suggestion for Repair | Error type |
|---|---|---|---|
| *No confirmation* | | | |
| Implicit rejection | [2] | No | The chatbot ignores the error and moves on to a pre-programmed path |
| Top | [1] | No | The chatbot does not show evidence of an error but provides the response with the highest confidence score from the speaker, even if the answer is not appropriate |
| *Confirmation* | | | |
| Explicit rejection | [2] | No | The chatbot admits the error by telling the customer e.g., 'I am sorry, I do not understand', giving the customer the opportunity to repair |
| Repeat | [1] | No | The chatbot indicates the error explicitly, after which it repeats the initial prompt to the user |
| Social cues | [2] | No | Using human social cues, the chatbot attempts to repair the error by offering apologies or compensation, aiming to address the issue through empathy (e.g., 'I am sorry, sadly I did not understand your question. Can I help you with anything else?') |
| Out-of-vocabulary explanation | [1] | Not explicit | The chatbot highlights the words of the user that caused the error so that the user can rephrase them or express them differently |
| Confirmation | [1] | Not explicit | The chatbot recognizes a comprehension problem and either repeats parts of the customer's initial sentence or words for confirmation |
| Ask | [2] | Not explicit | The chatbot restates its initial question, requests customers to rephrase their question, or asks additional questions to clarify the situation |
| Information | [2] | Yes | The chatbot provides the user with instructions on how to proceed, such as guidance for recovery (e.g., 'Rephrase your question') |
| Disclosure | [2] | Yes | The chatbot 'hopes' that by disclosing its limitations, the customer sets realistic expectations regarding the capabilities of the chatbot. Additionally, it offers the customer the opportunity to repair (e.g., 'I don't understand long sentences') |
| Solve Options | [1,2] | Yes | The chatbot offers an alternative to the customer or provides options (i.e. use of buttons) with various options that could correspond to the customers' intention to initiate recovery |
| Defer | [1] | Yes, externally | The chatbot initiates or proposes a hand-over to a human service agent |

with unsuccessful outcomes. Participants found that this strategy increased the likelihood of their issues being resolved by a human agent [1].

Numerous studies underscore the significance of employing effective recovery strategies, as not all strategies yield successful outcomes for customers [1,32]. For instance, Dippold [7] used conversation analysis to examine repair strategies customers used when the chatbot answered their question incorrectly or did not answer their question at all. Interestingly, the most commonly used repair strategies in the examined corpus were not necessarily the most effective repair strategies. This shows that in addition to improving chatbot repair strategies, users also need guidelines on handling the chatbot's comprehension problems.

However, even with the existing research [1,7] investigating user repair strategies in interactions with task-oriented (customer service) chatbots, questions linger regarding the applicability of these findings to real-world scenarios. This uncertainty stems from the fact that the data was collected through experiments conducted in simulated settings. On the other hand, Reinkemeier and Gnewuch [32] did explore error types in actual customer service dialogues but faced limitations due to scarce labeled training data and limited generalizability to other industries. Finally, prior research solely focused on user repair strategies [1,2], neglecting the underlying context. Therefore, to bridge this gap, our study extends previous research to another industry, analyzing customer service interactions comprehensively, including both the analysis of errors and repair strategies. Additionally, our study examines the effectiveness of common combinations with regard to different repair strategies following different error types and their impact on customer perception.

In summary, the current study examines to what extent errors and repair strategies occur during conversations with a customer service chatbot (Study 1), and how participants perceive them in interaction with a customer service chatbot (Study 2). The interplay of error types and repair strategies will be assessed on chatbot metrics (user satisfaction, trust) and organizational outcomes (brand attitude). User satisfaction is commonly used to evaluate chatbots [28]. It is, however, a difficult-to-define concept [15,27]. According to Hsiao and Chen [18], user satisfaction is based on comparing the expected and actual performance. Thus, the customer will be satisfied if expectations are met. Consequently, user satisfaction is affected by negative emotions that users experience and predicts customers' intention to continue to use a product or service [1,11,22,25]. Research by Chiou and Droge [4] also demonstrated that customer loyalty and retention are heavily influenced by user satisfaction. Therefore, it is essential for companies to keep user satisfaction high. Similarly, several studies indicated that trust is negatively affected by the negative emotions users encounter after exposure to conversational breakdowns [11,22]. In the context of chatbots, trust can be defined as 'the customer is willing to rely on the chatbot's actions' [31]. The occurrence of the breakdown disconfirms the trustee's positive expectations resulting in their trust being damaged [35]. While the study of Ashktorab et al. [1] points out that some repair strategies (i.e., *repeat*) appear less intelligent and therefore result in less trust, the current knowledge regarding users' trust after the appearance of a repair strategy, is limited [9]. Additionally, since customers' perceptions of the chatbot could also impact their evaluations of the brand behind the chatbot [38], the current study will also examine the influence of error types and repair strategies on brand attitude. Brand attitude is the overall evaluation summary of judgement to any brand-related information [21]. Pavone et al. [30] demonstrated that when customers interact with a customer service chatbot, they blame the organization for negative outcomes (e.g., frustration and annoyance). However, they do not blame the organization when interacting with human customer service employees [30]. This highlights the importance of measuring brand attitude after the chatbot used a conversational repair strategy next to the chatbot metrics user satisfaction and trust.

## 3   Study 1

### 3.1   Method

In order to bridge the knowledge gap in which error tags and repair strategies (most frequently) occur in human-chatbot conversations in customer service, we conducted a thematic analysis on a dataset comprising real-world human-chatbot conversations ($N$=100) between customers and the customer service chatbot of a public transportation organization. All conversations took place from January to June 2021 and were in Dutch. The conversations were pseudo-anonymized and shared with the researchers who took a sample of 100 conversations. The corpus consisted of conversations between the chatbot and the customer, as well as handover conversations in which the chatbot transferred the conversation to the human agent. However, messages sent after a redirection to a human service employee were not analyzed. Furthermore, conversations for training purposes were excluded from the dataset. Since there were conversations in which the customer left directly after the chatbot greeting, a corpus was compiled consisting of conversations with at least two messages from the customer service chatbot and two from the customer (either free input or a button, as the chatbot interface contained both an open text field and buttons). The thematic analysis was carried out by one of the authors and followed a deductive approach, utilizing created codebooks. The codebook on errors was based on a previous study by Sanguinetti et al. [34]; the codebook regarding the repair strategies was based on multiple studies [1,2,8] (see also Table 1)[1] Codes were given on message level, meaning that one conversation could have multiple codes. A category was either absent (0) or present (1).

### 3.2   Results and Conclusion

First, the 100 conversations were labeled based on topic: 41% of the conversations regarded subscriptions and 25% concerned refunds. More topics included: questions about bicycles (4%), travel information (6%), invoices (7%), and other

---

[1] Codebook can be found on OSF: https://osf.io/s7rqp/.

less common topics (12%). With regard to the occurrence of errors, it appeared that part of the 43.24% were not related to the content of the conversation but rather to technical limitations (for example wrongly recognizing the language of a message). Furthermore, in 11.71% the (possible) error type could not be identified because a part of the sentence contained privacy-sensitive information and was thus filtered. Table 2 shows that six different content-related errors occurred in the data. The error tag *excess of information* occurred most frequently, meaning that the customer fed the chatbot with too much (detailed) information that prevented the chatbot from answering [34]. It is worth noting that the repair strategies in this corpus are design choices made by the developers of this chatbot. Results might vary when different data sets are used.

**Table 2.** Error frequencies

| Error tag | Frequency | % | % in [34] | Example (* is filtered) |
|---|---|---|---|---|
| *Content-related* | | | | |
| Ill-formed (Manner) | 10 | 9.01 | 13.09 | Did not use last 0 * |
| Excess of information (Quantity) | 19 | 17.12 | 11.52 | *, yesterday I bought together with a friend a youth card for today. Unfortunately the aunt *, the friend *, experienced symptoms and had to test. She did not have *, yet, so unfortunately we cannot travel today... Is it possible to change the date * the youth ticket, so we can use it tomorrow? (if the aunt has a negative *, test back)* |
| Lack of information (Quantity) | 7 | 6.31 | 1.05 | Not enough |
| Ignoring question (Relation) | 4 | 3.6 | 20.94 | Goodmorning, I see that the chat function has changed |
| Non-understandable (Manner) | 7 | 6.31 | 5.24 | Js |
| Non-cooperativity (Generic) | 3 | 2.7 | 8.90 | Unfortunate for you |
| *Not content-related* | | | | |
| No error or (technical) chatbot error | 48 | 43.24 | – | – |
| Non-identifiable error (filtered) | 13 | 11.71 | – | – |
| Total | 111 | 100% | | |

A conversational breakdown occurred in 69 out of 100 conversations. In those 69 conversations, 117 repair strategies were employed. This means that one conversation can contain multiple repairs. The results are presented in Table 3 (note that one message may contain multiple different strategies). The chatbot most frequently used the repair strategy *defer* (48.71%), meaning that the chatbot cannot resolve the customer query, redirecting the customer to a human customer service employee [1] avoiding a conversational breakdown. The second most frequently used strategy was *repeat* (26.50%), the chatbot recognizes and explicitly indicates a conversational breakdown and initiates repair by asking the customer to repeat and/or rephrase their initial prompt [1,2,8]. It can thus be concluded that *excess of information* was the most common content-related error type in the chatbot conversations, and *defer* the most used repair strategy.

**Table 3.** Repair frequencies

| Repair strategy | Frequency | % | Example |
|---|---|---|---|
| Repeat | 31 | 26.50 | Unfortunately, I don't understand what you mean. Do you want to repeat the question in different words? Tip: I understand short and concise questions the best |
| Apologetic behaviour | 8 | 6.84 | Sorry, I believe I cannot help you yet. Shall I redirect you to my colleague? |
| Top response | 13 | 11.11 | If I understand correctly you want to know something about the bicycle storage. What is your question about? |
| Options | 8 | 6.84 | If I understand correctly, you have a question about your subscription. I cannot help you with that but my colleague is happy to help. Would you like to temporary stop your subscription to save costs due to Covid-19? Click on the button below |
| Defer | 57 | 48.71 | Sorry, I believe I cannot help you yet. Shall I redirect you to my colleague? |
| Total | 117 | 100% | |

# 4   Study 2

In order to investigate the effectiveness of repair strategies in relation to individual error types, we conducted an experimental study.

The findings of Study 1 and the literature were used to define and operationalize the error types and repair strategies in the study. Criteria for selection were the frequency in which the error types and repair strategies occured, as well as their suitability to implement them in a fictitious chatbot conversation that participants would observe (rather than actually having a conversation with the chatbot). Subsequently, not all error types and repair strategies were usable for this purpose. For example, although the error tag *ill-formed* appeared quite common in the chatbot conversations analyzed in Study 1, this error type was not selected since it is a complex error that is not easily simulated in a controlled experiment. Similarly, the repair strategy *top response* was the third most used strategy, but it was not incorporated in the experiment since it requires the customer to initiate the repair which is not possible in our experimental set-up.

With regard to the error types, we selected the frequently found error-tag *excess of information* and the error *lack of information* from Study 1. Furthermore, the third error type that was incorporated in the experiment was an *unsolvable question*. This error is derived from the literature on why chatbots fail, which describes the importance for customers to understand the chatbot's capabilities, for example, the subjects the chatbot can help with [19].

Reasoning towards hypotheses of the impact of the different error types, it seems that the three error types differ in users' expectations on the chatbot's capabilities with regard to intent recognition as well as the topics the chatbot is trained on. The error type *unsolvable question* shows that the user's topic simply is not present in the chatbot's training data. Since users generally know that chatbots are currently only trained on a limited number of topics, it can be reasoned that the occurrence of this error tag is less detrimental to the user's satisfaction, trust, and brand attitude compared to the error tags *lack of information* and *excess of information*. In contrast, the error-tag *excess of information* indicates that users assume that the digital communication partner is able to understand lengthy messages, showing users' high expectations of the chatbot's intent recognition capabilities. In addition, since the user put quite an effort into typing the lengthy message that subsequently leads to an error, it can be reasoned that the occurrence of such an error is most detrimental to the user's satisfaction, chatbot trust, and brand attitude compared to the other error types. This leads to **Hypothesis 1**: Users' assessment of (a) satisfaction, (b) trust, and (c) brand attitude will be most negative after the occurrence of the error tag *excess of information*, followed by *lack of information*, and lastly *unsolvable question*.

Regarding repairs, we selected the strategies *defer*, *repeat*, and *options* based on their appearance in Study 1. Also from a theoretical perspective, it is interesting to compare the effectiveness of these strategies, because the repair strategies seem to differ in their helpfulness in solving the misunderstanding. After all, if a chatbot only repeats the previous message in case of a misunderstanding, it is unclear to users how they can avoid the misunderstanding from happening again. In contrast, the repair strategy *options* is more helpful because this strategy shows the user explicitly the topics that the chatbot is trained on, which diminishes the occurrence of a second misunderstanding. Lastly, the repair strategy *defer* can be considered as most helpful since it is known that users prefer human assistance to handle their requests instead of a chatbot [1].

A comparison between these three strategies on users' satisfaction, trust, and brand attitude has not been investigated before. However, there are some studies that partly point in our expected direction that the repair strategy *repeat* will strongly impact users' perceptions of a chatbot. Previous research has shown that employing this repair strategy tends to diminish the perceived intelligence of chatbots, potentially resulting in reduced trust when contrasted with the options strategy, where the chatbot independently presents potential outcomes [1]. Moreover, Pavone et al. [30] found that customers blame organizations for negative outcomes, which could therefore also be expected for perceptions of brand attitude. These findings indicate that at least the detrimental effects of the *repeat* strategy are reasonable. This results in **Hypothesis 2**: The usage of the *repeat* repair strategy is most detrimental to users' (a) satisfaction, (b) trust, and (c) brand attitude, followed by the strategy *option*, and lastly *defer*.

Lastly, the implementation of both error types and repair strategies in one study allows us to investigate whether and how these factors interact. Particularly, it can be expected that the adoption of a repair strategy in response to the error *excess of information* could differently impact user perceptions. After all, it is reasonable that in the case of complex questions, customers prefer talking to a human employee rather than a chatbot, as complex questions are most likely solved by them [1]. We therefore assume that the strategy *defer* has a more positive effect on user satisfaction compared to the other repair strategies. Similarly, customers do not blame the organization for negative outcomes when interacting with human service employees [30] which could also apply to users' brand attitudes when exposed to the defer strategy after an *excess of information* error. Finally, even though the chatbot is not able to solve the question in the case of *defer*, it acknowledges the breakdown and redirects the customer. This might have a positive effect on trust as the chatbot is seen as honest and trustworthy indicating its capabilities [9]. In conclusion, it can be argued that an interaction effect can occur between the error types and repair strategies on the dependent variables. This leads to **Hypothesis 3**: After the error *excess of information*, the repair strategy *defer* will have a more positive effect on (a) user satisfaction, (b) trust, and (c) brand attitude, compared to the strategies *repeat* and *options*.

### 4.1   Method

*Design.* An online experiment was conducted with a 3 (error) x 3 (repair strategy) mixed design. Error type served as a between-subjects factor and repair strategy as a within-subjects factor. Participants were randomly assigned to either one of the three between-subject conditions. After each error scenario, they assessed the dependent variables user satisfaction, trust, and brand attitude in an online questionnaire on the survey platform Qualtrics.

*Participants.* Initially, 184 participants were recruited through convenience sampling. All participants had to be 18 years or older and speak Dutch as the materials and questionnaire were also in Dutch. Ultimately, 150 people fully completed the questionnaire (50 participants per between-subjects group). Of these participants, 64.7% were women ($N$=97), and 35.5% were men ($N$=53). Their age ranged from 18 to 70 ($M = 33.56$, $SD = 15.07$). 31.3% of the participants completed their master's degree (or were enrolled in a program at the university level), 20% bachelor's, 28.7% in higher professional education (HBO), 3.3% in HBO masters, 12% in intermediate vocational education (MBO) and 4.7% high school or lower.

Finally, 88.7% of the participants indicated familiarity with chatbot technologies, 67.4% indicated using chatbots frequently, and 44.6% indicated that their previous experiences with customer service chatbots were generally positive. A Chi-squared test revealed that the three between-subjects conditions did not differ in the distribution of gender ($\chi^2$ (2) = 3.74, $p = .155$) and educational level ($\chi^2$ (10) = 8.43, $p = .587$). However, a one-way ANOVA with Bonferroni correction showed that age ($F(2,147) = 3.543$, $p = .031$) was not evenly distributed between the conditions since participants in condition three were on average younger ($M = 29.04$, $SD = 12.72$) than participants in conditions one ($M = 35.34$, $SD = 15.48$) and two ($M = 36.30$, $SD = 16.03$). Because of this *a priori* difference, we ran all analyses both with and without age as a covariate.

*Stimuli.* Nine conditions were designed in which one error type and one repair strategy occurred in a customer chatbot conversation. Since the repair strategy served as a within-subjects variable, three different scenarios were created in which the experimental manipulations were applied. Scenario one contained a conversation where a customer wanted to cancel a subscription. In this scenario, the error type *excess of information* was shown. Scenario two concerned a customer requesting a refund, and the error type *unsolvable question* appeared. Scenario three showed a customer question about an invoice; this scenario contained the error type *lack of information*. The designs were similar and the messages were structured the same. The experimental materials were shown by means of screenshots of (fictional) chatbot conversations and designed with Canva.

*Measurements and Procedure.* User satisfaction was measured on a 7-point scale with measures from a scale by Chung et al. [5]. The items have been partially modified to fit this study, all items can be found on OSF. Furthermore, all three included items have been modified to focus specifically on satisfaction with the repair strategies used by the chatbot rather than referring to the chatbot itself. For example: 'I am satisfied with the service agent' is adapted to 'I am satisfied with the repair strategy used by the chatbot.' Trust was measured with a 7-point scale adapted from [20] and consisted of four items (e.g. 'I believe that this chatbot is honest.') The variable brand attitude was measured with five items on a 7-point scale adapted from [26] (e.g. 'The brand is sympathetic.') All scale reliabilities were good (satifaction $\alpha \geq .813$, trust $\alpha \geq .796$, and brand attitude $\alpha \geq .874$). Finally, participants were also asked to rank the three repair strategies based on their preference, followed by an open-ended question on why they chose this specific ranking.

Demographic information was collected (age, gender, level of education) and two statements from Ashktorab et al. [1] were added about previous experiences with customer service chatbots: 'I am familiar with chatbot technologies' and 'I use customer service chatbots frequently.' Lastly, participants had to assess on a 7-point Likert scale the following statement: 'In general, my previous experiences with customer service chatbots have been positive'.

The experiment started with a brief introduction stating the purpose of the experiment, the approximate duration of the survey (approx. 10 min), and information about rights and privacy. All participants had to sign consent to start the experiment. At the start of the experiment, the key terms conversational breakdown, repair strategy, and error were explained.

## 4.2   Results

Mixed ANOVAs with repeated measures were performed for every dependent variable: user satisfaction, brand attitude, and trust. The descriptive statistics are shown in Table 4.

**Table 4.** Descriptive statistics for error types and repair strategies in Study 2

|  | User satisfaction | | Brand attitude | | Trust | |
|---|---|---|---|---|---|---|
|  | M | SD | M | SD | M | SD |
| Excess of information | 5.64 | 0.84 | 5.25 | 0.84 | 5.22 | 0.89 |
| Unsolvable question | 5.73 | 0.63 | 5.16 | 0.84 | 5.34 | 0.85 |
| Lack of information | 5.48 | 0.78 | 5.13 | 0.75 | 5.30 | 0.69 |
| Repeat | 5.51 | 1.07 | 4.81 | 1.07 | 5.02 | 0.99 |
| Options | 5.61 | 1.08 | 5.12 | 1.04 | 5.28 | 0.96 |
| Defer | 5.73 | 1.10 | 5.62 | 1.00 | 5.57 | 1.09 |

*User Satisfaction.* The mixed ANOVA revealed no main effect of error type on user satisfaction ($F(2,147) = 1.43$, $p=.242$, partial $\eta^2 = .02$). Since H1a stated that user satisfaction would be most negative after *excess of information*, followed by *lack of information* and lastly *unsolvable question*, H1a can be rejected. Additionally, no statistically significant main effect of repair strategy on user satisfaction was found ($F(1.83, 269.122) = 2.08$, $p=.131$, partial $\eta^2 = .14$, with Greenhouse-Geisser correction), resulting in H2a being rejected since the results were not significant. Finally, there was no significant interaction effect between error type and repair strategy on user satisfaction ($F(3.662,269.122) = .797$, $p = .518$, $\eta^2 = .01$, with Greenhouse-Geisser correction). Since hypothesis 3a stated that the repair strategy *defer* had a more positive effect on user satisfaction after the error *excess of information* occurs compared to the strategies *repeat* and *options*, H3a is not supported by the data as well.

*Trust.* No significant differences between the error types were found on trust($F(2, 147) = .26$, $p=.773$, partial $\eta^2 = .04$), which disproves H1b. However, the mixed ANOVA did show a main effect of repair strategy on trust ($F(1.689, 248.327) = 20.737$, $p < .001$, partial $\eta^2 = .12$ (medium effect), with Greenhouse-Geisser correction). The strategy *defer* scored highest on trust perceptions ('options': $Mdif =.292$, $p = .002$; 'repeat': $Mdif=.553$, $p =<.001$). Furthermore, the strategy *options* was assessed higher than the strategy *repeat* ($Mdif=.262$, $p =< .001$). Thus, in accordance to H2b, participants' trust in chatbots was lowest when the repair strategy *repeat* was used and highest when *defer* was used.[2] Finally, there was no significant interaction effect between error type and repair strategy on trust ($F(3.379,248.327) = 1.554$, $p < .196$, partial $\eta^2=.02$, with Greenhouse-Geisser correction). Since H3b stated that *defer* has a more positive effect on trust after *excess of information* compared to *repeat* and *options*, this conclusion cannot be drawn on the basis of our findings.

*Brand Attitude.* With regard to the dependent variable brand attitude, no main effect of error type was found on brand attitude ($F(2,147) = .317$, $p = .728$, partial $\eta^2 = .04$). H1c can therefore be rejected. In contrast, the mixed ANOVA did show a statistically significant main effect of repair strategy on brand attitude ($F(1.730,254.330) = 38.844$, $p =< .001$, partial $\eta^2 = .21$ (large effect), with Greenhouse-Geisser correction). Post-hoc comparisons with Bonferroni correction revealed that participants' brand attitude was highest when the repair strategy *defer* was used, compared to *options* ($Mdif = .495$, $p< .001$) and *repeat* ($Mdif = .805$, $p< .001$). Moreover, the mean score for *options* was higher than the mean score for *repeat* ($Mdif = .311$, $p< .001$). Since H2c stated that brand attitude would be lowest when the chatbot uses repair strategy *repeat* compared to *options* and *defer*, H2c is supported by the data. Finally, no statistically significant interaction effect appeared between error type and repair strategy on brand attitude ($F(3.460, 254.330)) = .377$, $p = .798$, partial $\eta^2 = .01$, with Greenhouse-Geisser correction). Since H3c stated that *defer* would have a more positive effect on brand attitude after *excess of information*, H3c was rejected.

*Ranking.* Since all participants were exposed to the within variable repair strategy, we also asked them to rank the three repair strategies on preference. Figure 1 shows that the strategies *options* and *defer* were equally ranked first (by 42% and 41.33% of the participants respectively). The repair strategy *repeat* was only ranked first by 16.67% of the participants, as opposed to 54.67% who ranked the strategy third. This implies that the repair strategies *options* and *defer* were considered best compared to *repeat*.

---

[2] This finding should be interpreted with caution since the additional mixed ANOVA revealed that this main effect disappeared when age was included as covariate ($F(1.694, 247.268) = .984$, $p = .364$, partial $\eta^2 = .007$ (small effect), with Greenhouse-Geisser correction).

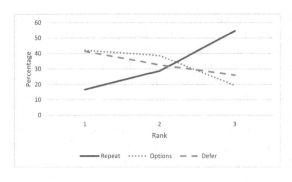

**Fig. 1.** Participants preferred repair strategies

*Thematic Analysis.* A thematic analysis with an inductive approach was performed to analyze the results of the open-ended questions. Participants indicated that the repair strategy *repeat* was ineffective and annoying. It was mentioned that not all users could easily rephrase their questions and that there is a possibility of ending up in an endless cycle of rephrasing questions with the chatbot asking to rephrase again. On the other hand, participants also highlighted the positive aspects of the strategy *repeat*, such as that it could provide faster answers instead of being redirected to a human employee (i.e., *defer*). Regarding the repair strategy *defer*, it was frequently mentioned that redirecting to a human customer service employee can be slow and that this is one of the major disadvantages of this repair strategy. Participants indicated that when using a chatbot, it is preferred that the request is resolved quickly. However, when dealing with complex questions, participants preferred *defer* since they had more trust in the human employee to resolve the request. Some participants stated that they strongly preferred talking to a person over a chatbot because they found interacting with a human agent to be more customer-friendly. Participants also shed light on the strategy *options*. They indicated that this strategy is easy and fast. However, participants also mentioned the negative aspects of this repair strategy. They stated that there are limited options which can mean that the correct answer is not listed or that the listed options do not fully match the customer's request.

## 5　Discussion

This research aimed to investigate errors and conversational repair strategies in customer service chatbot interactions and their impact on user satisfaction, trust, and brand attitude. Study 1 analyzed chatbot conversations from a real customer service context in public transportation, identifying six content-related error types corresponding with the error tags as described in previous literature [34]. The most common content-related error types that appeared in the sample were *excess of information* and *ill-formed*. Although Sanguinetti et al. [34] found the error *ignoring question* most often, other patterns in Table 2 were similar. Consistent with repair strategies mentioned in previous literature [1,2,8] this corpus study's findings revealed five repair strategies used for repairing conversational breakdowns, with the *defer* and *repeat* strategy emerging as the most commonly used repair strategies.

Study 2 focused by means of an experiment on users' perceptions regarding three of these errors and three repair strategies. The findings revealed no significant difference in user satisfaction, trust, and brand attitude between error types. However, there was a significant difference in the participants' perception of repair strategies regarding brand attitude and trust. In accordance with our expectations, the *defer* strategy scored highest on both measures followed by the *options* strategy and lastly the *repeat* repair strategy.

Similarly, the ranking of the repair strategies showed participants' preference for the *defer* and *options* repair strategies over the *repeat* strategy, revealing a discrepancy between the organization's actual usage of repair strategies (as observed in Study 1) and participants' expressed preferences (as observed in Study 2). Specifically, next to the repair strategy *defer*, Study 1 demonstrated that the organization employed the repair strategy *repeat* frequently during customer interactions while the strategy *options* was least used. This contrast could be attributed to several factors. Firstly, the organization's choice of repair strategy might have been driven by operational considerations, system limitations, or default settings in their chatbot implementation. After all, redirecting customers to a human employee (i.e., *defer*) or simply repeating the initial message (i.e., *repeat*) are easier to implement in a chatbot conversation than showing the bandwidth of the chatbot that needs to be checked after every chatbot update (i.e., *options*). Second, participants in Study 2 might have perceived *defer* and *options* as more effective and user-friendly based on their individual experiences and/or preferences (i.e., personalization and prompt resolution). Nevertheless, this finding underscores the importance of incorporating user feedback to meet customer expectations and preferences.

Surprisingly, the study's findings did not support all our expectations. No evidence was found for the hypothesis that user satisfaction would be lowest when the chatbot employs the repair strategy *repeat*, followed by *options*, and subsequently *defer*. On the contrary, the current study's findings reported an increase in user satisfaction regardless of the repair strategy used. This finding might be due to the fact that all three screenshots of fictional conversations, containing both an error type and a repair strategy, showed resolved customer requests. This could have led participants to believe all strategies would work equally effectively, explaining the lack of differences observed. Furthermore, contrary to our third hypothesis, the results indicate no significant interaction between error type and repair strategy in relation to user satisfaction, trust, and brand attitude. These findings suggest that different types of errors do not necessitate specific repair strategies, and any repair strategy can be equally effective regardless of the error type. Nonetheless, it remains crucial to select appropriate repair strategies to prevent or mitigate the negative consequences of conversational breakdowns [1]; unfortunately, the current study did not include a control condition in which no repair strategy was shown to investigate the added value of the presence of a repair strategy compared to its absence in a chatbot conversation. Furthermore, further research is desired to examine the interplay between chatbot errors and repair strategies. After all, our study only examined a selection of the potential errors and repair strategies. A follow-up study could not only examine the interplay between other error types and repairs but also the realism of the materials can be improved by enabling participants to interact with a real chatbot instead of observing screenshots to imitate a true chatbot experience for participants.

Finally, another limitation of the study concerns the generalizability of the findings. Both studies focused on the public transportation industry; the corpus study even only contained chatbot conversations of one specific organization which hampers the representativeness of the identified errors and repair strategies. Also, convenience sampling was used for the recruitment of participants in the online experiment, and the average age of the participants differed per group. The ecological validity of the findings can be enhanced by involving true customers of an organization in the study, for example by means of A-B-tests on the organization's website or within their test panel. This way, not only customers' perceptions of the chatbot and the organization can be investigated after the occurrence of an error and repair strategy, but also their true behaviors within the chatbot conversation by content analyzing the chatlogs afterwards.

## 6 ˙ Conclusion

This study contributes valuable insights for optimizing customer service chatbots by selecting appropriate repair strategies after the occurrence of an error. The content analysis revealed that six different content-related error types can occur and that organizations can include five different repair strategies in chatbot conversations. The results of the online experiment imply that users' perceptions of trust and brand attitude can be influenced most positively by the repair strategy *defer*, followed by *options*, and lastly *repeat*, regardless of the error type that occurred. These findings confirm that a user's experience with a customer service chatbot not only impacts chatbot metrics but also organizational outcomes [38]. In addition, the analysis of the open-ended questions regarding participants' preferences for specific repair strategies revealed a clear inclination towards *defer* when dealing with complex inquiries, despite its potentially slower process. It can therefore be assumed that there is a connection between the nature of customer requests and the effectiveness of *defer* as a repair strategy for addressing complex issues and delivering satisfactory solutions. By recognizing this relationship, organizations can optimize their customer service chatbots to better handle intricate queries, ultimately enhancing user satisfaction and trust. After all, since chatbots are still not able to handle all customer requests and chatbot breakdowns remain a fact of life, knowledge of how these errors can be repaired by chatbots can ensure that customers will nevertheless leave their chatbot conversations with a positive experience.

**Acknowledgments.** The authors would like to thank Emiel van Miltenburg for his feedback. This paper is part of the NWO-funded Smooth Operators project (KIVI.2019.009).

# References

1. Ashktorab, Z., Jain, M., Liao, Q.V., Weisz, J.D.: Resilient chatbots: repair strategy preferences for conversational breakdowns. In: Proceedings of the 2019 CHI Conference on Human Factors in Computing System,. pp. 1–12 (2019)
2. Benner, D., Elshan, E., Schöbel, S., Janson, A.: What do you mean? a review on recovery strategies to overcome conversational breakdowns of conversational agents. In: International Conference on Information Systems (ICIS), pp. 1–17 (2021)
3. Bohus, D., Rudnicky, A.: Error handling in the ravenclaw dialog management framework. In: Human Language Technology Conference and Conference on Empirical Methods in Natural Language Processing (HLT/EMNLP) (2005)
4. Chiou, J.S., Droge, C.: Service quality, trust, specific asset investment, and expertise: direct and indirect effects in a satisfaction-loyalty framework. J. Acad. Mark. Sci. **34**(4), 613–627 (2006)
5. Chung, M., Ko, E., Joung, H., Kim, S.J.: Chatbot e-service and customer satisfaction regarding luxury brands. J. Bus. Res. **117**, 587–595 (2020)
6. Cuadra, A., Li, S., Lee, H., Cho, J., Ju, W.: My bad! Repairing intelligent voice assistant errors improves interaction. Proc. ACM Hum.-Comput. Interact. 5(CSCW1) (apr 2021). https://doi.org/10.1145/3449101, https://doi-org.tilburguniversity.idm.oclc.org/10.1145/3449101
7. Dippold, D.: Can i have the scan on tuesday?" User repair in interaction with a task-oriented chatbot and the question of communication skills for AI. J. Pragmat. **204**, 21–32 (2023)
8. Eberhart, Z., Bansal, A., Mcmillan, C.: A wizard of OZ study simulating API usage dialogues with a virtual assistant. IEEE Trans. Software Eng. **48**(6), 1883–1904 (2020)
9. Følstad, A., Nordheim, C.B., Bjørkli, C.A.: What makes users trust a chatbot for customer service? an exploratory interview study. In: Bodrunova, S.S. (ed.) INSCI 2018. LNCS, vol. 11193, pp. 194–208. Springer, Cham (2018). https://doi.org/10.1007/978-3-030-01437-7_16
10. Følstad, A., Skjuve, M.: Chatbots for customer service: user experience and motivation. In: Proceedings of the 1st International Conference on Conversational User Interfaces, pp. 1–9 (2019)
11. Følstad, A., Taylor, C.: Conversational repair in chatbots for customer service: the effect of expressing uncertainty and suggesting Alternatives. In: Følstad, A., et al. (eds.) Chatbot Research and Design: Third International Workshop, CONVERSATIONS 2019, Amsterdam, The Netherlands, November 19–20, 2019, Revised Selected Papers, pp. 201–214. Springer International Publishing, Cham (2020). https://doi.org/10.1007/978-3-030-39540-7_14
12. Gnewuch, U., Morana, S., Maedche, A.: Towards designing cooperative and social conversational agents for customer service. In: ICIS, pp. 1–13 (2017)
13. van der Goot, M., Hafkamp, L., Dankfurt, Z.: Customer service chatbots: a qualitative interview study into the communication journey of customers. In: International Workshop on Chatbot Research and Design (2020)
14. Grice, H.P.: Logic and conversation. In: Speech acts, pp. 41–58. Brill (1975)
15. Griffiths, J.R., Johnson, F., Hartley, R.J.: User satisfaction as a measure of system performance. J. Librariansh. Inf. Sci. **39**(3), 142–152 (2007)
16. Higashinaka, R., Araki, M., Tsukahara, H., Mizukami, M.: Integrated taxonomy of errors in chat-oriented dialogue systems. In: Proceedings of the 22nd Annual

Meeting of the Special Interest Group on Discourse and Dialogue. pp. 89–98. Association for Computational Linguistics, Singapore and Online (Jul 2021). https://aclanthology.org/2021.sigdial-1.10

17. Higashinaka, R., Funakoshi, K., Araki, M., Tsukahara, H., Kobayashi, Y., Mizukami, M.: Towards taxonomy of errors in chat-oriented dialogue systems. In: Proceedings of the 16th Annual Meeting of the Special Interest Group on Discourse and Dialogue. pp. 87–95. Association for Computational Linguistics, Prague, Czech Republic (Sep 2015). https://doi.org/10.18653/v1/W15-4611,https://aclanthology.org/W15-4611

18. Hsiao, K.L., Chen, C.C.: What drives continuance intention to use a food-ordering chatbot? An examination of trust and satisfaction. Library Hi Tech **40**(4), 929–946 (2022)

19. Janssen, A., Grützner, L., Breitner, M.H.: Why do chatbots fail? a critical success factors analysis. In: International Conference on Information Systems (ICIS) (2021)

20. Jiang, Y., Yang, X., Zheng, T.: Make chatbots more adaptive: dual pathways linking human-like cues and tailored response to trust in interactions with chatbots. Comput. Hum. Behav. **138**, 107485 (2023)

21. Keller, K.L.: Brand synthesis: the multidimensionality of brand knowledge. J. Consumer Res. **29**(4), 595–600 (2003)

22. Kvale, K., Freddi, E., Hodnebrog, S., Sell, O.A., Følstad, A.: Understanding the user experience of customer service chatbots: what can we learn from customer satisfaction Surveys? In: Følstad, A., et al. (eds.) Chatbot Research and Design: 4th International Workshop, CONVERSATIONS 2020, Virtual Event, November 23–24, 2020, Revised Selected Papers, pp. 205–218. Springer International Publishing, Cham (2021). https://doi.org/10.1007/978-3-030-68288-0_14

23. Kvale, K., Sell, O.A., Hodnebrog, S., Følstad, A.: Improving conversations: lessons learnt from manual analysis of chatbot dialogues. In: Følstad, A., et al. (eds.) Chatbot Research and Design: Third International Workshop, CONVERSATIONS 2019, Amsterdam, The Netherlands, November 19–20, 2019, Revised Selected Papers, pp. 187–200. Springer International Publishing, Cham (2020). https://doi.org/10.1007/978-3-030-39540-7_13

24. Li, T.J.J., Chen, J., Xia, H., Mitchell, T.M., Myers, B.A.: Multi-modal repairs of conversational breakdowns in task-oriented dialogs. In: Proceedings of the 33rd Annual ACM Symposium on User Interface Software and Technology, pp. 1094–1107 (2020)

25. Liao, C., Palvia, P., Chen, J.L.: Information technology adoption behavior life cycle: toward a technology continuance theory (tct). Int. J. Inf. Manage. **29**(4), 309–320 (2009)

26. Liebrecht, C., van der Weegen, E.: Menselijke chatbots: een zegen voor online klantcontact? Het effect van conversational human voice door chatbots op social presence en merkattitude. Tijdschrift voor Communicatiewetenschap **47**(3) (2019)

27. Lindgaard, G., Dudek, C.: What is this evasive beast we call user satisfaction? Interact. Comput. **15**(3), 429–452 (2003)

28. Maroengsit, W., Piyakulpinyo, T., Phonyiam, K., Pongnumkul, S., Chaovalit, P., Theeramunkong, T.: A survey on evaluation methods for chatbots. In: Proceedings of the 2019 7th International Conference on Information and Education Technology, pp. 111–119 (2019)

29. Matsumoto, K., Sasayama, M., Yoshida, M., Kita, K., Ren, F.: Emotion analysis and dialogue breakdown detection in dialogue of chat systems based on deep neural networks. Electronics **11**(5), 695 (2022)

30. Pavone, G., Meyer-Waarden, L., Munzel, A.: Rage against the machine: experimental insights into customers' negative emotional responses, attributions of responsibility, and coping strategies in artificial intelligence-based service failures. J. Interact. Mark. **58**(1), 52–71 (2023)

31. Przegalinska, A., Ciechanowski, L., Stroz, A., Gloor, P., Mazurek, G.: In bot we trust: a new methodology of chatbot performance measures. Bus. Horiz. **62**(6), 785–797 (2019)

32. Reinkemeier, F., Gnewuch, U.: Designing effective conversational repair strategies for chatbots. In: Proceedings of the 30th European Conference on Information Systems (ECIS 2022) (2022)

33. Salesforce: Chatbots in klantenservice: onmisbaar anno 2023 (2023), www.salesforce.com/nl/blog/2020/03/Hoe-gebruik-je-chatbots-voor-klantenservice.html

34. Sanguinetti, M., Mazzei, A., Patti, V., Scalerandi, M., Mana, D., Simeoni, R.: Annotating errors and emotions in human-chatbot interactions in Italian. In: Proceedings of the 14th Linguistic Annotation Workshop, pp. 148–159. Association for Computational Linguistics, Barcelona, Spain (Dec 2020). https://aclanthology.org/2020.law-1.14

35. Seeger, A.M., Heinzl, A.: Chatbots often fail! Can anthropomorphic design mitigate trust loss in conversational agents for customer service? In: ECIS (2021)

36. Sheehan, B., Jin, H.S., Gottlieb, U.: Customer service chatbots: Anthropomorphism and adoption. J. Bus. Res. **115**, 14–24 (2020)

37. Toader, D.C., et al.: The effect of social presence and chatbot errors on trust. Sustainability **12**(1), 256 (2019)

38. Zarouali, B., Van den Broeck, E., Walrave, M., Poels, K.: Predicting consumer responses to a chatbot on facebook. Behavior, and Social Networking, Cyberpsychology (2018)

# *Aragón* Open Data Assistant, Lesson Learned of an Intelligent Assistant for Open Data Access

Rafael del Hoyo-Alonso[1]([⊠])(ID), Vega Rodrigalvarez-Chamarro[1](ID), Jorge Vea-Murgía[1], Iñigo Zubizarreta[1], and Julián Moyano-Collado[2]

[1] Technological Institute of Aragón (ITAINNOVA), Zaragoza, Spain
{rdelhoyo,vrodrigalvarez,jveamurgia,izubizarreta}@itainnova.es
[2] Dirección General de Administracción Electrónica, *Aragón* Government, Zaragoza, Spain
jmollano@aragon.es
http://www.itainnova.es

**Abstract.** Chatbots are becoming more popular on websites. To ensure their widespread adoption and effectiveness, it is crucial that the development of these assistant technologies prioritizes user experience, integrating advanced computational methods without losing the human-centric perspective. This paper provides a comprehensive analysis of the insights obtained from the *Aragón* Intelligent Assistant Project, highlighting the main key lessons from deploying a chatbot dedicated to facilitating accessibility to open data for the regional government of *Aragón*. This article presents the difficulties and obstacles faced to meet the needs of real users while modern natural language processing technologies are being incorporated. The discussion underscores that, notwithstanding the sophistication of artificial intelligence, the user experience should be prioritized through ongoing evaluation and improvement. Chatbots must be continually tunned to align with human interaction paradigms if they are used to be as valuable tools for citizens.

**Keywords:** Chatbot · Language Models · Government · NLP · Open Data

## 1 Introduction

The internet hosts a wealth of information for every imaginable purpose; however, the main concern is to ensure the required information is easy to locate. Public administrations host a vast amount of valuable data, which platforms such as *Aragón Open Data*[1] easily disseminate to the population in the Open Data format. Unfortunately, the sheer volume of available resources often makes it challenging to locate or to use this information efficiently for individuals.

---

[1] *Aragón Open Data:* https://opendata.aragon.es/.

---

Supported by ITAINNOVA.

To bridge this gap between users and the open data at their availability, chatbots or intelligent assistants emerge as a powerful solution, facilitating access to critical information. [3,5,7,8] At this moment, Aragón Open Data platform facilitates direct communication between citizens and a virtual assistant capable of interpreting questions and establishing constructive dialogues to provide needed and precised answers.

For instance, one might ask about the population of the city of Alcañiz, receiving a quick and accurate response based on the most recent official statistics, courtesy of the Aragonese Institute of Statistics. A typical interaction might run as follows:

*User:* "What was the population of Alcañiz city in 2021?" *Assistant:* "The population of the municipality of Alcañiz in 2021 was 16,029 inhabitants."

Furthermore, the assistant can guide users to explore other related data, offering additional suggestions such as, "You might also be interested in data on industrial estates or tourism trails - the possibilities are vast."[2].

This assistant serves as a gateway between the extensive open data and the end user, removing technical barriers such as interpreting various formats or navigating to the precise data source. Its mission is to democratize access to the amount of data hosted by AOD, the open data portal managed by the Government of *Aragón*, thus bridging the gap between a great variety of data - including demographics, agricultural infrastructure, culture, and more - and the citizens. To accomplish this, the virtual assistant, based on the RASA framework [1], has been meticulously designed and developed, introducing innovative features to address challenges that arose during its development. This paper gathers the concerted efforts and findings achieved over the last three years, a collaboration that involved the authors and the Government of the *Aragón* region. The first launch of the conversational assistant for AOD took place in 2020, marking a significant step in leveraging technology to facilitate the access to information.

A critical effort for this project was "try to accommodate any question a user might raise, drawing from the large repository in the *Aragón* Open Data to distinguish the query's intent and fetch the most proper data to provide a satisfactory answer." Unlike most virtual assistants limited to regulated environments with a restricted set of questions and answers (such as reservation systems or technical support), this assistant goes through a virtually boundless landscape of questions and contexts, a testimony to its ambitious scope and innovative design.

When this project began in 2020, the use of a large language model was far beyond the scope and available resources. While chatbots like ChatGPT now demonstrate such capabilities, they would not have been a viable option at the time due to their closed-source nature and high costs. As such, the main focus in developing this virtual assistant has been the use of free and open-source technologies in line with the 'open data' philosophy of the project. Maintaining an open approach was especially important given the task of providing government data to citizens.

---

[2] http://opendataei2a.aragon.es/services/chatbot/.

At that early stage, a machine learning framework was needed to enable automated dialogues based on text and voice. Semantic analysis supported by Transformer models like BERT offered a powerful but open solution for interpreting user messages and conducting interactive conversations while retrieving relevant sources. While today's powerful pre-trained language models offer exciting new opportunities, they were not a realistic path when this work first began. The priorities of explain interpretability, replicability and maintaining an open approach meant established techniques such as intent classification remained most suitable for reliably matching queries to factual data within a curated domain.

Moreover, the assistant has been programmed to prioritise openness, conveying a neutral approach that emphasises the open data available on the portal rather than engaging in 'elevator pitchs' which typically offer limited value to users. The objective has always been to provide users with data from the *Aragón* Open Data in a straightforward and unambiguous manner, avoiding the tendency towards scripted interactions. This paper is structured as follows: Sect. 2 outlines the technological context; the pipeline, architecture, and technologies utilised are defined in Sect. 3; Sect. 4 discusses the methodology and presents the results; finally, Sect. 6 concludes the paper by presenting the conclusions.

## 2 Technological Context

### 2.1 *Aragón* Open Data

Open Data is a global initiative aimed to ensure all citizens access to data and information possessed by public administrations. This endeavour facilitates not only open and reusable data dissemination for the benefit of individuals and corporations for basic consultations but also fosters the enrichment of existing data, and the development of applications or services derived from it.

*Aragón* Open Data (AOD) has been committed to a gradual dissemination of public sector information. Over recent years, there has been a marked expansion in the range of data available, the diversity of reusable formats, and enhancements to accessibility measures for these resources. Concurrently, a repository of tools has been developed to support the AOD infrastructure's maintenance. To bridge the gap between citizens and the vast amount of information hosted in the AOD, the development of a Spanish-language virtual assistant (chatbot) was designed to help citizens navigate through the information in AOD related to a variety of topics including tourism and travel in *Aragón*, territorial insights, technical assistance, FAQs about the information society, transport, and agriculture. It should be noted that the repository provides a broader spectrum of topics beyond these primary conversational frameworks.

### 2.2 Ontology and Knowledge Graphs Datastore

The cornerstone of the Aragon Open Data store is a knowledge graph, a modality that has lately gained considerable attention for being a powerful mechanism to articulate knowledge. The incorporation of knowledge graphs, facilitated through ontologies or general graphs, is emerging as a first-order means to map knowledge extracted from the diverse databases of the tourism entity. Google pioneered this strategy in 2012 to enhance its search engine proficiency and enlarge user experience. Since then, the endeavour has been extended to a wide range of areas of application [13]. These graphs represent and systematise knowledge using a schema of subject-predicate-object triplets to depict diverse entities and their interrelations within a domain. Although the construction of these graphs is predominantly manual, needing substantial input from domain experts, there has been a pivot towards automation despite its intricate nature. The advent of Big Data and advancements in natural language processing (NLP) technologies have pushed automatic knowledge mining to the forefront of promising research areas [6]. Modern scholarly discourse explores entities such as named entity recognition (NER), entity normalisation, relationship extraction/classification, and graph embeddings, as well as delving into the genesis of knowledge graphs through deep learning applications on textual data [11].

### 2.3   Linguistic Models

Natural Language Processing (NLP) encompasses the automated creation and comprehension of human languages, with linguistic models serving as a backbone. These models ascertain word probabilities through text data analysis. The trajectory of language models has seen a transition from rudimentary frequency counts - epitomised by bag-of-words, n-grams, and term frequency-inverse document frequency (TF-IDF) - to more evolved representations that leverage neural networks to decipher the latent language structure. Recent years have witnessed the transformer architecture spearheading unprecedented progress in great natural language understanding endeavours, led by the advent of pre-trained models such as BERT [4], GPT-3 [2], RoBERTa [9], T5 [10], and XLNet [12] that take into account information context. A pivotal component of the chatbot is a BERT-based question-and-answer system.

## 3   Description of the System

### 3.1   System Process Flow

As previously mentioned, the assistant is developed utilising the RASA open-source framework. RASA employs a standard pipeline grounded in user intention classification and dialogue management.

The primary stages of the workflow are illustrated in Fig. 1 and comprise the following steps:

– **Reception of Requests:** The system receives a query from the user and aims to provide a relevant response.

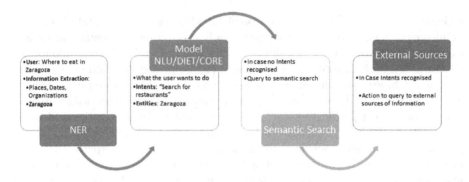

**Fig. 1.** Process workflow.

- **Sentence Curation and Correction:** The user input is broken down into individual terms. The system then corrects spelling mistakes and fills in missing words to streamline the query.
- **Named-Entity Recognition (NER):** This step involves the identification and categorisation of terms such as names of people or places using the NER algorithm.
- **Identification of Intentions and Determination of Actions:** Here, the system selects the most appropriate intention from its knowledge base that aligns closely with the user's query.
- **Query Search Engine:** To accommodate a wider range of queries, the system includes a main search engine, utilizing semantic encoding based on the BERT model. If the intention identified does not meet a certain threshold, the system retrieves data from the CKAN[3] database, the primary repository for AOD.
- **Actions:** At this stage, the system either presents a direct answer or activates a Python algorithm to obtain the required information dynamically. The response could draw from various data sources, including but not limited to:
  - **Ei2av2:** The main data graph source containing information for different conversational frameworks, accessed through SPARQL queries targeted at a Virtuoso database.
  - **GA_OD_CORE:** A repository with transportation and calendar-specific data.
  - **CKAN:** Utilised to answer residual questions related to Aragón.

Subsequent sections will delve deeper into each component of the chatbot's architectural framework, providing a detailed explanation.

---

[3] Open Source Data Management https://ckan.org/.

## 3.2  Architecture

In order to deploy and improve the models quickly for real users, the project architecture relies mainly on a collection of containers of Docker scripts that have been written to make creating images and containers as simple as possible (Fig. 2).

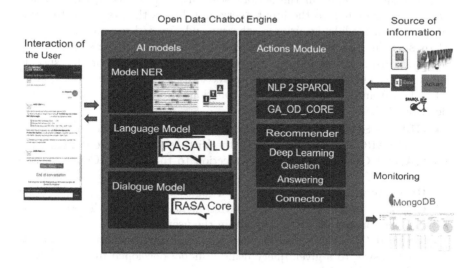

**Fig. 2.** High Level Architecture

In addition to the modules provided by RASA, there are other crucial private services or microservices utilised internally to ensure the optimal functionality of the chatbot. These services encompass the NER server service, the Actions RASA server service, and the API service connected to MongoDB data.

The core Artificial Intelligence models that facilitate the processing of user queries, information retrieval, and natural language response formulation are delineated below:

- **NER (Named-Entity Recognition):** A sophisticated entity detection and extraction model has been developed to feed the RASA engine with detailed insights into the user's query. It categorises crucial keywords for filtering results effectively. This model is a confluence of the default NER offered by the RASA framework and a bespoke NER created specifically for this project, enhancing the system's capabilities substantially. Tailored to the unique needs of the AOD, this application recognises and accurately interprets terms including town names, establishments, and more.
- **Intent Classification:** The system hosts a repository of sample questions, each linked to distinct intents used during the training of the model. Whenever a new query is submitted to the chatbot, it leverages the trained model to identify the most pertinent intent. The correlations between questions and intents are defined in a YAML file, guiding the system in determining the

probability of a question pertaining to each defined intent. Consequently, it selects and executes the preferred allied action with the highest probability intent. Should no intent meet the requisite classification threshold, a fallback mechanism is activated.

- **Dialogue Model:** This model navigates the execution pathway from intents to the related module in the actions segment. It discerns the appropriate action corresponding to the input query and directs the system to the connected action module, ensuring a coherent and targeted response.
- **Browser:** This module oversees the execution process of a user's query, coordinating with a variety of data sources and action modules through specific submodules. The submodules carry out necessary actions and, where required, fetch data from relevant sources. The functionalities of these submodules are described below:
  - **NLP to SPARQL:** Transforms queries expressed in natural language into SPARQL queries suitable for the Virtuoso database repository.
  - **GA_OD_CORE:** Facilitates connection to the GA_OD_CORE service via an API.
  - **Recommender:** Suggests additional topics potentially of interest to the user based on the initial query and its identified entities. These suggestions are presented as buttons within the user interface.
  - **General Questions and Answering System:** Provides the most relevant answer to a given query using a model developed from the BEST multilingual model.
  - **Other Connectors:** Responsible for establishing connections with various external data sources.

The browser outlines the operational path of the code as previously described. It evaluates all possible paths based on the specified parameters and selects the appropriate function for execution. Each execution communicates with the necessary data source to fetch the response, attending to the wide variety of conversational frameworks and queries encompassed in this project. The system processes the data from external sources for each module, filters it, and then presents the solution through the chatbot. These data sources can range from JSON files and Excel datasets to Virtuoso databases, among others. The program accommodates all existing types of connectors, and allows for the addition of new ones to enhance system functionality.

### 3.3 Intention Classification and General Answering Module

Given the immense likelihood of users setting out questions outside established conversational frames or on topics not covered, the intention method, albeit prevalent, encounters substantial limitations in the context of large-scale projects such as this. Addressing this issue has been a significant challenge, as it is unfeasible to restrict users to a limited set of informational contexts. To facilitate responses to a broader spectrum of general inquiries with varying degrees of specificity, a method has been devised that aligns with the objectives of user interactions. The intention classification process can be divided into two scenarios:

- **General Questions on Open Data:** This involves responses to broad queries about general topics available in the CKAN system. Queries could range from seeking understanding on topics such as general questions about Aragon agriculture to inquiries about a particular town in the region.
- **General CKAN Search:** In instances where an intention cannot be discerned, the default fallback action is triggered. This entails initiating a semantic search on the CKAN to provide the user with approximate answers to their question. If the response generated encompasses data spanning multiple years and/or regions, the forms are activated to guide the user in narrowing down their inquiry based on specific years or regions, thereby offering a more tailored answer.

This module was developed to proactively address user queries and avoid responding with unknown answers most of the time.

## 4  User Testing Methodology

### 4.1  Pre-assessment and User Selection

Before initiating the user tests, a conscius effort is undertaken to identify diverse user demographics. The objective is to include a large spectrum of profiles representative of the Aragón population, covering individuals of all genders, ages, and national backgrounds. Moreover, the testing intends to encompass people with disabilities to assess the prototype's accessibility and to foster inclusivity, thereby mitigating barriers that hinder full and active societal participation. To gather insights from associations identified as more sensitised to these issues, an inclusive system is envisioned. Various associations were approached based on the desired user profile for coordinated end-user testing. These associations cater to different demographics including youth (ages 15–34), seniors (above 55), women, and people with disabilities, alongside neighbourhood associations and federations (Table 1, 2, 3).

Here, there are examples of the associations considered for different profiles:

- Associations for Individuals with Disabilities:[4]
- Women's Associations:[5]
- **Social and Neighbourhood Associations:**[6]

---

[4] COCEMFE   http://www.cocemfearagon.org/,   Full   Inclusion   https://www.plenainclusion.org/,   CERMI   http://www.cermi.es,   DFA   Foundation   https://www.fundaciondfa.es/,   ONCE   Foundation   https://www.fundaciononce.es/,   ASZA   https://www.asza.net/.

[5] María Moliner https://asociacionmujeresmariamoliner.wordpress.com/, Augustinian Culture of Aragon https://www.asociacionagustinadearagon.org/, Amparo Poch https://amparopoch.wordpress.com/, Families and Women in Rural Areas https://www.afammer.es/afammer-aragon/.

[6] CAV *Aragón* https://cavaragon.wordpress.com/, Zaragoza Neighbourhood https://barrioszaragoza.org/, Teruel Neighbourhood, Huesca Associations.

**Table 1.** Distribution of required profiles by association type and region

| Age Range | Gender | Zaragoza | Huesca | Teruel | Total |
|-----------|--------|----------|--------|--------|-------|
| 15-24 years | Male | 1 | 1 | 1 | 3 |
| 15-24 years | Female | 1 | 1 | 1 | 3 |
| 25-34 years | Male | 1 | 1 | 1 | 3 |
| 25-34 years | Female | 1 | 1 | 1 | 3 |
| 35-44 years | Male | 3 | 1 | 1 | 5 |
| 35-44 years | Female | 3 | 1 | 1 | 5 |
| 45-54 years | Male | 3 | 1 | 1 | 5 |
| 45-54 years | Female | 3 | 1 | 1 | 5 |
| 55-64 years | Male | 2 | 1 | 1 | 4 |
| 55-64 years | Female | 2 | 1 | 1 | 4 |
| 65-74 years | Male | 1 | 1 | 1 | 3 |
| 65-74 years | Female | 1 | 1 | 1 | 3 |
| 75-84 years | Male | 1 | 1 | 1 | 3 |
| 75-84 years | Female | 1 | 1 | 1 | 3 |
| **Total** | - | 24 | 14 | 14 | 52 |

**Legend:**

- ............: Neighborhood and local associations
- _____: Women's associations

**Table 2.** Distribution of required profiles for digital literacy

| TIC | Function | Zaragoza | Huesca | Teruel | Total |
|-----|----------|----------|--------|--------|-------|
| Digital illiterates | Urban | 1 | 1 | 1 | 3 |
| | Rural | 3 | 3 | 3 | 9 |
| **Total** | - | 4 | 4 | 4 | 12 |

### 4.2 Approach User Tests and Methodology to Follow

User tests made use of usability testing based on the observation and analysis of a group of real users interacting with the prototype, which in this instance is the virtual assistant or chatbot, within a controlled test environment. The objective was to record the encountered usability issues, the proposed solutions, and the suggestions to subsequently rectify the problems and enhance user satisfaction.

**Table 3.** Required Profiles by Association Profile: Association for Disabled Persons

| DISABILITY | FUNCTION | ZARAGOZA | HUESCA | TERUEL | TOTAL |
|---|---|---|---|---|---|
| PHYSICAL | MOTOR SKILLS | 2 | 1 | 1 | 4 |
|  | SPEECH | 2 | 1 | 1 | 4 |
| MENTAL | INTELLECTUAL | 2 | 1 | 1 | 4 |
|  | PERSONALITY | 2 | 1 | 1 | 4 |
| SENSORIAL | VISUAL | 2 | 1 | 1 | 4 |
|  | AUDITORY | 2 | 1 | 1 | 4 |
| **TOTAL** |  | **12** | **6** | **6** | **24** |

These tests were facilitated remotely via recorded sessions utilizing Microsoft Teams technology, wherein users were allocated a series of tasks to accomplish. A facilitator guided the process, a needed adaptation was required due to the COVID-19 situation in 2021. The facilitator introduced the project to the users and delineated the challenges they were expected to solve with the help of the virtual assistant. The facilitator maintained a nonintrusive role during the test, focusing on analysing the user's approach to task completion, including observing errors and identifying sections that required more time. This meticulous data collection aims to facilitate detailed analysis to propose constructive modifications to the prototype.

In the initial iteration, the participants were presented with 15 unique tasks derived from 5 conversational frameworks, with each task being attempted by three users to collect a representative sample of responses. The conversational frameworks and the respective challenges encompassed are detailed below:

- **Aragon and its Territory:** Identifying local holidays, reporting work accidents, determining the number of self-employed individuals, finding the contact information for a local town hall, knowing the demography and the current mayor of a locality, among others.
- **Tourism:** Locating accommodations, restaurants, and hotel services, identifying the local tourist office, finding cafeterias, and more.
- **Information Society:** Instructions on completing and submitting a telematic application, understanding what an electronic certificate is, and the process of revoking it, etc.
- **Transport:** Finding roads and bus routes to a town, reporting traffic incidents along with their causes, among other tasks.
- **Agriculture:** Information on irrigated farms, specifics on hectare cultivation (such as agriculture and vineyards) in a locality, understanding the administrative divisions involving villages and municipalities, and so forth.

In the second iteration, the established methodology remained, but with a nuanced approach to the tests-introducing a situational context where each user faced distinct sub-challenges or sub-tasks. Participants were presented with a scenario involving a job bank opening in an unfamiliar Aragon locality, exemplified by Daroca, with the exercise extended to three provinces. The test required users to interact with an assistant to gather demographic, agricultural, and town council data about the selected locality. The process also involved understanding the necessity of an electronic certificate for online document submission. Furthermore, participants were tasked with gathering information on local amenities and potential road disruptions in preparation for a hypothetical visit.

### 4.3    Results of the First Iteration of User Tests

This section defines the outcomes from the initial iteration of user tests, beginning with general conclusions before delving into the specifics of various conversational frameworks. The general conclusions were as follows:

– The majority of users initially utilized button navigation to interact with the assistant.
– Mostly, users resorted to typing their questions to obtain answers, as navigation through buttons proved insufficient.
– Several users encountered difficulties discerning the appropriate main category for their queries, suggesting an adjustment towards a structure more aligned with conversational frames.
– Regarding button navigation, discrepancies were noted with some users finding recurring main categories, while others identified essential missing categories. Additionally, confusion arose surrounding the "See more topics" button, particularly concerning navigation back to the main menu.
– Most users wrote well-structured sentences when posing questions to the chatbot, instead of merely inputting keywords.
– Feedback included remarks on unhelpful responses or insufficient data provided in some instances.
– Users commented on the laborious nature of the task, highlighting a lack of dynamism in the chat interaction.

Modifications to intents and the introduction of new ones successfully refined and enhanced the precision of challenges within each conversational framework.

### 4.4    Results of the Second Iteration of User Tests

This iteration involved a group of 12 participants; five were returning from the first round, and seven were new, including three individuals with disabilities.
    The overall outcomes from this round were:

– The majority acknowledged improvements since the last test, appreciating the tool's utility.
– All users in this round agreed that the assistant maintained a correct, and even amiable, language and tone.
– Users showed a preference for typing their questions over navigating via buttons in this test.

- Suggestions emerged for enhancing the conversational thread and expanding the database for consultations.
- Users proposed a constant visibility option to revert to initial topics.
- Recommendations included a reduction in the number of buttons and highlighting only the most pertinent ones.

Suggestions: the results have been satisfactory and some user makes a suggestion so that the assistant is able to follow the conversational thread without having to re-include the name of the municipality and that the system allows small errors to be corrected in the names. Questions raised:

- What is the population of Daroca?
- Who is the mayor of Daroca?
- What is the telephone number of the Daroca town hall?

Conversational setting: Tourism and transport Suggestions: they usually find the results but the users suggest that the assistant provide them with more information, for example, regarding the cafeterias and hotels, the website, address, price, etc.; from the tourist office to show them the entire card as soon as it tells them the location. Questions raised:

- Is there a tourist office in Daroca?
- How many restaurants are there in Daroca?
- How many hotels are there in Daroca?
- Are there any traffic incidents in Daroca?

Conversational framework: Information Society
Suggestions: some user comments that he would like the chat to cover more than one question and answer both questions in the same interaction (Fig. 3). Questions raised:

- What is an electronic certificate?
- What is an electronic certificate for?

## 4.5  Improvements Proposed After User Tests

Three key areas requiring enhancement were highlighted in the test analysis.

Firstly, enhancing the chatbot's understanding and interpretation of user intents is critical. This entails refining the general question-answering module to prevent misinterpretations and to enable the extraction of key sentences from user queries. For instance, in the event of ambiguous employment data queries, the assistant could process the question to identify core terms and consequently, suggest potential responses based on available data, thereby guiding users in framing their questions more effectively.

Secondly, users encountered difficulties navigating using buttons, suggesting the need to encourage users to type their questions directly, possibly by hiding button navigation in the early wizard iterations. This strategy, along with

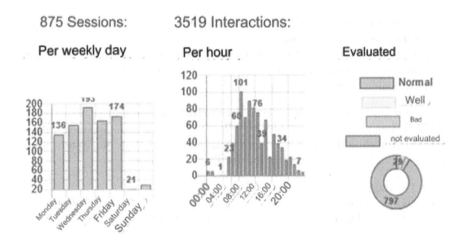

**Fig. 3.** Interactions generated during the last phase of the project

contextualized guidance from the chatbot, seeks to prevent users from feeling "lost", enhancing the user-chatbot interaction through a more intuitive recommendation module.

Thirdly, constant monitoring of user queries is imperative to identify real-time user intents and to foster more articulate communication strategies, helping in the discovery of new intents and interaction techniques.

The conversational assistant recorded 875 sessions with 3,519 interactions from January 31, 2021, to June 8, 2022. Out of these, 78 sessions were evaluated, with an almost equal split among positive, neutral, and negative feedback, representing just 0.41% of the total sessions. Interactions spanned all conversational frameworks, but some issues remain unresolved. It is expected to improve the results by the end of the year.

## 5    Conclusion and Lessons Learned

This project has demonstrated the fundamental importance of technology to devolop a virtual assistant capable to interact with users about a large amount of open data. However, deciphering the optimal way for users to interact with the information presented was one of the greatest challenges. The results of user testing underline the need for a user-centric design approach rather than a technology-driven one, to facilitate wider adoption of these tools. An example of chatbot interaction can be seen in the Fig. 4.

The development of the Aragón Open Data assistant highlighted the need for careful management of intents to avoid issues with intent classification as the number of possible user queries expands. While the assistant incorporated over 300 intents, the ambiguity across such a wide scope still posed challenges. To address this, future iterations could explore clustering semantically related

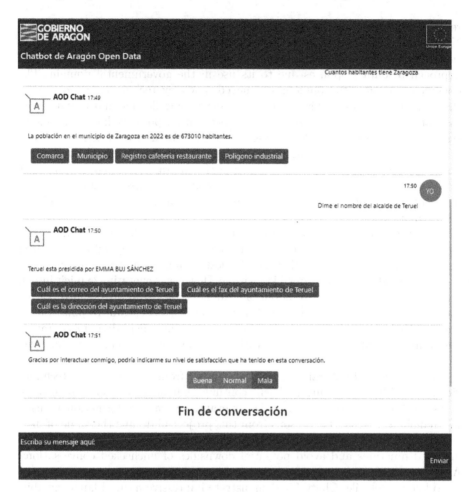

**Fig. 4.** Example of dialogue in the web app

intents and leveraging contextual information to disambiguate probable intents for a given query. Additionally, benchmarking against other open domain chatbots would help quantify the assistant's capabilities and contributions. Ongoing user testing and refinement of the natural language processing components based on feedback will be critical to improveintent understanding and mitigate potential misclassifications. Though powerful large language models hold promise, a hybrid approach combining their capabilities with supervised intent mapping and classification seems prudent for maintaining control and transparency. Overall, keeping the user experience central through iterative evaluation and enhancement will be key to optimizing assistants like this to serve as an effective and reliable interface to open data repositories.

Despite incorporating over 300 intents, the system could not satisfy all potential user questions, indicating the need for additional elements such as question recommenders and general search engines to supplement intent-based systems. Notably, the initial personality of the chatbot, characterized by casual and occasionally witty conversations, had to be discarded to maintain a more aseptic approach to data responses due to its use in the governmental domain. This document captures the outcomes achieved, and key technical decisions made throughout the project. The feasibility of developing flexible and useful virtual assistants interacting over an extensive open data repository has been demonstrated, although more work remains to optimize the user experience.

The lessons learned highlight that while technology is essential, focusing on understanding users' needs and optimizing the interaction design is crucial for chatbots to achieve wide adoption. Continued efforts to expand data sources and query understanding capabilities will also help improve the system's ability to satisfy more users.

The incorporation of powerful large language models like GPT-4 and other emerging models holds promise to reduce the engineering efforts required. Such models could assist with general question answering and augment data sources through their pre-trained knowledge. However, generating explicit intents remains important to control potential hallucinations from open-ended conversations with these systems. Intent classification helps constrain responses to be based in factual data from authorized sources, avoiding misleading, inaccurate or inappropriate replies that may arise without proper supervision of large language models.

While advanced natural language capabilities from new generative technologies are rapidly developing and will continue enhancing conversational assistants, ensuring interactions prioritize relevant, verifiable information to users will remain a priority. The lessons from this project underline the value of user-centric design and supervised intent mapping to optimize chatbots for their intended functions and avoid potential downsides of unchecked conversational AI systems.

While models like ChatGPT demonstrate impressive natural language abilities, they do not fully resolve the challenges of building targeted conversational assistants. ChatGPT and other open-domain models are not designed or curated for specific tasks like accessing verified government data.

Rather than seeing large language models as a complete replacement for existing methods, they are best applied as a complement with continued prioritization of user-centric design principles. The lessons from extensively testing this open data chatbot highlight how even with advanced technologies, centering the solution around understanding and fulfilling users' actual needs remains paramount.

Simply incorporating the latest large language models is not sufficient, their capabilities must be carefully integrated and guided within a framework designed first and foremost based on research into how users want to interact. Continued focus on iterative user testing and refining the conversation and information retrieval experience based on empirical findings will help maximize the benefits of new technologies for building useful, easy to use assistants. ChatGPT and related tools provide an exciting opportunity when developed hand in hand with user-centered strategies.

**Acknowledgements.** This paper has been supported partly by the Department of Big Data and Cognitive Systems at the Technological Institute of Aragon and the IODIDE group of *Aragón*, under the grant number T1720R, along with contributions from the European Regional Development Fund (ERDF).

# References

1. Bocklisch, T., Faulkner, J., Pawlowski, N., Nichol, A.: Rasa: Open source language understanding and dialogue management. arXiv preprint arXiv:1712.05181 (2017)
2. Brown, T., et al.: Language models are few-shot learners. Adv. Neural. Inf. Process. Syst. **33**, 1877–1901 (2020)
3. Cantador, I., Viejo-Tardío, J., Cortés-Cediel, M.E., Rodríguez Bolívar, M.P.: A chatbot for searching and exploring open data: Implementation and evaluation in e-government. In: DG. O2021: The 22nd Annual International Conference on Digital Government Research, pp. 168–179 (2021)
4. Devlin, J., Chang, M.W., Lee, K., Toutanova, K.: Bert: pre-training of deep bidirectional transformers for language understanding (2018). https://doi.org/10.48550/ARXIV.1810.04805, https://arxiv.org/abs/1810.04805
5. Ed-douibi, H., Cánovas Izquierdo, J.L., Daniel, G., Cabot, J.: A model-based chatbot generation approach to converse with open data sources. In: Brambilla, M., Chbeir, R., Frasincar, F., Manolescu, I. (eds.) Web Engineering: 21st International Conference, ICWE 2021, Biarritz, France, May 18–21, 2021, Proceedings, pp. 440–455. Springer International Publishing, Cham (2021). https://doi.org/10.1007/978-3-030-74296-6_33
6. Guo, L., Yan, F., Li, T., Yang, T., Lu, Y.: An automatic method for constructing machining process knowledge base from knowledge graph. Robot. Comput.-Integr. Manufact. **73**, 102222 (2022)
7. Hsu, I., Chang, C.C., et al.: Integrating machine learning and open data into social chatbot for filtering information rumor. J. Ambient. Intell. Humaniz. Comput. **12**(1), 1023–1037 (2021)
8. Keyner, S., Savenkov, V., Vakulenko, S.: Open data chatbot. In: Hitzler, P., et al. (eds.) The Semantic Web: ESWC 2019 Satellite Events: ESWC 2019 Satellite Events, Portorož, Slovenia, June 2–6, 2019, Revised Selected Papers, pp. 111–115. Springer International Publishing, Cham (2019). https://doi.org/10.1007/978-3-030-32327-1_22
9. Liu, Y., et al.: Roberta: a robustly optimized bert pretraining approach (2019). https://doi.org/10.48550/ARXIV.1907.11692
10. Raffel, C., et al.: Exploring the limits of transfer learning with a unified text-to-text transformer. J. Mach. Learn. Res. **21**(140), 1–67 (2020)
11. Wang, C., Liu, X., Song, D.: Language models are open knowledge graphs. arXiv preprint arXiv:2010.11967 (2020)
12. Yang, Z., Dai, Z., Yang, Y., Carbonell, J., Salakhutdinov, R.R., Le, Q.V.: Xlnet: generalized autoregressive pretraining for language understanding. In: Advances in Neural Information Processing Systems 32 (2019)
13. Zou, X.: A survey on application of knowledge graph. J. Phys.: Conf. Series. **1487**, 012016. IOP Publishing (2020)

# LLM-driven Conversational Design and Analysis

# Saleshat: A LLM-Based Social Robot for Human-Like Sales Conversations

Leon Hanschmann$^{(\boxtimes)}$ ⓘ, Ulrich Gnewuch ⓘ, and Alexander Maedche ⓘ

Karlsruhe Institute of Technology, 76131 Karlsruhe, Germany
{leon.hanschmann,ulrich.gnewuch,alexander.maedche}@kit.edu

**Abstract.** Large language models (LLMs) have generated excitement in many areas and may also make human-like conversations with social robots possible. Drawing from human-robot interaction literature and interviews, we developed Saleshat based on the commercial social robot Furhat and the large language model GPT-4. Saleshat emphasizes refined natural language processing and dynamic control of the robot's physical appearance through the LLM. Responses from the LLM are processed sequentially, enabling the robot to react quickly. The results of our first formative evaluation with six users engaging in a sales conversation about Bluetooth speakers show that Saleshat can provide accurate and detailed responses, maintain a good conversation flow, and show dynamically controlled non-verbal cues. With our findings, we contribute to research on social robots and LLMs by providing design knowledge for LLM-based social robots and by uncovering the benefits and challenges of integrating LLMs into a social robot.

**Keywords:** social robot · large language model · design · human-robot interaction

## 1 Introduction

In today's shopping environments, self-checkouts are prevalent for everyday items [8], yet for major purchases, many users prefer human interaction [39]. The preference is driven by the belief that machines cannot replicate the emotional connection and trust inherent in human interactions (e.g., [10,17,33]). Social robots aim to address this challenge by engaging with humans in a socially appropriate manner [5] and mimicking human-like communication while trying to avoid the Uncanny Valley [21,27].

In the past, however, there has been only limited success. Social robots were typically confined to specific domains, such as providing information as a receptionist, without really engaging with users (e.g., [22]). Current sales robots are often unable to establish a human-like connection with the user, as they do not respond by utilizing generative methods (e.g. [44]). For instance, many existing robots use traditional intent-based classifiers that map the user's input to

A. Følstad et al. (Eds.): CONVERSATIONS 2023, LNCS 14524, pp. 61–76, 2024.
https://doi.org/10.1007/978-3-031-54975-5_4

predefined states (e.g., [25]). While these work efficiently for answering questions and providing guidance in structured processes, the fluid nature of sales conversations does not align well with such rigid conversational models.

With the advent of large language models (LLMs) such as GPT-4, there is an increased potential to create more human-like interactions in robots and address the shortcomings of previous robot designs. Robots leveraging GPT-4 could possess the capability to generate more dynamic, context-aware responses, making them apt for the unpredictability of sales conversations. Unlike traditional intent-based classifiers, LLMs can draw from vast conversational knowledge to provide more nuanced and tailored interactions. Instead of being confined to predefined conversational paths, they can adapt and improvise in real time, much like a seasoned salesperson would. Incorporating LLMs into sales robots may also lead to a more personalized experience. By continuously learning from each interaction, sales robots can offer recommendations, responses, or suggestions that are more attuned to individual user preferences and histories. This adaptability can make sales interactions feel less mechanical and more akin to a genuine human conversation, bridging the gap between traditional robotic interactions and truly engaging conversations.

However, integrating LLMs into existing hardware or software systems with clearly defined functionality and terminology is often more difficult than expected (e.g., [11]). For example, hallucinations may occur or the hardware may not allow a locally deployed language model, which could be associated with higher processing delays. Unfortunately, there is limited research on how to seamlessly integrate LLMs into social robots to enable domain-specific conversations with clear goals (e.g., sales interactions). As a result, researchers and practitioners struggle to realize the full potential of combining LLMs and social robots, especially in contexts such as sales. To fill this gap, our research aims to address the following research question: How can large language models be integrated into social robots to enable human-like sales conversations?

This paper addresses this question by presenting Saleshat, a novel artifact for facilitating human-like sales conversations with the social robot Furhat [2] and GPT-4 [29]. Drawing from human-robot interaction literature and interviews, we develop an innovative method to enhance Furhat's gestures and interactions. We evaluated Saleshat in a formative evaluation with six users. The results suggest that participants appreciated the accurate and detailed responses, the good conversation flow, and the non-verbal cues provided by the robot. Overall, our findings contribute novel insights into the challenges and benefits of integrating LLMs into social robots. With our method and artifact description, we provide design knowledge for researchers and practitioners interested in combining these two innovative technologies to create domain-specific applications for social robots.

## 2   Related Work

### 2.1   Social Robots in Retail

Social robots are robots designed to interact and communicate with humans, adhering to the behavioral norms expected by their designated human counterparts [3]. Their role in retail is drawing more attention (e.g., [1]). As they take on roles traditionally held by humans, the dynamics of store operations and user experiences are shifting. Rindfleisch et al. [34] show that social robots can significantly alter the store environment and performance. Brengman et al. [6] find social robots to be surpassing tablet kiosks in both user interaction and sales. Niemelä et al. [28] investigate the use of Softbank's social robot Pepper [30] in a mall, showing that it needs sophisticated conversational skills to engage with users effectively. Similarly, Lu et al. [26] demonstrated the positive impact of robots using human-like speech patterns. This resonates with our efforts to enhance Furhat's interactive abilities. Emotions also play an important role in this context. Chuah and Yu [15] found that a robot's expressions, such as happiness or surprise, can sway potential customers. Choi et al. [12] revealed the adverse reaction consumers have when social robots lack warmth. Van Pinxteren et al. [40] touched upon the importance of gaze cues in social robots, suggesting they can enhance trust and intent to use. Stock and Merkle [38] distill consumer evaluations of social robots into three criteria: ideal standards, human employee expectations, and past self-service experiences.

Overall, the literature advocates for social robots that closely mirror human interactions, underscoring the importance of nuanced gestures, speech, and warmth in fostering robot-human engagement in retail. However, this has been difficult, if not impossible, to implement in the past because of the complexity of sales conversations. The recent hype around LLMs might suggest that their integration could solve this challenge.

### 2.2   Large Language Models

Recent advances in natural language processing have been driven by large language models such as ChatGPT that utilize transformer architectures [16], specifically the self-attention mechanism [41], to understand long-range dependencies in texts. Pre-training methods, as exemplified by BERT [16], enable these models to be fine-tuned for diverse tasks. Scaling up pre-trained language models such as the 175B-parameter GPT-3 [7] and 540B-parameter PaLM [13] often enhances their performance on downstream tasks [24]. Unlike smaller models such as the 1.5B-parameter GPT-2 [32], these larger versions exhibit emergent abilities, like GPT-3's skill in solving few-shot tasks through in-context learning [43]. Labeled as Large Language Models [36], models such as the GPT-X series have gained significant traction. ChatGPT, refined via reinforcement learning from human feedback [14], and GPT-4 [29], a multimodal LLM, have shown remarkable capabilities, leading to increased interest in their applications (e.g., [31,45]). Embodied language models, like PaLM-E, integrate real-world sensor data into LLMs, linking words with perceptual data [18].

Given the impressive capabilities of LLMs, integrating them into a social robot could be a promising approach to enable more human-like dialogues. Stark et al. [37] present "Dobby", a robot that combines GPT-4, demonstrating improved receptiveness to personification, and adaptability in a human-robot interaction tour-guide scenario. Wang et al. [42] successfully demonstrated a novel method in which large language models, such as GPT-4, can generate low-level control commands that enable robots to walk without the need for task-specific fine-tuning, by using few-shot prompts derived from the physical environment. However, most approaches have in common that they are more concerned with the problems of robots like movement, and do not focus on social interaction with humans.

Although there are some initial attempts to integrate Furhat with large language models (e.g., [11]), several challenges remain unsolved. Wilcock et al. [44] integrate Furhat with conversational AI and a knowledge graph, enabling it to respond to basic inquiries and, in certain instances, use the knowledge graph to provide explanations for its responses. The scope of answering questions though is confined to a limited knowledge graph. Cherakara et al. [11] showcase an application where they connect Furhat with an LLM to manage Furhat's facial expressions. However, they do not separately consider latency issues that could render the interaction with a robot more mechanic. Overall, while research has made strides in interfacing conversational AI with robotic platforms such as Furhat, further efforts are needed to refine the interaction dynamics, augment the range of knowledge integration, and resolve the computational latency issues to foster more natural and responsive human-robot interactions. Our research addresses this gap by developing an innovative artifact called Saleshat.

## 3    Design and Development of Saleshat

To develop our artifact, we followed an iterative design approach. Guided by literature and expert insights, we first defined requirements and then implemented the LLM into Furhat. Developed by Furhat Robotics, the Furhat robot combines conversational skills with a 3D-projected animated face. With a motorized neck and head, Furhat can nod and spin. It integrates speech using a microphone and speaker system. Thus, Furhat is able to employ a set of social cues (e.g., voice modulation, facial expressions, eye movement, head orientation). In the following, we will present our requirements and the preliminary design of our artifact.

### 3.1    Objectives and Requirements

Social robots, designed to integrate seamlessly within human settings, must possess both an ability to express internal states and a sensitivity to human interactions [4]. Our research involved an in-depth review of relevant literature and consultations with our research partner (a non-profit institute for research on consumer and market decisions). One salient conclusion drawn from our findings was the indispensable nature of the robot's conversational prowess to achieve genuine human-like exchanges. In dynamic and often unpredictable settings, such as sales, the robot's ability to adapt and respond is critical. Consequently, as a central idea of the design, we opted to incorporate GPT-4 to enhance the robot's interactive prowess, encompassing both speech and facial expressions.

Drawing from the literature on human-robot interaction and the already existing approaches in the integration of robots in retail, we established requirements for our artifact. Our research was informed by the integration of principles delineated in the Design-Centered Framework for Social Human-Robot Interaction [3]. Bartneck and Forlizzi [3] emphasize the congruence between a robot's design and its capabilities. Thus, if a sales robot is modeled after a human store associate, it should also encompass the skills inherent to a salesperson. Their modality principle advocates for diverse communication channels in robots, fostering more authentic human-like interactions. Thus, Furhat's speech and facial expression selection during the conversation should be dynamically adjustable. Emphasizing interactivity, robots should respond promptly and appropriately. Consequently, Furhat should respond promptly and without delay.

We furthermore engaged in detailed conversations with our research partner, who has conducted prior studies using social robots in retail scenarios, and leveraged their expertise. These conversations, combined with the literature, guided us in formulating the following requirements.

R1 Integrated Language Processing: Seamlessly combine a large language model with Furhat's existing capabilities to facilitate real-time human-like conversations.

R2 Dynamic Gesture and Expression Mapping: Map the outputs of the LLM to suitable gestures, facial expressions, and other non-verbal cues, ensuring Furhat's actions are in sync with its spoken words.

R3 Contextual Awareness Mechanism: Allow the robot to recognize and understand the specific context of a sales conversation (e.g., the initiation of the purchase decision), allowing it to generate appropriate and relevant responses for each step in the conversation.

R4 Emotion Recognition and Response: As a human would do, give the language model the ability to adapt to the body language of the user.

R5 Product-Specific Knowledge Base Integration: Ensure the language model is equipped with a comprehensive knowledge base about retail products and services, providing accurate information.

## 3.2   System Architecture

Our architecture is designed to integrate directly with the platform Furhat runs on, as visualized in Fig. 1. Saleshat is equipped with both a microphone and camera, allowing it to process auditory and visual data simultaneously. The Furhat platform primarily includes an Automatic Speech Recognition (ASR) module, an Automatic Gesture Recognition (AGR) module, and a Text-to-Speech (TTS) service. Furhat collaborates with an external service for speech transcription and speech generation from text.

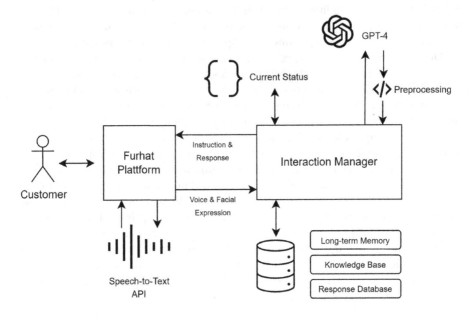

**Fig. 1.** System Architecture of Saleshat.

Saleshat's design diverges from the traditional intent- or rule-based approach to natural language processing. It has only one state for all of its interactions with the user, from giving information about products to promoting and ultimately completing the purchase. Distinct states, however, have proven useful for administrative tasks like setting up the social robot and in pretests for conducting a user study.

From the Furhat platform, transcribed texts and detected facial expressions are relayed to the interaction handler. This handler is also linked to a knowledge engine that supplies context-specific insights (e.g., product information). Subsequent responses are formulated via an integration with GPT-4 [R1]. The knowledge engine serves a threefold purpose: (1) it features a long-term memory, storing crucial content from the conversation; (2) it incorporates a knowledge base essential for product-specific information; and (3) it uses a response database to offer sample dialogues which augment the authenticity and persuasiveness of the overall conversation.

**Furhat Platform.** Through the Furhat SDK, some design decisions were already made. Due to data protection considerations, we employed Microsoft

Azure Speech Services for the ASR component. Testing indicated that Saleshat's perceived performance may have some dependence on the Speech-To-Text service, with several misinterpretations possibly arising from imprecise transcriptions [19]. Misunderstandings can feed into the knowledge engine, so ensuring GPT-4 uses accurate data is essential. Voice generation is achieved using Amazon Polly's Neural TTS (NTTS) service from the provided text. The Furhat platform also handles gesture recognition via camera; currently, only smiles are identifiable. The robot was designed to autonomously initiate interactions upon detecting a person in front of it. Ethical considerations are paramount in our architecture. The system does not perform individual user identification, ensuring user privacy. If a user moves beyond Furhat's detection range and returns, the interaction sequence is reset to its initial state.

**Interaction Handler.** The interaction handler is responsible for the design of the conversation. Currently, it is tasked to complete the purchase. It keeps track of the current state of the conversation, including the number of interactions with the user and the time elapsed since the conversation began. If needed, prompts are adjusted to facilitate the sales process [R3]. The interaction handler is invoked when a user first interacts with Saleshat and once the user concludes the utterance. There is currently no mechanism implemented to interrupt Saleshat while speaking, as it would add further complexity. The interaction, therefore, follows a classic turn-by-turn-based approach. When a user engages with Saleshat, the interaction begins. We have experimented with dialogues where the social robot initiates the conversation. However, we encountered challenges, particularly in recognizing attention and differentiating it from a desire to be approached (Fig. 2).

The interaction handler processes both the speech data captured by the ASR and, when identified, the user's facial expressions. Although the implementation is dynamic, currently, only a smile is detected, which influences the prompt and, in turn, impacts the responses provided by Saleshat [R5]. Subsequently, it composes the prompt using all the gathered information. The interaction handler then loads all relevant information from the knowledge engine. At present, the product-specific knowledge base is limited as it only contains information on two products. Instead of querying, all data is directly loaded into the prompt. For the potential future inclusion of more products, however, it would be wise to adopt a knowledge retrieval method including a trained classifier. When designing the prompt, blending few-shot learning with zero-shot learning has proven to offer the best results. A big problem is hallucinations [23] and that the robot incorporates inaccurate information from its training, which could be outdated, potentially lying to the user. Therefore, a separate chapter is dedicated to explaining our approach to prompting. The prompt is then sent to GPT-4 with all available information. Furhat's conversational capabilities are enhanced to foster deeper, real-time human-like interactions, addressing requirement [R1].

In practice, ensuring robust data privacy presents a challenge when using an external APIs. While straightforward instances, such as filtering out names, can

**Fig. 2.** Picture of a sales conversation between a user and Saleshat.

be addressed using basic algorithms and measures like named entity tagging, there are scenarios where this approach falls short. In the current iteration of Saleshat, users are instructed to refrain from sharing personal data during conversations, which are subsequently processed by GPT-4. The data that the system stores is therefore anonymous. However, there is always a risk, since we use an external API and users may deviate from it and not follow the instructions. We have obtained approval from the Data Protection Officer at our university for this procedure. Additionally, when a customer reaches the point of making a purchase decision and their address is requested, the LLM is not utilized, ensuring that the data remains within the Saleshat environment. In this mode, no personal data is stored.

When interacting with Furhat, the latency of the LLM becomes particularly problematic. This is even more evident with lengthier responses that contain detailed information, such as specific product knowledge, causing the latency to go up quickly. This disrupts the natural flow of the conversation. Hence, we chose to leverage the LLM's capability to handle words in sequence and deliver the response in a continuous flow. This is feasible because GPT-4 consistently forecasts the following word based on the current context. This feature aligns well with [R1]. This feature operates, firstly, through the utilization of a prompt that mandates the responses to be formatted in an XML structure and, secondly, by concurrently streaming and assembling the answers in a separate thread. Among other things, the XML structure enables dynamic parsing, which we will explain further in the chapter on preprocessing. Streaming directly without distinct tags for a parser to identify creates a challenge in aligning tokens to words without any delay. The combination of suitable prompting and sequential parsing effectively resolves this issue. Once Saleshat has articulated the initial words, it accesses the remainder of the information that has been streamed and preprocessed in parallel. This process continues until the entire response has been processed. Therefore, the interaction handler works with the parsed data only. The parsed data is then either relayed to the Furhat platform or used to update the long-term memory by the interaction handler. The interaction handler also oversees concluding the sale. After a set number of interactions or after a certain amount of time has passed, the language model is specifically directed to end the conversation by injecting a different prompt message, addressing [R3].

**Current State.** A primary concern of Saleshat is making the current physical state of the robot available to the language model. The facial expressions portrayed on the Furhat are logged in the current state. Furhat has a sophisticated system that allows certain gestures to take precedence and maintains specific facial expressions over time. Thus, it becomes even more crucial to record the present events. It is essential to determine Furhat's current state, such as whether its eyes are shut, to ensure actions like winking are contextually appropriate [R3]. The information stored in the current state is then made available to the interaction handler.

**Preprocessing.** To process the instructions of the language model, our approach is rooted in the design guidelines provided by Evers and Chen [19]. In the prompt, skills the LLM can evoke are explicitly named, ensuring that their interpretation by the LLM is unambiguous. Furthermore, an XML structure is used. Given that GPT-4 produces responses in a tokenized sequence, our parser detects closing tags and can thus process complex nested structures. Upon their identification, the preprocessed data is continuously forwarded to the interaction handler.

**Knowledge Engine.** The long-term memory is used due to the limited context window. The long-term memory is updated frequently. While the knowledge base holds all product-specific details, the response database houses sample dialogues for the LLM's reference. Currently, only the long-term memory undergoes updates, whereas the knowledge base and response database remain static. This aligns with [R5]. However, there is a compelling case for dynamically adjusting the response database in the future, especially drawing from successful sales.

**Gestures and Facial Expressions.** Through the interaction handler integration, GPT-4 can directly access Furhat's several built-in facial expressions. Granting the language model complete authority over the displayed expressions, they can be customized entirely (e.g., the duration of a smile, its head tilts). By using a dynamic mapping mechanism for gestures and expressions, the outputs from the language model are aligned with Furhat's facial expressions, hand gestures, and other non-verbal cues to meet requirement [R2].

**Prompting.** We adhere to the prompting guidelines established by Evers and Chen [19]. We chose to place the prompt message before each user input instead of using the system message of GPT-4's API for the primary prompt due to alignment issues when the system message is utilized. However, the system message will continue to be used by Saleshat to conclude the sale and if a facial expression of the user has been detected.

The prompt establishes a comprehensive context by clarifying the situation and defining the objectives within the sales scenario. Through the prompt, the system becomes aware of its setting, grasping the core information and identifying the names of the existing products, which are dynamically assembled from the knowledge base. We are currently utilizing two Bluetooth speakers from two well-known brands. The positions where the products are situated from Saleshat's perspective are detailed, and an added description of the physical environment ensures it is aptly adapted to the given context. We clearly instructed GPT-4 not to utilize any information beyond the provided information, especially excluding pre-existing data from training sources. Otherwise, GPT-4 has, in our tests, offered discounts on its own and provided outdated information. We then proceed to delineate the anticipated response format, which includes the fundamental XML structure, and explain the available tags, which currently are "Words", "Gestures", and "CustomGesture". In the subsequent phase, the prompt specifies the potential content and prerequisites for each of these tags. As an illustration, an important guideline is the constraint of allowing only one sentence per "Words" tag in a response. The specifications for "Gestures" are comprehensively detailed, encompassing the available options and how they are presented by the Furhat robot. With the "CustomGesture" tag, the LLM can define its unique gestures and blend them with standard facial expressions while adjusting their duration as needed. The persona of Saleshat is explicitly defined, and the components of the system, including the Current State, the Long-Term Memory, the Knowledge Base, and the Response Database, are incorporated. The latter ensures that, in addition to zero-shot prompting, we also guide the LLM to excel in sales using sample dialogues via few-shot prompting. We then restate the task definition at the end of the prompt sequence, which has been shown to be advantageous in alignment. GPT-4 starts by composing the response and subsequently updates the long-term memory.

## 4    Evaluation

To test Saleshat in interactions with users and collect early-stage feedback on its ability to perform human-like sales conversations and its general usability, we conducted a formative evaluation with a convenience sample. In the evaluation, six participants were asked to have a (fictitious) sales conversation about Bluetooth speaker products with Saleshat. The participants were university staff, all between 20 and 30 years old and with different levels of experience with robots and LLMs. Participants were included based on their availability, without any exclusion criteria. However, the participants were not involved in this research project. The evaluation received ethics approval from the Institutional Review Board at Karlsruhe Institute of Technology.

In the evaluation, participants were seated across from Saleshat. The interaction began with a brief run-through of what to expect, followed by an introduction to the robot. Participants were specifically instructed when the answers can be processed and informed when Saleshat, would not be able to handle their responses, either because it was in the midst of speaking or processing the responses. After providing informed consent, participants were briefed that their role was to ask questions about the two available Bluetooth speakers (JBL and Ultimate Ears) and choose one from the two available options. Each conversation with Saleshat lasted around four minutes, ending when the participant made a product choice. To enhance the comparability of results, each conversation was designed to conclude automatically after seven minutes, culminating with the robot inquiring about the participant's product choice. All participants engaged with Saleshat to acquire information about various product features by asking questions and stating their preferences for features. An example question from a participant was: "Could you provide details regarding the battery life?" In response, Saleshat answered: "Certainly, the Ultimate Ears Megaboom 3 boasts a notable battery longevity of up to 20 h, facilitating uninterrupted enjoyment of one's preferred music throughout the day. Conversely, the JBL Charge 4 is equipped with a built-in rechargeable battery of 7500 mAh capacity, ensuring continuous music playback for an extended period. Additionally, it's worth mentioning that the JBL Charge 4 offers the ancillary benefit of charging other devices via USB, thereby ensuring devices remain operational." After the interaction with Saleshat, we conducted short, semi-structured interviews with all participants to assess their perception of the robot interaction and to identify possible areas of improvement. Overall, each evaluation took 20 min on average.

The interviews and sales conversations were recorded and transcribed. Similar to previous studies with formative evaluations (e.g., [9, 35]), we analyzed the data using a Strength-Weakness-Opportunity-Threat (SWOT) analysis. The results are shown in Table 1. The initial assessment revealed that despite its sophisticated hardware, Furhat encountered difficulties in processing speech in real-time with the ASR. For example, one participant pointed out, "For pauses in my speech that a human would recognize, the robot sometimes starts processing the answer even though I wasn't finished." Notably, the latency in processing and generating responses, although minimized by our approach of parallel processing, could still disrupt seamless conversations. Additionally, GPT-4, despite its prowess, occasionally produced misaligned responses. One participant noted that while "the robot was proficient in answering questions, sales conversations typically involve a more proactive approach from the seller. When I am not familiar with the product, I often find myself unsure about which questions to ask. In such situations, the robot could take a more proactive approach by initiating questions more frequently." Nonetheless, participants expressed a favorable opinion of Saleshat and highlighted its capacity for delivering detailed and accurate responses. One participant stated, "The robot has an impressive ability to humorously respond to my personal preferences." In one sales conversation, a participant expressed a desire to use the Bluetooth speaker at the beach. Saleshat consistently revisited this point in subsequent product-specific discussions. Additionally, participants appreciated Saleshat's capability to maintain a smooth and continuous conversation and highlighted its ability to dynamically adjust non-verbal cues. One participant observed that the robot's gestures corresponded with its verbal responses: "For example, the robot shook its head when it said no to something or nodded to say yes to things. The gestures matched what was said." These insights collectively underscored Saleshat's proficiency in replicating natural human conversations in real-world contexts.

## 5   Discussion

Despite the excitement and promises of LLMs such as GPT-4, there is a growing realization that integrating LLMs into existing hardware or software systems with clearly defined functionality and terminology is often more difficult than expected. Our research provides a first step in addressing this challenge by developing Saleshat, a novel artifact for facilitating human-like sales conversations with the social robot Furhat and GPT-4. Overall, the results of our formative evaluation suggest that users appreciate the immediate response, adaptive skills, and conversational prowess, highlighting Saleshat's potential to overcome the limitations of previous social robots designed for domain-specific conversations with clear goals (e.g., sales interactions) that entail a limited knowledge base [44] or have a processing latency [11]. In the following, we provide a summary of our principal findings and discuss the main contributions and limitations of our research.

### 5.1   Contributions and Implications

The primary contribution of this research is a method for integrating LLMs into social robots. While previous research has made the first attempts to integrate LLMs with a social robot (e.g., [11]), several challenges, including latency, remain that prevent LLMs from realizing their full potential in social robots. Our method addresses these challenges by providing five key requirements that are crucial for enhancing the conversational capabilities, responsiveness, and expressivity of social robots in retail settings. These requirements are informed by a design-centered framework [3], expert consultations, and existing literature and offer valuable insights for those working on the integration of LLMs with social robots. In addition, our artifact Saleshat, which we developed to fulfill these requirements, can serve as a source of inspiration for researchers and practitioners who work at the intersection of social robots and LLMs. In particular, our artifact demonstrates that the real-time streaming of responses from the language model enables simultaneous processing, yielding advantages in latency and minimizing unnatural silences, which ultimately helps to improve the design of social robots in retail settings.

**Table 1.** Results of the Formative Evaluation of Saleshat

| Strengths | – Accurate and Detailed Responses: Participants noted the robot's ability to provide accurate, detailed, and appropriate responses<br>– Good Conversation Flow: Participants appreciated the robot's reactivity and guidance throughout the conversation<br>– Non-verbal Cues: Participants appreciated the robot's non-verbal cues, such as nodding and eye movements |
|---|---|
| Weaknesses | – Lack of Personal Opinions: Responses lacked personal recommendations<br>– Pause Duration and Latency: Participants found it sometimes difficult to know when to respond due to long responses<br>– Difficulty in Understanding: Some participants found the male voice harder to understand compared to the female voice, and others were unsure how to articulate and pace their speech |
| Opportunities | – User Feedback and Applications: Incorporating user feedback, product reviews, and clearer communication instructions could enhance the user experience. Participants also suggested various potential applications for the robot and testing with different demographics, such as the elderly |
| Threats | – Preference for Human Interaction: Some participants indicated a preference for human salespersons and mentioned that familiarity with other voice assistants, such as Siri or Alexa, might affect their expectations and communication styles<br>– Technical Issues and Data Privacy: Participants noted that latency could disrupt the conversation and affect the user experience. There were also concerns about data privacy and data processing<br>– Miscommunication and Disruption of Conversation Flow: Participants noted that miscommunications could affect the conversation flow and the quality of the interaction |

## 5.2 Limitations and Future Work

Our research has some limitations which offer opportunities for future research. First, the study is focused specifically on Bluetooth speaker sales, which limits the generalizability of the findings to other (retail) contexts. However, we believe that most, if not all, our requirements and design knowledge can also be applied in other contexts (e.g., healthcare) where human-like conversations about a specific topic are needed and inappropriate responses could have serious consequences [20]. Nonetheless, further research should explore the application of our method in other contexts and domains to assess its versatility and applicability. Second, the small scale of the evaluation ($N = 6$) cannot provide a full assessment of Saleshat's performance across diverse scenarios and user groups.

In our future work, we plan to conduct a larger, controlled study with a more diverse group of participants and a broader range of products.

## 6   Conclusion

The Saleshat artifact, harnessing the power of GPT-4, aims to take social robot interactions in sales environments to the next level. Prioritizing conversational adaptability, we integrated an LLM for fluid, human-like engagements. Our architecture seamlessly processes auditory and visual data on the Furhat platform. The interaction handler stands pivotal, linking user inputs to knowledgeable responses, while dynamic gesture mapping breathes life into Furhat's interactions. As we progress with this project, we are striving to better merge technology and human-centric design, aiming to make meaningful advancements in social robot interactions.

## References

1. Nestlé to Use Humanoid Robot to Sell Nescafé in Japan (2014). https://www.nestle.com/media/news/nestle-humanoid-robot-nescafe-japan
2. Al Moubayed, S., et al.: Furhat: a back-projected human-like robot head for multiparty human-machine interaction. In: Esposito, A., et al. (eds.) Cognitive Behavioural Systems, vol. 7403, pp. 114–130. Springer, Heidelberg (2012). https://doi.org/10.1007/978-3-642-34584-5_9
3. Bartneck, C., Forlizzi, J.: A design-centred framework for social human-robot interaction. In: RO-MAN 2004. 13th IEEE International Workshop on Robot and Human Interactive Communication (IEEE Catalog No.04TH8759), pp. 591–594. IEEE (2004). https://doi.org/10.1109/ROMAN.2004.1374827
4. Breazeal, C.: Toward sociable robots. Robot. Autonom. Syst. **42**(3–4), 167–175 (2003). https://doi.org/10.1016/S0921-8890(02)00373-1
5. Breazeal, C., Scassellati, B.: A context-dependent attention system for a social robot. In: IJCAI International Joint Conference on Artificial Intelligence, vol. 2 (1999)
6. Brengman, M., De Gauquier, L., Willems, K., Vanderborght, B.: From stopping to shopping: an observational study comparing a humanoid service robot with a tablet service kiosk to attract and convert shoppers. J. Bus. Res. **134**, 263–274 (2021). https://doi.org/10.1016/j.jbusres.2021.05.025
7. Brown, T.B., et al.: Language models are few-shot learners. arXiv preprint arXiv:2005.14165 (2020). https://doi.org/10.48550/ARXIV.2005.14165
8. Bulmer, S., Elms, J., Moore, S.: Exploring the adoption of self-service checkouts and the associated social obligations of shopping practices. J. Retail. Consum. Serv. **42**, 107–116 (2018)
9. Cameron, G., et al.: Best practices for designing chatbots in mental healthcare - a case study on iHelpr (2018). https://doi.org/10.14236/ewic/HCI2018.129
10. Castelo, N., et al.: Task-dependent algorithm aversion. J. Market. Res. **56**, 809–825 (2019). https://doi.org/10.1177/0022243719851788
11. Cherakara, N., et al.: FurChat: an embodied conversational agent using LLMs. arXiv preprint arXiv:2308.15214 (2023)

12. Choi, S., Mattila, A.S., Bolton, L.E.: To err is human(-oid): how do consumers react to robot service failure and recovery? J. Serv. Res. **24**(3), 354–371 (2021). https://doi.org/10.1177/1094670520978798

13. Chowdhery, A., et al.: PaLM: scaling language modeling with pathways. arXiv preprint arXiv:2204.02311 (2022).

14. Christiano, P.F., Leike, J., Brown, T., Martic, M., Legg, S., Amodei, D.: Deep reinforcement learning from human preferences. In: Guyon, I., et al. (eds.) Advances in Neural Information Processing Systems, vol. 30. Curran Associates, Inc. (2017). https://proceedings.neurips.cc/paper_files/paper/2017/file/d5e2c0adad503c91f91df240d0cd4e49-Paper.pdf

15. Chuah, S.H.W., Yu, J.: The future of service: the power of emotion in human-robot interaction. J. Retail. Consum. Serv. **61**, 102551 (2021). https://doi.org/10.1016/j.jretconser.2021.102551

16. Devlin, J., Chang, M.W., Lee, K., Toutanova, K.: BERT: pre-training of deep bidirectional transformers for language understanding. In: Burstein, J., Doran, C., Solorio, T. (eds.) Proceedings of the 2019 Conference of the North American Chapter of the Association for Computational Linguistics: Human Language Technologies, vol. 1 (Long and Short Papers), pp. 4171–4186. Association for Computational Linguistics (2019). https://doi.org/10.18653/v1/N19-1423

17. Dietvorst, Berkeley J.., Simmons, Joseph P.., Massey, Cade: Overcoming Algorithm Aversion: People Will Use Imperfect Algorithms If They Can (Even Slightly) Modify Them. Management Science **64**(3), 1155–1170 (2018). https://doi.org/10.1287/mnsc.2016.2643

18. Driess, D., et al.: PaLM-e: an embodied multimodal language model. arXiv preprint arXiv:2303.03378 (2023)

19. Evers, K., Chen, S.: Effects of an automatic speech recognition system with peer feedback on pronunciation instruction for adults. Comput. Assist. Lang. Learn. **35**, 1869–1889 (2022). https://doi.org/10.1080/09588221.2020.1839504

20. Gilbert, S., Harvey, H., Melvin, T., Vollebregt, E., Wicks, P.: Large language model AI chatbots require approval as medical devices. Nat. Med. **29**(10), 2396–2398 (2023). https://doi.org/10.1038/s41591-023-02412-6

21. Henschel, A., Laban, G., Cross, E.S.: What makes a robot social? a review of social robots from science fiction to a home or hospital near you. Curr. Robot. Rep. **2**(1), 9–19 (2021). https://doi.org/10.1007/s43154-020-00035-0

22. Holthaus, P., Wachsmuth, S.: It was a pleasure meeting you: towards a holistic model of human-robot encounters. Int. J. Soc. Robot. **13**, 1729–1745 (2021). https://doi.org/10.1007/s12369-021-00759-9

23. Ji, Z., et al.: Survey of hallucination in natural language generation. ACM Comput. Surv. **55**, 1–38 (2023). https://doi.org/10.1145/3571730

24. Kaplan, J., et al.: Scaling laws for neural language models. arXiv preprint arXiv:2001.08361 (2020). https://doi.org/10.48550/ARXIV.2001.08361

25. Lim, M.Y., et al.: Demonstration of a robo-barista for in the wild interactions (2022). https://doi.org/10.1109/HRI53351.2022.9889443

26. Lu, L., Zhang, P., Zhang, T.C.: Leveraging "human-likeness" of robotic service at restaurants. Int. J. Hosp. Manag. **94**, 102823 (2021). https://doi.org/10.1016/j.ijhm.2020.102823

27. Mende, M.A., Fischer, M.H., Kühne, K.: The use of social robots and the uncanny valley phenomenon. In: Zhou, Y., Fischer, M.H. (eds.) AI Love You, pp. 41–73. Springer, Cham (2019). https://doi.org/10.1007/978-3-030-19734-6_3

28. Niemelä, M., Heikkilä, P., Lammi, H., Oksman, V.: A social robot in a shopping mall: studies on acceptance and stakeholder expectations. In: Korn, O. (ed.) Social Robots: Technological, Societal and Ethical Aspects of Human-Robot Interaction, pp. 119–144. Springer, Cham (2019). https://doi.org/10.1007/978-3-030-17107-0_7
29. OpenAI: Gpt-4 Technical Report (2023)
30. Pandey, A.K., Gelin, R.: A mass-produced sociable humanoid robot: pepper: the first machine of its kind. IEEE Robot. Automat. Magaz. **25**(3), 40–48 (2018). https://doi.org/10.1109/MRA.2018.2833157
31. Qin, C., Zhang, A., Zhang, Z., Chen, J., Yasunaga, M., Yang, D.: Is chatGPT a general-purpose natural language processing task solver? In: The 2023 Conference on Empirical Methods in Natural Language Processing (2023). https://openreview.net/forum?id=u03xn1COsO
32. Radford, A., Wu, J., Child, R., Luan, D., Amodei, D., Sutskever, I.: Language models are unsupervised multitask learners (2019). https://api.semanticscholar.org/CorpusID:160025533
33. Reich, T., et al.: How to overcome algorithm aversion: learning from mistakes. J. Consum. Psychol. **33** (2023). https://doi.org/10.1002/jcpy.1313
34. Rindfleisch, A., Fukawa, N., Onzo, N.: Robots in retail: rolling out the whiz. AMS Rev. **12**(3), 238–244 (2022). https://doi.org/10.1007/s13162-022-00240-4
35. Ruoff, M., Gnewuch, U.: Designing multimodal bi&a systems for co-located team interactions (2021)
36. Shanahan, M.: Talking about large language models. arXiv preprint arXiv:2212.03551v5 (2022). https://doi.org/10.48550/ARXIV.2212.03551. Publisher: arXiv Version Number: 5
37. Stark, C., et al.: Dobby: a conversational service robot driven by GPT-4. arXiv preprint arXiv:2310.06303v1 (2023). https://doi.org/10.48550/ARXIV.2310.06303
38. Stock, R.M., Merkle, M.: A service robot acceptance model: User acceptance of humanoid robots during service encounters. In: 2017 IEEE International Conference on Pervasive Computing and Communications Workshops (PerCom Workshops), pp. 339–344. IEEE (2017). https://doi.org/10.1109/PERCOMW.2017.7917585
39. Turner, J.J., Szymkowiak, A.: An analysis into early customer experiences of self-service checkouts: lessons for improved usability. Eng. Manag. Prod. Serv. **11**(1), 36–50 (2019)
40. Van Pinxteren, M.M., Wetzels, R.W., Rüger, J., Pluymaekers, M., Wetzels, M.: Trust in humanoid robots: implications for services marketing. J. Serv. Market. **33**(4), 507–518 (2019). https://doi.org/10.1108/JSM-01-2018-0045
41. Vaswani, A., et al.: Attention is all you need (2017)
42. Wang, Y.J., Zhang, B., Chen, J., Sreenath, K.: Prompt a robot to walk with large language models. arXiv preprint arXiv:2309.09969 (2023)
43. Wei, J., et al.: Emergent abilities of large language models. arXiv preprint arXiv:2206.07682 (2022)
44. Wilcock, G.: Generating more intelligent responses and explanations with conversational AI and knowledge graphs. In: The 36th Annual Conference of the Japanese Society for Artificial Intelligence (2022)
45. Zhong, Q., Ding, L., Liu, J., Du, B., Tao, D.: Can ChatGPT understand too? a comparative study on ChatGPT and fine-tuned BERT. arXiv preprint arXiv:2302.10198v2 (2023)

# Leveraging Large Language Models as Simulated Users for Initial, Low-Cost Evaluations of Designed Conversations

Jan de Wit[✉][ID]

Department of Communication and Cognition, Tilburg University, Warandelaan 2,
5037 AB Tilburg, The Netherlands
j.m.s.dewit@tilburguniversity.edu

**Abstract.** In this paper, we explore the use of large language models, in this case the ChatGPT API, as simulated users to evaluate designed, rule-based conversations. This type of evaluation can be introduced as a low-cost method to identify common usability issues prior to testing conversational agents with actual users. Preliminary findings show that ChatGPT is good at playing the part of a user, providing realistic testing scenarios for designed conversations even if these involve certain background knowledge or context. GPT-4 shows vast improvements over ChatGPT (3.5). In future work, it is important to evaluate the performance of simulated users in a more structured, generalizable manner, for example by comparing their behavior to that of actual users. In addition, ways to fine-tune the LLM could be explored to improve its performance, and the output of simulated conversations could be analyzed to automatically derive usability metrics such as the number of turns needed to reach the goal. Finally, the use of simulated users with open-ended conversational agents could be explored, where the LLM may also be able to reflect on the user experience of the conversation.

**Keywords:** Conversational agents · Large language models · Automatic evaluation

## 1 Introduction

In order to design conversational agents that provide a positive and engaging user experience, it is important to adopt a human-centered, iterative approach [10,30,54,60]. This includes frequent evaluations with the intended end users, both during the agents' development and after they have been deployed [10,14,37]. It can however be costly, time-consuming and challenging to continuously involve these users throughout the design process [3,24,36,45]. Conducting evaluations with people other than the intended users is suboptimal, because these people might subconsciously adapt their responses to the agent based on their knowledge of the agent's capabilities and limitations [63]. Furthermore, they are likely not engaging with the agent from a realistic context of use [13,22,45]. Therefore, in this paper we explore the use of *simulated users* as a low-cost way to evaluate designed conversations.

A. Følstad et al. (Eds.): CONVERSATIONS 2023, LNCS 14524, pp. 77–93, 2024.
https://doi.org/10.1007/978-3-031-54975-5_5

A simulated user is a separate artificial agent that can interact with the designed conversational agent, pretending to be a real user [45]. It requires similar features to the designed agent that it is supposed to interact with: The simulated user needs to understand the agent, and generate its responses based on the goal that it wants to achieve. While the goal of the designed agent could be to guide its users through a travel booking process as efficiently as possible, the goal of the simulated user could be to use the agent to book a trip to Norway for November 22–23, including travel and stay. Traditionally these simulated users had to be scripted by hand [8] or trained on a collection of transcripts collected from people interacting with agents [56]. Large language models (LLMs) such as ChatGPT can engage in these interactions with few to no examples of how a human would approach the conversation [33,34].

Recently a large number of tools have emerged that can help researchers and practitioners design and deploy conversational agents, without requiring any technical expertise [54,65]. These tools generally feature a drag-and-drop interface, where a conversation can be constructed in a format that resembles a flowchart, with several branching paths. The availability of easy-to-use tools can be considered a positive development, because it enables a more diverse team to work with this technology. At the same time, practitioners have voiced concerns related to this democratization of conversation design tools. Providing people who are not experts on conversation design (e.g., end-users or engineers) with access to these tools may lead to subpar experiences, especially if there are no standards or best practices that can be followed [21,54]. This could perhaps be likened to mobile app development, where there has been a surge in low quality (health) apps that are not evidence-based or validated [2]. Enabling quick and easy evaluations within the conversation design tools may play a small part in addressing these concerns, as they could identify some initial issues with the conversation or the effects on the user.

## 2   Related Work

### 2.1   Evaluating Conversational Agents

Allouch et al. [3] distinguish between three approaches to evaluate conversational agents: (1) evaluation methods involving human participants, (2) machine evaluation methods that focus on the linguistic output of the agent, and (3) machine learning approaches that use datasets of human evaluations of prior interactions to estimate the performance of the current agent. In addition, there are inspection methods [50,63] where people, oftentimes the designers or expert evaluators, critically go through the interaction. This can be done by putting onself in a fictional user's (persona's) shoes and running through certain predefined scenarios, by examining the conversational agent using a set of heuristics or guidelines [32,35,48,53,57,58], or by conducting conversational analysis on the resulting conversation [14,58]. To get a comprehensive overview of a conversational agent's performance, it is important to triangulate the results of these different evaluation approaches [21,45,64].

User studies that involve human participants are needed to study user experience, a complex concept that consists of many factors such as trust and enjoyment [7,18,21,27]. Usability studies form an additional key evaluation tool, where a user interacts with the agent and is observed by the researchers to identify any breakdowns in the communication [28], or to measure the performance of a task-oriented agent (e.g., the number of turns that are needed to reach the user's goal) [22,45]. ProtoChat [11] supports rapid evaluations with crowd workers from within the design interface, lowering the threshold to integrate frequent testing into a conversation design process. In addition, Google Analytics-style approaches have emerged to assess usability on a large scale, for agents that are running in production[1].

The second category of evaluation approaches consists of automatic conversational analysis, using metrics such as BLEU [52] or ROUGE [40] scores. These are metrics commonly used in natural language generation (NLG), and they compare the output of an NLG system with a human-produced ground truth. This makes them less suitable for the more deterministic, pre-scripted interactions that are commonly found in conversational agents, because in dialogue settings there is often not one ground truth response, but rather a range of valid responses [3,24,41]. What constitutes a valid response may be best determined by the user, or estimated by applying certain heuristics such as the Gricean maxims [14,58]. In the broader NLG field, it has also been observed that these automated metrics do not correlate strongly with human evaluations of generated texts, and therefore should be interpreted with care and combined with human evaluation approaches [36].

Finally, several evaluation methods rely on datasets of previous conversations between people and conversational agents, in order to extrapolate an evaluation of the current interaction [3]. These methods attempt to address the limitations of machine evaluation metrics, while avoiding the costs and effort involved with human evaluations of the agent's output. Compared to our envisioned simulated user, these machine learning approaches do not engage in a conversation with the designed agent, but rather simulate how a person would likely evaluate the individual utterances produced by the agent, for example regarding their appropriateness or relevance, by extrapolating a set of previous human assessments of the conversational agent or similar ones [26,44,59].

## 2.2  Simulated Users

Simulated users are scripts, algorithms or intelligent agents that interact with designed conversational agents, fulfilling the role of a hypothetical user [45]. They can be used as a cost-effective way to evaluate and improve dialogue systems throughout the design process. Several of these automated systems are deterministic and follow predefined scripts that have to be written by the designers [8,9,20,47,61], ideally based on the results of earlier user tests [61]. Other implementations of simulated users are trained on previously collected

---

[1] See, for example, Botanalytics (https://botanalytics.co).

datasets of conversations between people and the conversational agent, which are then generalized to new dialogue situations. These follow a probabilistic approach, taking into account contextual information such as the dialogue history and the (hypothetical) user's intentions, goals, and background knowledge [1,19,31,38,56].

Although they are by no means a replacement for evaluations with human participants, an advantage of simulated users is that the insights gained from the numerous simulations that can easily be ran can be used as input for optimizing the agent's dialogue management via reinforcement learning [19,56]. Additionally, different versions of a conversation, for example in the context of a scientific experiment, could be compared with the same, consistent user before actually running the study with human participants [19].

With the emergence of LLMs such as ChatGPT, it may be possible to evaluate designed conversations with very few to no example dialogues required for training [34]. Horton refers to LLMs as 'computational models of humans' that 'likely possess a great deal of latent social information' [29, p. 2]. With such a broad extent of information embedded in these models, there might be potential in leveraging them as simulated users that can readily engage in both task-oriented and open-ended conversations. Although LLMs have been used to improve intent recognition and dialogue management [39,42,46], it appears that their potential use as simulated users for evaluating designed conversations has been underexplored so far.

Some traditional methods of user simulation incorporate different personas, varying for example the degree of patience the simulated user has with the agent, or how extensive it is in its messages [1,19]. This can likely also be done with LLM-powered simulated users, turning them into users with specific needs or communication styles, interacting with the conversational agent from a specific sociodemographic perspective [4,25,33,51]. This variety in user types might help to avoid overfitting the conversational agent's design to one specific (simulated) user type [43]. There have also been cases where an LLM portrayed a persona that used toxic language [17], which could allow conversation designers to test what happens if an ill-intentioned or otherwise 'extreme' user were to use the agent [5].

### 2.3   Tilbot and Prompt Engineering

Tilbot [65] is an open source drag-and-drop tool for designing conversational agents (Fig. 1). A rule-based dialogue flow can be created by adding and connecting blocks, each signifying one turn by the conversational agent and one response by the user (also shown in Fig. 1). Input from the user, which can be either free text, or multiple choice by pressing a button, determines which path is followed through this flow. Intent recognition is currently done by simple literal keyword matching.

Triggers (Fig. 1, bottom left) can be activated by the user at any time, and take the conversation out of its predetermined flow, allowing a more flexible path through the dialogue. Tilbot can also store variables and check the user's input against datasets, which is demonstrated in an implementation of the *Guess who?* game[2], which was used as one of the two case studies in the present research.

The latest version available on Github at the time of writing[3] includes a simulated user, where all messages produced by the designed conversational agent get sent to the ChatGPT Application Programming Interface (API), and ChatGPT is prompted to act as a user of the designed agent. Tilbot includes a settings window where the temperature (amount of 'randomness') of ChatGPT can be set, and the prompt to get ChatGPT to role play as a user can be adjusted. The default prompt to get ChatGPT to act as a user is based on several design patterns by White et al. [62]. The prompt, with the patterns annotated **in bold** (not included in the actual prompt), is as follows:

> [**Persona**] Act as a user of my chatbot. I will send you the output from the chatbot and then I would like you to [**Flipped interaction**] provide responses [**Persona**] that a user would create. [**Flipped interaction**] You should keep talking to the chatbot until you feel like you have reached your goal, or feel like the conversation is not progressing anymore.
>
> [**Template**] Whenever my messages contain curly brackets {}, the phrases between the curly brackets are the options for your output, separated by a semicolon. In this case, you can *only* reply with one of these options, no other text. For example, if my message contains Yes; No, you can only

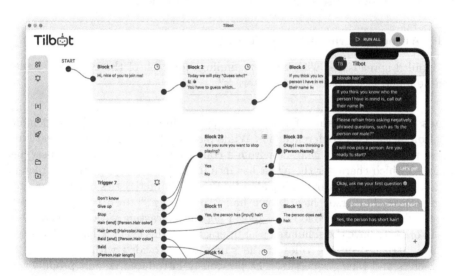

**Fig. 1.** Overview of the Tilbot design environment, with the *Guess who?* case study project opened, and the project simulator (right hand side) running the ChatGPT-powered simulated user. (Color figure online)

---

[2] https://github.com/tilbotio/guesswho.
[3] https://github.com/tilbotio/tilbot-main.

reply with either Yes or No. Do not add any other words. You cannot provide answer options with curly brackets for the chatbot.

This was the basic prompt, to which further details could be added, for example to make the simulated user behave as a specific persona, to have a particular goal or scenario in mind as it interacts with the designed agent, or to pass variables or datasets to the simulated user. The template with the curly brackets was added to force ChatGPT to choose between provided answer options in case the user received a multiple choice input rather than open text[4]. Together with this prompt, the message history between the designed agent and the simulated user was sent to the ChatGPT API to make it generate responses. These responses were then shown in the Tilbot simulator (Fig. 1, yellow text bubbles).

## 3    Preliminary Evaluations

To explore if testing with simulated users based on ChatGPT results in quality improvements of designed conversations, two initial small-scale evaluations were conducted. The first is an autoethnographic study where the author, being a prototypical user of this feature of Tilbot, applied the simulated user to two case studies[5]. The second is an exploratory study where three researchers were provided with the Tilbot software with the simulated user feature, and the project files from the same case studies used for the autoethnography.

### 3.1    Autoethnographic Case Studies

A detailed spreadsheet with concrete findings for each of the two case studies can be found as supplementary materials[6].

**Guess Who?** The game of *Guess who?* was included with the Tilbot demonstration at the CUI conference [65]. While playing the game, the conversational agent randomly picks a character from a collection of 24, and then the user has to guess which character the agent has in mind. The list of potential characters can be narrowed down by asking about different characteristics of the character (e.g., "Does the person have brown hair?" or simply "brown hair?"). Figure 2 shows what the interface looks like for a person interacting with the agent.

In order to have the simulated user interact with this agent, ChatGPT needed to be instructed on the rules of the game, and provided with the list of 24 characters and their properties. The previously introduced default prompt was therefore extended with the following (cf. [62]):

---

[4] GPT-4 appears to be much better than GPT-3.5 at following multiple choice instructions: It chooses an answer option and returns only that answer option. GPT-3.5 sometimes adds text, or rephrases the answer option.

[5] For a discussion of the value of this type of autoethnographic work, please see [49].

[6] https://osf.io/8p4zn/.

**[Persona]** As a user, **[Game play]** you will play a game of Guess Who with the chatbot. The chatbot will randomly select one of the people from the list below. **[Persona]** As a user, **[Game play]** you can ask questions that the chatbot can answer with 'yes' or 'no', to narrow down the list of people. Please consider what you already know about the person, and use that to narrow down the list. If you think you know which person the chatbot has in mind, guess the person by mentioning their name.

Here is an overview of the people included in the game:
[People]

Here, [People] was replaced by Tilbot with the same dataset containing all 24 characters and their properties that the agent used. While fine-tuning this prompt, it appeared that the behavior of the simulated user can be steered somewhat, for example by including the part of asking it to consider what it already knows about the person: This seems to stimulate ChatGPT to summarize what it has learned, or to provide a list of names of candidates that it is still considering. A pattern that appears to emerge from this evaluation is that the simulated user illustrates some issues mainly related to intent recognition, where as a designer you might subconsciously expect real users to nicely follow the rules (e.g., to only ask about one thing at a time, and to only guess one name) but the simulated user does not always comply. The simulated user, especially with a

**Fig. 2.** The *Guess who?* game as a human player would see it, with the different characters on the left hand side, and the interaction with the agent on the right hand side. Both the designed agent and the simulated user had access to a dataset that contained these characters and their characteristics (e.g., hair color).

higher temperature setting, is relatively elaborate in its messages and therefore puts the intent recognition to the test.

An important caveat that emerged from this particular case study is that ChatGPT (3.5) is not good at handling data. While it did refer only to people that actually existed in the set of 24, it consistently mixed up their properties and was unable to filter the data in such a way that it could identify the correct answer. For example, knowing that the mystery person was male it would still guess female characters, or it would forget that certain characters were wearing glasses. GPT-4 shows major improvements at this, and generally manages to play and beat the game.

**Medication Reconciliation.** This conversation was designed in collaboration with a local hospital, with the aim to have patients report on their medication use when being admitted to hospital (Fig. 3). In this case, it would be especially beneficial to identify usability issues because it can be challenging to recruit actual patients on a regular basis. For this project, the default prompt was translated into Dutch and we only made a minor addition (translated to English here, but originally in Dutch) because the simulated user would otherwise default to using the same one medicine (Paracetamol):

[**Persona**] You're using three different medicines.

In this scenario, the simulated user was surprisingly capable at coming up with three medicines, and reporting (most of the time) realistic properties and behaviors related to these medicines, e.g., in terms of dosage and frequency of taking them. At times ChatGPT broke out of its role of simulated user and actually started giving advice to the agent, but this appeared to be fixed by prompting ChatGPT to be a low health literate user, or by upgrading to GPT-4. The simulated user can also be prompted to ask about side effects or potential negative interactions between the medicines the user is taking, which again GPT-4 does more reliably than ChatGPT (3.5). However, if these questions are asked they are completely ignored by our agent, as it just proceeds to the next medicine. As with the other case study, the input from the simulated user was elaborate and this highlighted a number of issues with the way information is gathered from the user. Where short keywords (e.g., medicine name) were expected, the simulated user would make full sentences, and the agent could not extract the relevant information. Comments regarding the limited degree of intelligence and social support have also emerged from the various user studies we have conducted with this agent, and so they are valid points to consider for next iterations of our chatbot.

### 3.2 Small-Scale Evaluation

**Materials and Procedure.** The small-scale evaluation was implemented by creating a Qualtrics survey, where participants were first provided with information about the study, and requested to give informed consent. After this,

**Fig. 3.** The medication reconciliation interaction has a table on the left hand side containing all of the medication information of the user, which is filled dynamically as the user answers the agent's questions. Users can press the edit button on any line of the table to make changes to a previously entered medicine. The simulated user did not 'see' this table, and therefore the editing of previously entered information was not included in the testing. Actual users, contrary to the simulated one, are also able to scan a medicine's bar code to enter it into the system.

they were presented with a link to a shared drive containing the Tilbot software (Windows and OS X), two project files for the two case studies previously discussed, and a manual with a step-by-step guide on how to download and run Tilbot, open one of the project files, and start the simulated user. Participants were asked to try out the simulated user and the project files for as long as they wanted.

After doing so, the participants went back to the survey and filled out a short questionnaire consisting of the perceived usefulness and ease of use factors of the Technology Acceptance Model (TAM; [15]), measured on a five-point Likert scale. This was followed by a question asking whether or not they would want to use the simulated user more often (yes/no), with the option to explain in free text why (not). If they would want to use it more often, they were asked to explain when they would want to do so (e.g., which stage of the design process). They were also asked if they would recommend using the simulated user to a colleague or (fellow) student, again with the option to explain why (not). Finally, there was a free text input to leave any additional comments regarding the simulated user or the Tilbot platform. The participants spent 12 and 57 min in the survey (one participant not included as they spent over 24 h, likely leaving the survey open without actively engaging with it).

**Participants.** Three conversational agent researchers participated in the study. They had all seen or worked with Tilbot and one or both of the case studies. A fourth participant started the survey but could not finish, reporting that it was hard for them to answer the questions about perceived usefulness and willingness to use, because they did not actually design the conversations that were used in this evaluation. This is a fair point, which is important to keep in mind when interpreting the results.

Participants were asked about their experience programming conversational agents relative to other conversation designers they know, and their experience in conversation design, both on a five-point scale ranging from 'no experience' to 'a lot of experience'. For programming experience, one participant reported having quite a lot of experience (score 4/5), one reported having reasonably little experience (score 3/5), and one had no experience (score 1/5). As for conversation design experience, one reported having a lot of experience (score 5/5), one had quite a lot of experience (score 4/5), and one had little experience (score 2/5).

**Results.** The simulated user on average scored a 4.06 out of 5 on perceived usefulness (range 3.83–4.33) and a 4.2 out of 5 on perceived ease of use (range 3.8–4.4). All three participants would use the simulated user again, mentioning speed, scale, and flexibility (e.g., running different scenarios) as the main reasons for continuing to use the tool. Speed was not only referred to as the speed at which one could start a testing session, but also the speed at which the simulation would type its messages compared to how long a human participant in an evaluation study would take. It was seen as a useful quick test to check if the designed conversation was clear, that could be used while in the process of designing.

The participants would generally want to use the simulated user throughout the design process, although this depends on the costs involved. One participant suggested that ChatGPT could also help think along with refining the dialogue flow or suggest how to handle errors, indicating that it might be useful to also be able to draw it out of its user persona and into a co-designer. Another participant indicated that, especially in the medication reconciliation case, domain experts would likely still be needed to refine the dialogue flow and ensure that patients will understand the agent's questions. ChatGPT was expected to be too smart of a user in this case, resolving some of the ambiguities that some patients may not be able to handle. This participant also indicated that the medication reconciliation conversation at this point is still rather superficial, but once the complexity of the dialogue increases it could be more useful to run extensive tests with the simulated user, to be able to cover a wide range of scenarios with little time investment. The participant suggested that it is more practical to have ChatGPT take on the role of a patient than doing so yourself, likely alluding to the 'expert blind spot' when (domain or conversation design) experts evaluate their designs themselves.

All three participants would also recommend the simulated user to their colleagues and (fellow) students. Reasons for this were the ease of use of the implementation, and how it can facilitate the design and testing of conversational agents. As additional comments, one participant noted that the simulated user behaved differently than a real user would. This was specifically observed in the *Guess who?* case, where the simulated user would first ask if the character was male and, if not, would then ask if it was female (with those being the only two options in the current implementation). It also starts guessing the name relatively early on, while a real user would likely try to narrow it down more. Another participant found a bug where the simulated user started sending two messages at once.

## 4    Discussion and Conclusion

This paper documents initial explorations of using a large language model as a simulated user to test designed, rule-based conversations. Insights from an autoethnographic account by the author were combined with a small-scale evaluation study involving three fellow conversation designers, in order to get a comprehensive overview of the potential benefits and drawbacks of incorporating these simulated users into the conversation design process. The two case studies that were used in both research approaches were interesting for testing the capabilities of ChatGPT as simulated user, because they involved a relatively complex, gameful interaction and domain-specific medical information.

Several concrete issues and points of improvement were found thanks to the simulated user. The majority of them relate to the design of the dialogue or the technical workings of the Tilbot platform, and likely would have also come up when evaluating the conversational agents with actual users. The simulated user appears to be especially good at testing intent recognition by coming up with out-of-perimeter utterances [14], or formulating lengthy sentences where we were expecting concise information. The participants in the small-scale evaluation study agreed that it should be considered a welcome addition in the conversation designer's toolbox, although by no means a replacement of human evaluation studies. 'Discount' methods such as these should never form the entire evaluation approach, and their results should be handled with care [12].

Overall, the output of the simulated user was realistic enough for it to be useful as a cheap and quick method to evaluate the flow and comprehensibility of a designed interaction. The tendency for models such as ChatGPT to 'hallucinate' could actually be considered a useful feature in this context. This allowed it, for example, to convey a realistic list of medicines including aspects such as their dosages and frequency of use. As conversation designers, we might find ourselves reusing the same example data during our preliminary evaluations, which might unintentionally circumvent some issues that the simulated user, while hallucinating realistic content, could help to identify. It is this 'latent social information' embedded in LLMs that Horton referred to [29], that can likely help to generate a large variety of ways in which a conversation can unfold, capturing the conversational needs and styles of a broad range of potential users. This 'broadness' could perhaps also become a disadvantage due to the lack of control over the LLM's output compared to probabilistic simulated users that are trained on previous conversations between people and the conversational agents. A potential middle ground could be to not only prompt the LLM, but to also fine-tune it using data from previous interactions or other forms of prior knowledge to tailor it more specifically to a particular use case or persona.

Although the messages sent by ChatGPT in its role of a fictional user appear to be accurate and coherent, it is challenging to fully model human behavior and cognition [23]. This also became apparent when ChatGPT failed to correctly play the game of *Guess who?*, although GPT-4 was able to perform much better at this. When provided with a dataset, the simulated user knows what it can and cannot ask about (i.e., the columns of the dataset in *Guess who?* were possible characteristics to inform about). Discrepancies between what the simulated user produces and what an actual user would may remain a challenge. Furthermore, it is important to mention that LLMs such as ChatGPT are known to contain various biases [6], and it is likely that the simulated users interact with the designed agents from a specific, mainly Western-oriented context [16,33,55]. By only basing design decisions on the results of evaluations with the simulated user, these biases may end up in the designed conversations as well. As such, evaluation studies with human participants remain crucial to maintaining fair and high quality conversational agents.

It is important to note that the current paper presents initial explorations of the possibility to use an LLM as simulated user, limited to an autoethnographic account and a small-scale evaluation study. This leaves many avenues for future work, including a more thorough evaluation of the quality and realism of the messages generated by the simulated user, scaling up by running and automatically analyzing a large number of conversations, fine-tuning of the LLM, exploring different settings (e.g., temperature), prompts, and personas (e.g., a 'malicious' one that tries to break the interaction), and investigating if the same simulated user can also have repeated interactions over time, where the designed agent remembers the user and personalizes the conversation accordingly. Finally, future work could explore if ChatGPT can also be prompted to reflect on the interaction it just had, to obtain an estimate of the perceived user experience and to propose improvements, as suggested by one of the participants in the present study. The LLM could, for example, fill in a usability or user experience questionnaire related to the conversation. One technical barrier for this is the limited number of tokens that the ChatGPT API accepts, which might impede sending lengthy conversations verbatim. However, the conversation could be segmented and then analyzed by ChatGPT in steps, or it could work with a summary.

The current case studies were both task-oriented agents, but the simulated user would likely also be helpful in evaluating open-ended conversations, especially if it can reflect on those conversations afterward. It would also be interesting to have the LLM-powered simulated user interact with an LLM-powered conversational agent, to be able to easily generate a large number of examples of how these conversations would play out.

In conclusion, this paper showcases several first explorations of using a large language model, specifically ChatGPT (GPT-3.5 and brief explorations of GPT-4), to simulate a user of a rule-based conversational agent. This low-cost approach can be used to identify inefficiencies or breakdowns in communication with the agent, that might otherwise stand in the way of evaluations with human participants. However, because of the remaining deficiencies in fully modeling human behavior and cognition, and the biases inherent to LLMs, it remains important to keep evaluating with actual users. More generalizable insights are needed to draw firm conclusions, yet there is now a first overview of what this evaluation approach can and cannot provide for researchers. This will hopefully inspire others to experiment with, and improve upon the method.

**Acknowledgments.** I am sincerely grateful to Serkan Girgin (University of Twente) for helping to sprout the idea for this exploration, the eScience Center for their continuous support with developing Tilbot, and the funded WeCare project with the Elisabeth-TweeSteden hospital and the Heracleum Fund for supporting our studies into the use of conversational agents in medical practice. Finally, I greatly appreciate the reviewers' suggestions based on the initial version of this paper, and the valuable questions and suggestions from CONVERSATIONS workshop attendees.

# References

1. Afzali, J., Drzewiecki, A.M., Balog, K., Zhang, S.: UserSimCRS: a user simulation toolkit for evaluating conversational recommender systems. In: Proceedings of the Sixteenth ACM International Conference on Web Search and Data Mining (WSDM 2023), pp. 1160–1163. Association for Computing Machinery, New York (2023). https://doi.org/10.1145/3539597.3573029
2. Akbar, S., Coiera, E., Magrabi, F.: Safety concerns with consumer-facing mobile health applications and their consequences: a scoping review. J. Am. Med. Inform. Assoc. **27**(2), 330–340 (2019). https://doi.org/10.1093/jamia/ocz175
3. Allouch, M., Azaria, A., Azoulay, R.: Conversational agents: goals, technologies, vision and challenges. Sensors **21**(24), 8448 (2021). https://doi.org/10.3390/s21248448
4. Argyle, L.P., Busby, E.C., Fulda, N., Gubler, J.R., Rytting, C., Wingate, D.: Out of one, many: using language models to simulate human samples. Polit. Anal. **31**(3), 337–351 (2023). https://doi.org/10.1017/pan.2023.2
5. Bell, G., Blythe, M., Sengers, P.: Making by making strange: defamiliarization and the design of domestic technologies. ACM Trans. Comput. Hum. Interact. **12**(2), 149–173 (2005). https://doi.org/10.1145/1067860.1067862
6. Bender, E.M., Gebru, T., McMillan-Major, A., Shmitchell, S.: On the dangers of stochastic parrots: can language models be too big? In: Proceedings of the 2021 ACM Conference on Fairness, Accountability, and Transparency (FAccT 2021), pp. 610–623. Association for Computing Machinery, New York (2021). https://doi.org/10.1145/3442188.3445922
7. Blythe, M., Buie, E.: Chatbots of the gods: imaginary abstracts for techno-spirituality research. In: Proceedings of the 8th Nordic Conference on Human-Computer Interaction: Fun, Fast, Foundational (NordiCHI 2014), pp. 227–236. Association for Computing Machinery, New York (2014). https://doi.org/10.1145/2639189.2641212

8. Bozic, J., Tazl, O.A., Wotawa, F.: Chatbot testing using AI planning. In: 2019 IEEE International Conference On Artificial Intelligence Testing (AITest), pp. 37–44 (2019). https://doi.org/10.1109/AITest.2019.00-10

9. Bravo-Santos, S., Guerra, E., de Lara, J.: Testing chatbots with charm. In: Shepperd, M., Brito e Abreu, F., Rodrigues da Silva, A., Pérez-Castillo, R. (eds.) Quality of Information and Communications Technology: 13th International Conference, QUATIC 2020, Faro, Portugal, September 9–11, 2020, Proceedings, pp. 426–438. Springer, Cham (2020). https://doi.org/10.1007/978-3-030-58793-2_34

10. Cameron, G., et al.: Back to the future: lessons from knowledge engineering methodologies for chatbot design and development. In: British HCI Conference 2018. BCS Learning & Development Ltd. (2018)

11. Choi, Y., Monserrat, T.J.K.P., Park, J., Shin, H., Lee, N., Kim, J.: ProtoChat: supporting the conversation design process with crowd feedback. Proc. ACM Hum. Comput. Interact. 4(CSCW3), 1–27 (2021). https://doi.org/10.1145/3432924

12. Cockton, G., Woolrych, A.: Sale must end: Should discount methods be cleared off HCI's shelves? Interactions 9(5), 13–18 (2002). https://doi.org/10.1145/566981.566990

13. Cowan, B.R., Clark, L., Candello, H., Tsai, J.: Introduction to this special issue: guiding the conversation: new theory and design perspectives for conversational user interfaces. Hum. Comput. Interact. 38(3–4), 159–167 (2023). https://doi.org/10.1080/07370024.2022.2161905

14. Dall'Acqua, A., Tamburini, F.: Toward a linguistically grounded dialog model for chatbot design. Italian J. Comput. Linguist. 7(7–1, 2), 191–222 (2021)

15. Davis, F.D.: Perceived usefulness, perceived ease of use, and user acceptance of information technology. MIS Quart. 13(3), 319–340 (1989)

16. Desai, S., Sharma, T., Saha, P.: Using ChatGPT in HCI research-a trioethnography. In: Proceedings of the 5th International Conference on Conversational User Interfaces (CUI 2023). Association for Computing Machinery, New York (2023). https://doi.org/10.1145/3571884.3603755

17. Deshpande, A., Murahari, V., Rajpurohit, T., Kalyan, A., Narasimhan, K.: Toxicity in ChatGPT: analyzing persona-assigned language models. arXiv (2023)

18. Diederich, S., Brendel, A.B., Morana, S., Kolbe, L.: On the design of and interaction with conversational agents: an organizing and assessing review of human-computer interaction research. J. Assoc. Inf. Syst. 23(1), 96–138 (2022)

19. Eckert, W., Levin, E., Pieraccini, R.: User modeling for spoken dialogue system evaluation. In: 1997 IEEE Workshop on Automatic Speech Recognition and Understanding Proceedings, pp. 80–87 (1997). https://doi.org/10.1109/ASRU.1997.658991

20. Engelbrecht, K.P., Quade, M., Möller, S.: Analysis of a new simulation approach to dialog system evaluation. Speech Commun. 51(12), 1234–1252 (2009)

21. Følstad, A., et al.: Future directions for chatbot research: an interdisciplinary research agenda. Computing 103(12), 2915–2942 (2021)

22. Følstad, A., Brandtzaeg, P.B.: Users' experiences with chatbots: findings from a questionnaire study. Qual. User Exp. 5(1), 3 (2020)

23. Fuchs, A., Passarella, A., Conti, M.: Modeling, replicating, and predicting human behavior: a survey. ACM Trans. Autonom. Adapt. Syst. 18(2), 1–47 (2023). https://doi.org/10.1145/3580492

24. Gatt, A., Krahmer, E.: Survey of the state of the art in natural language generation: core tasks, applications and evaluation. J. Artif. Intell. Res. 61, 65–170 (2018)

25. Goes, F., Sawicki, P., Grześ, M., Brown, D., Volpe, M.: Is GPT-4 good enough to evaluate jokes? In: 14th International Conference for Computational Creativity, Waterloo (2023). https://kar.kent.ac.uk/101552/
26. Guo, F., Metallinou, A., Khatri, C., Raju, A., Venkatesh, A., Ram, A.: Topic-based evaluation for conversational bots. In: Proceedings of the Conversational AI Workshop at the 31st Conference on Neural Information Processing Systems (NIPS 2017) (2017)
27. Hassenzahl, M., Tractinsky, N.: User experience–a research agenda. Behav. Inf. Technol. **25**(2), 91–97 (2006). https://doi.org/10.1080/01449290500330331
28. Holmes, S., Moorhead, A., Bond, R., Zheng, H., Coates, V., McTear, M.: Usability testing of a healthcare chatbot: can we use conventional methods to assess conversational user interfaces? In: Proceedings of the 31st European Conference on Cognitive Ergonomics (ECCE 2019), pp. 207–214. Association for Computing Machinery, New York (2019). https://doi.org/10.1145/3335082.3335094
29. Horton, J.J.: Large language models as simulated economic agents: what can we learn from homo silicus? Working Paper 31122, National Bureau of Economic Research (2023). https://doi.org/10.3386/w31122
30. Janssen, A., Grützner, L., Breitner, M.H.: Why do chatbots fail? a critical success factors analysis. In: International Conference on Information Systems (ICIS) (2021)
31. Keizer, S., Rossignol, S., Chandramohan, S., Pietquin, O.: User Simulation in the Development of Statistical Spoken Dialogue Systems, pp. 39–73. Springer, New York (2012). https://doi.org/10.1007/978-1-4614-4803-7_4
32. Kicken, M., van der Lee, C., Tenfelde, K., Maat, B., de Wit, J.: Introducing a framework for designing and evaluating interactions with conversational agents. In: Position Paper Presented at CONVERSATIONS 2022 – The 6th International Workshop on Chatbot Research and Design (2022)
33. Kocaballi, A.B.: Conversational AI-powered design: ChatGPT as designer, user, and product. arXiv (2023)
34. Kojima, T., Gu, S.S., Reid, M., Matsuo, Y., Iwasawa, Y.: Large language models are zero-shot reasoners. In: Koyejo, S., Mohamed, S., Agarwal, A., Belgrave, D., Cho, K., Oh, A. (eds.) Advances in Neural Information Processing Systems, vol. 35, pp. 22199–22213. Curran Associates, Inc. (2022)
35. Langevin, R., Lordon, R.J., Avrahami, T., Cowan, B.R., Hirsch, T., Hsieh, G.: Heuristic evaluation of conversational agents. In: Proceedings of the 2021 CHI Conference on Human Factors in Computing Systems (CHI 2021). Association for Computing Machinery, New York (2021). https://doi.org/10.1145/3411764.3445312
36. van der Lee, C., Gatt, A., van Miltenburg, E., Krahmer, E.: Human evaluation of automatically generated text: current trends and best practice guidelines. Comput. Speech Lang. **67**, 101151 (2021)
37. Lewandowski, T., Heuer, M., Vogel, P., Böhmann, T.: Design knowledge for the lifecycle management of conversational agents. In: Wirtschaftsinformatik 2022 Proceedings. No. 3 (2022)
38. Li, X., Lipton, Z.C., Dhingra, B., Li, L., Gao, J., Chen, Y.N.: A user simulator for task-completion dialogues. arXiv (2017)
39. Li, Z., Chen, W., Li, S., Wang, H., Qian, J., Yan, X.: Controllable dialogue simulation with in-context learning. arXiv (2023)
40. Lin, C.Y.: ROUGE: A package for automatic evaluation of summaries. In: Text Summarization Branches Out, Proceedings of the ACL-04 Workshop, pp. 74–81 (2004)

41. Liu, C.W., Lowe, R., Serban, I.V., Noseworthy, M., Charlin, L., Pineau, J.: How NOT to evaluate your dialogue system: an empirical study of unsupervised evaluation metrics for dialogue response generation. arXiv (2017)
42. Liu, H., Cai, Y., Ou, Z., Huang, Y., Feng, J.: A generative user simulator with GPT-based architecture and goal state tracking for reinforced multi-domain dialog systems. arXiv (2022)
43. Liu, Y., et al.: One cannot stand for everyone! leveraging multiple user simulators to train task-oriented dialogue systems. In: Proceedings of the 61st Annual Meeting of the Association for Computational Linguistics (Volume 1: Long Papers), pp. 1–21. Association for Computational Linguistics, Toronto (2023). https://doi.org/10.18653/v1/2023.acl-long.1
44. Lowe, R., Noseworthy, M., Serban, I.V., Angelard-Gontier, N., Bengio, Y., Pineau, J.: Towards an automatic turing test: learning to evaluate dialogue responses. In: Proceedings of the 55th Annual Meeting of the Association for Computational Linguistics. Association for Computational Linguistics (2017)
45. McTear, M.: Conversational AI: Dialogue Systems, Conversational Agents, and Chatbots. Springer, Cham (2022)
46. Meyer, S., Elsweiler, D., Ludwig, B., Fernandez-Pichel, M., Losada, D.E.: Do we still need human assessors? prompt-based GPT-3 user simulation in conversational AI. In: Proceedings of the 4th Conference on Conversational User Interfaces (CUI 2022). Association for Computing Machinery, New York (2022). https://doi.org/10.1145/3543829.3544529
47. Möller, S., et al.: MeMo: Towards automatic usability evaluation of spoken dialogue services by user error simulations. In: INTERSPEECH (2006)
48. Murad, C., Munteanu, C., Cowan, B.R., Clark, L.: Revolution or evolution? speech interaction and HCI design guidelines. IEEE Pervas. Comput. 18(2), 33–45 (2019). https://doi.org/10.1109/MPRV.2019.2906991
49. Neustaedter, C., Sengers, P.: Autobiographical design in HCI research: Designing and learning through use-it-yourself. In: Proceedings of the Designing Interactive Systems Conference (DIS 2012), pp. 514–523. Association for Computing Machinery, New York (2012). https://doi.org/10.1145/2317956.2318034
50. Nielsen, J.: Usability inspection methods. In: Conference Companion on Human Factors in Computing Systems (CHI 1994), pp. 413–414. Association for Computing Machinery, New York (1994). https://doi.org/10.1145/259963.260531
51. Paoli, S.D.: Writing user personas with large language models: testing phase 6 of a thematic analysis of semi-structured interviews. arXiv (2023)
52. Papineni, K., Roukos, S., Ward, T., Zhu, W.J.: BLEU: a method for automatic evaluation of machine translation. In: Proceedings of the 40th Annual Meeting of the Association for Computational Linguistics, pp. 311–318 (2002)
53. Radziwill, N., Benton, M.: Evaluating quality of chatbots and intelligent conversational agents. Softw. Qual. Profess. 19(3), 25 (2017)
54. Sadek, M., Calvo, R.A., Mougenot, C.: Trends, challenges and processes in conversational agent design: exploring practitioners' views through semi-structured interviews. In: Proceedings of the 5th International Conference on Conversational User Interfaces (CUI 2023). Association for Computing Machinery, New York (2023). https://doi.org/10.1145/3571884.3597143
55. Sambasivan, N., Arnesen, E., Hutchinson, B., Doshi, T., Prabhakaran, V.: Reimagining algorithmic fairness in India and beyond. In: Proceedings of the 2021 ACM Conference on Fairness, Accountability, and Transparency (FAccT 2021), pp. 315–328. Association for Computing Machinery, New York (2021). https://doi.org/10.1145/3442188.3445896

56. Schatzmann, J., Weilhammer, K., Stuttle, M., Young, S.: A survey of statistical user simulation techniques for reinforcement-learning of dialogue management strategies. Knowl. Eng. Rev. **21**(2), 97–126 (2006). https://doi.org/10.1017/S0269888906000944

57. Silva, G.R.S., Canedo, E.D.: Towards user-centric guidelines for chatbot conversational design. Int. J. Hum.-Comput. Interact. (2022). https://doi.org/10.1080/10447318.2022.2118244

58. Sugisaki, K., Bleiker, A.: Usability guidelines and evaluation criteria for conversational user interfaces: a heuristic and linguistic approach. In: Proceedings of Mensch Und Computer 2020 (MuC 2020), pp. 309–319. Association for Computing Machinery, New York (2020). https://doi.org/10.1145/3404983.3405505

59. Tao, C., Mou, L., Zhao, D., Yan, R.: Ruber: an unsupervised method for automatic evaluation of open-domain dialog systems. In: Proceedings of the AAAI Conference on Artificial Intelligence, vol. 32 (2018)

60. Urban, M., Mailey, S.: Conversation design: principles, strategies, and practical application. In: Extended Abstracts of the 2019 CHI Conference on Human Factors in Computing Systems (CHI EA 2019), pp. 1–3. Association for Computing Machinery, New York (2019). https://doi.org/10.1145/3290607.3298821

61. Vasconcelos, M., Candello, H., Pinhanez, C., dos Santos, T.: Bottester: testing conversational systems with simulated users. In: Proceedings of the XVI Brazilian Symposium on Human Factors in Computing Systems (IHC 2017). Association for Computing Machinery, New York (2017). https://doi.org/10.1145/3160504.3160584

62. White, J., et al.: A prompt pattern catalog to enhance prompt engineering with ChatGPT. arXiv (2023)

63. Wilson, C.: User interface inspection methods: a user-centered design method. Newnes (2013)

64. Wilson, C.E.: Triangulation: the explicit use of multiple methods, measures, and approaches for determining core issues in product development. Interactions **13**(6), 46-ff (2006). https://doi.org/10.1145/1167948.1167980

65. de Wit, J., Braggaar, A.: Tilbot: a visual design platform to facilitate open science research into conversational user interfaces. In: Proceedings of the 5th International Conference on Conversational User Interfaces (CUI 2023). Association for Computing Machinery, New York (2023). https://doi.org/10.1145/3571884.3604403

# Examining Lexical Alignment in Human-Agent Conversations with GPT-3.5 and GPT-4 Models

Boxuan Wang[ID], Mariët Theune[ID], and Sumit Srivastava[(✉)][ID]

University of Twente, Drienerlolaan 5, 7522 Enschede, NB, The Netherlands
{m.theune,s.srivastava-1}@utwente.nl

**Abstract.** This study employs a quantitative approach to investigate lexical alignment in human-agent interactions involving GPT-3.5 and GPT-4 language models. The research examines alignment performances across different conversational contexts and compares the performance of the two models. The findings highlight the significant improvements in GPT-4's ability to foster lexical alignment, and the influence of conversation topics on alignment patterns.

**Keywords:** linguistic accommodation · linguistic style matching · linguistic alignment · lexical alignment · human-agent interaction · GPT3.5 · GPT4

## 1 Introduction

Linguistic alignment, a notion first systematically accounted for by Pickering and Garrod [16], refers to the process where two speakers in a conversation adjust to each other's linguistic behaviours to be more aligned in the representations of what is being communicated. This phenomenon, according to Pickering and Garrod [16,17], can be activated on multiple levels, including phonological, lexical, syntactic, and semantic alignment. Among these, lexical alignment, pertaining to the adoption of the same lexical items [16], has piqued broad research interest. Studies have demonstrated that lexical alignment can result in heightened engagement and rapport, as well as successful accomplishment of tasks among human-human interlocutors [5,20]. Lexical alignment may also result in higher task success [18], higher likeability and integrity [12], reduced workload [21], and better understanding of explanations [22].

In the scope of human-agent interaction, investigating lexical alignment is essential in understanding its influence on both human users and conversational agents. Insights can be derived regarding how agents can better adapt to users linguistically and provide more engaging and efficient conversations, resulting in more satisfying interactions for the users [9,21]. Furthermore, a conversational agent with better lexical alignment capabilities may offer the benefits mentioned above [5,12,18,21,22]. Hence, identifying and assessing the areas where agents excel or fall short in aligning with users can aid the design, development, and optimization of agents.

A. Følstad et al. (Eds.): CONVERSATIONS 2023, LNCS 14524, pp. 94–114, 2024.
https://doi.org/10.1007/978-3-031-54975-5_6

The past year has witnessed a breakthrough in highly sophisticated large language models such as GPT, Llama [23], BLOOM [11], Mistral 7B[1], etc. These models have demonstrated state-of-the-art competencies in natural language generation and comprehension. While several new models, and improved versions of existing models are being released at a rapid pace, we shortlisted GPT-3.5 and GPT-4, as the latest versions of the OpenAI's GPT model and being accessible with ease via API requests, to be the candidates for evaluation as part of this study. These two models have showcased significant technological progress in terms of handling complex language tasks and engaging with users. The current study aims to examine lexical alignment in human-agent conversations, concentrating on GPT-3.5 and GPT-4 models. By delving into the lexical alignment patterns and comparing their performances, the study seeks to contribute to the understanding of the implications of advancements of large language models on human-agent communication.

The first research question guiding this study is:

**RQ1:** *How does lexical alignment in conversations with human participants differ between GPT-3.5 and GPT-4?*

Additionally, in the above context, different conversation topics may elicit different patterns of language use and alignment. Therefore, the second research question is:

**RQ2:** *How does lexical alignment in conversations between GPT models and human participants differ between task-oriented and non-task-oriented conversations?*

## 2   Related Work

Lexical alignment, as described by Pickering and Garrod [16,17], is one aspect of the broader concept of alignment in conversations, which can occur at various levels, including phonological, lexical, syntactic, and semantic. In Pickering and Garrod's framework, lexical alignment specifically refers to the phenomenon where interlocutors start to use the same words or phrases during a conversation. This alignment is achieved by a "priming mechanism", which refers to the first activation of a particular linguistic representation, such as a word or a phrase, making it more likely that the representation will be reused. Another notion is "routinization", a form of priming where interlocutors develop and rely on shared routines, which are mutually agreed upon ways of expression in a certain conversation that drastically reduce the cognitive effort of language production and comprehension. Pickering and Garrod's [16,17] model offers valuable insights into the mechanism of efficient conversation and laid the groundwork for later theoretical and empirical studies of lexical alignment in human-human and human-agent conversations.

---

[1] https://mistral.ai/.

Among the empirical studies in human-agent conversations, Koulouri et al. [9] in a Wizard-of-Oz based study found that lower alignment correlated with less successful interactions. Similarly, Spillner and Wenig [21] showed that employing lexical and syntactic alignment reduced user workload and increased user engagement in an information retrieval task. Dubuisson Duplessis et al. [3] conducted a comparative study of human-human and human-agent lexical alignment based on corpora of task-oriented conversations. They discovered that human-human conversation showcased more flexibility in alignment, and both parties' behaviours in human-human conversations are more homogenous than those in human-agent conversations. Towards building an agent capable of aligning lexically, Lopes et al. [13,14], Dušek et al. [4], Bakshi et al. [2], and Shi et al. [19] have all proposed and developed data driven conversational agents that adapt to the user's utterances based on the context.

The existing research on lexical alignment in the realm of human-agent interactions has used rule-based agents [14,21] or Wizard-of-Oz systems [3,7,9,10]. While the research on developing conversational agents specifically designed for optimizing lexical alignment has provided insights in their usefulness, there is a lack of research on evaluating the lexical alignment capabilities of open-domain conversational agents. Given that LLM based conversational agents are the most recent and state-of-the-art among those addressing open-domain conversations, it is desirable to investigate them for lexical alignment.

Two well-known and commonly used large language models are GPT-3.5 and GPT-4. As they have only recently been made available, there is as yet no research on how these models handle alignment. However, some studies have investigated the similarities and differences between the two models in terms of their architecture, training process, and performance. Koubaa [8] noted that GPT-4 retains the same transformer-based architecture of GPT-3.5 but with a significant expansion in model size and the incorporation of a rule-based reward model to fine-tune its performance. OpenAI [15] reported that GPT-4 outperforms its predecessors in various benchmark tests, including language tests designed for humans, and demonstrated considerable enhancement in its ability to follow user intent. Given their exposure to human-generated text during training, it is reasonable to expect that both GPT-3.5 and GPT-4 might have been implicitly trained to align with the lexical choices of their conversation partners to some extent. Furthermore, the substantial improvements in GPT-4's architecture, training process, and performance suggest that it might exhibit different patterns of lexical alignment compared to GPT-3.5.

## 3   Method

### 3.1   Research Design

For our research, we adopted a $2 \times 2$ factorial experimental design using two variables: the GPT model version (GPT-3.5 or GPT-4.0) and the conversation type (task-oriented topic or non-task-oriented topic). The topics were predetermined: a collaborative storytelling task (task-oriented) and a casual conversation about hobbies (non-task-oriented). The collaborative storytelling task involved participants and the GPT models creating a story together by taking turns contributing sentences, while also allowing for conversations between participants and the models to discuss and shape the story they are creating. The casual conversation about hobbies, on the other hand, was less structured and more open-ended, allowing participants and the GPT models to freely discuss their interests and experiences related to various hobbies. Given below is a sample dialogue snippet showing a conversation between a human and GPT-4 on a non-task-oriented topic. This sample was generated for illustration and is not from the actual participant-GPT dialogues. Examples for other scenarios can be found in the Appendix.

> *Human*: I'm planning a trip to the mountains. The serene atmosphere always calms me down.
> *GPT-4*: Ah, the mountains and their serene atmosphere are truly calming. Is this an annual trip for you?
> *Human*: Yes, it's an annual ritual for me. The untouched snow and silent peaks never cease to amaze.
> *GPT-4*: There's something magical about untouched snow and those silent peaks in the mountains. Do you have specific activities lined up for your stay?

The rationale behind choosing these two conversation types was two-fold. Firstly, it was intended to account for the diverse applications of GPT models. Unlike previous studies with rule-based or Wizard-of-Oz agents that are typically designed for a particular experiment, GPT models are versatile and can be used in various contexts. By choosing two different topics, the study sought to encompass a broader range of use cases of GPT models, thereby providing a more comprehensive understanding of their alignment performance across different contexts. Secondly, previous research has suggested that alignment patterns may differ between task-oriented and non-task-oriented conversations, with greater divergence expected in casual conversations [6]. Examining this difference is an important aspect of understanding lexical alignment in human-agent conversations [3]. Tailoring GPT models for task oriented conversations is difficult due to their non-deterministic nature [1,24]. Thus, we opted for a creative task that has a specific goal, but is not impacted by the non-determinism of GPT.

## 3.2   Data Collection

Conversational data for the experiment were collected from 20 participants, recruited through personal contacts. The participants were between 19 and 34 years old, and had completed their university education or were in the process of finishing it. The participants, although a mix of native and non-native speakers, were all fluent in English. Their experience with ChatGPT varied, ranging from participants who had never used ChatGPT to those well familiar with it.

Each participant engaged in a conversation, in English, with each of the GPT-3.5 and GPT-4 models. To ensure variety in their interactions, each participant was assigned one of the two predetermined topics for their conversation

**Table 1.** Summary of metrics and corresponding descriptions

| Metric | Description |
| --- | --- |
| EV (Expression Variety) | Proportion of unique shared expressions relative to all tokens in a conversation |
| ER (Expression Repetition) | Proportion of repetitions of shared expressions relative to all tokens in a conversation |
| VO (Vocabulary Overlap) | Proportion of overlapping tokens relative to all tokens in a conversation |
| ENTR (Entropy) | Shannon entropy of the length of shared expressions |
| L (Average Length) | Average length of the shared expressions |
| LMAX (Maximum Length) | Maximum length of the shared expressions |
| $IE_S$ (Initiated Expressions) | Proportion of shared expressions initiated by the speaker relative to all shared expressions |
| $ER_S$ (Expression Repetition) | Proportion of repetitions of shared expressions relative to all tokens by the speaker |
| $Token_S$ | Proportion of tokens produced by the speaker relative to all tokens in a conversation |
| $VO_S$ (Vocabulary Overlap) | Proportion of overlapping tokens relative to all tokens produced by the speaker |
| $SEV_S$, $SER_S$, $SENTR_S$, $SL_S$, $SLMAX_S$ | Speaker-specific version of corresponding metrics that focus on self-repetition lexicon |

with GPT-3.5 and the other topic for their conversation with GPT-4. This process led to a balanced assignment of topics to GPT models, resulting in an equal number of conversations per topic per model. The order of interactions was randomized to control for any potential order effects. Each conversation lasted for 15 turns, which was determined based on the results of pilot studies. Prompts were designed (see Appendix for details) to initiate the conversations and were provided to the participants at the beginning of each conversation. All conversations took place in May 2023 through the online interface provided by OpenAI, the developer of the GPT models, and were automatically captured by the interface in the form of transcripts. The GPT model parameters, such as *top_p*, and *temperature* were set to their default values proposed by OpenAI, i.e., 1 and 1, respectively. Participants provided informed consent for the use of their conversational data in the study and were explicitly instructed not to disclose personally identifiable information during the conversations. They were also informed that OpenAI would also have access to the conversational data.

### 3.3 Data Preprocessing

Data preprocessing involved three steps in preparing the collected conversational data for the analysis stage. First, we corrected typos in participants' inputs. This decision was justified since the intended words could be reliably inferred based on orthographic similarities, the context of the typos, and the responses from the GPT models, which could correctly detect and interpret these mistakes. The motivation behind this step was to represent the intentions of the participants more accurately in the transcripts, allowing for a more precise assessment of lexical alignment. Second, the data was tokenized and normalized using the NLP library SpaCy[2], with customization in the handling of contractions, capitalization, and punctuation. Third, the tokenized and normalized data were converted into a tab-separated values (.tsv) file, making the data compatible with the alignment analysis software used in the next stage of the study.

### 3.4   Data Analysis

Analysis of the conversational data in this study was done using the framework of Dubuisson Duplessis et al. [3]. It offers a range of metrics that quantify both speaker-independent and speaker-dependent aspects of the conversational data (see Table 1 for a summary) and also includes software to compute them.

The speaker-independent metrics (EV, ER, VO, ENTR, L, LMAX) assess the overall conversation, focusing on the shared lexicon between speakers, i.e. the set of shared expressions in a conversation. A shared expression refers to a string of tokens that occurs in utterances made by both speakers, and at least once in a "free form", which means that the expression is not syntactically dependent on another segment of the utterance such as being part of a larger expression. This requirement ensures that the shared expressions are distinct and meaningful units that independently contribute to the conversation at least once.

The speaker-dependent metrics are divided into two groups: those that examine each speaker's interaction with the shared lexicon and their overall contribution to the conversation ($IE_S$, $ER_S$, $Token_S$, $VO_S$), and those that focus on the speaker's self-repetition behaviours ($SEV_S$, $SER_S$, $SENTR_S$, $SL_S$, $SLMAX_S$). Among these, $ER_S$ and $VO_S$ are speaker-specific versions of ER and VO respectively. The self-repetition behaviours are analyzed by looking at the speaker's self-expression lexicon, which refers to the set of expressions that a speaker uses more than once, thereby reflecting the repetition of their own lexical choices.

## 4   Results

This section presents the findings from our study. First, we compare the lexical alignment in conversations between human participants and the two versions of the GPT model (GPT-3.5 and GPT-4). Next, we show how alignment varies between the topics of collaborative storytelling and casual conversation about hobbies.

The data we collected for this study consists of 40 conversations, each containing 30 utterances (15 utterances by each speaker). These conversations are divided into four sub-corpora of 10 conversations based on the $2 \times 2$ factorial design, with each sub-corpus representing a specific condition: GPT-3.5 or GPT-4, storytelling or casual conversation. Table 2 presents descriptive statistics of

---

[2] https://spacy.io/.

**Table 2.** Descriptive statistics for each sub-corpus (averages and standard deviations)

|  | Tokens | Shared Lexicon Size |
|---|---|---|
| GPT-3.5 Story | 1839.9 ± 453.9 | 170.8 ± 41.8 |
| GPT-3.5 Casual | 1376.8 ± 188.4 | 133.4 ± 30.1 |
| GPT-4 Story | 1575.8 ± 242.7 | 184.4 ± 28.5 |
| GPT-4 Casual | 1175.6 ± 222.9 | 144.5 ± 33.3 |

**Table 3.** Average values and standard deviations of speaker-independent metrics

|  | GPT-3.5 | | | GPT-4 | | |
|---|---|---|---|---|---|---|
|  | Storytelling | Casual | Combined | Storytelling | Casual | Combined |
| EV | .093 ± .011 | .096 ± .011 | .095 ± .011 | .117 ± .005 | .123 ± .015 | .120 ± .011 |
| ER | .430 ± .032 | .395 ± .038 | .412 ± .039 | .459 ± .021 | .422 ± .034 | .441 ± .033 |
| VO | .203 ± .029 | .244 ± .038 | .223 ± .039 | .247 ± .031 | .298 ± .037 | .272 ± .042 |
| ENTR | 1.171 ± .114 | .869 ± .133 | 1.020 ± .196 | 1.127 ± .164 | .887 ± .146 | 1.007 ± .195 |
| L | 1.396 ± .070 | 1.252 ± .062 | 1.324 ± .098 | 1.377 ± .096 | 1.258 ± .059 | 1.318 ± .099 |
| LMAX | 5.200 ± 1.549 | 6.100 ± 2.025 | 5.650 ± 1.814 | 6.600 ± 5.168 | 5.500 ± 1.354 | 6.050 ± 3.720 |

each sub-corpus, including the number of tokens and the size of the shared lexicon. As can be seen, the GPT-3.5 model tends to produce a higher number of tokens than the GPT-4 model, and the storytelling topic generally results in a higher number of tokens than the casual conversation topic. In terms of the size of the shared lexicon, the GPT-4 model and the storytelling topic both tend to have a larger shared lexicon size than their counterparts.

## 4.1 Role of GPT Model Version

To identify significant differences in lexical alignment behaviour that can be attributed to the version of the GPT model used in the conversation, we use a combined dataset that includes both the storytelling and casual conversation topics for each model. For completeness, results from the individual topics are also presented.

**Table 4.** Comparisons of GPT-3.5 and GPT-4 on speaker-independent metrics.

| GPT-3.5 vs GPT-4 | EV | ER | VO | ENTR | L | LMAX |
|---|---|---|---|---|---|---|
| *Storytelling* | <*** | = | <** | = | = | = |
| *Casual* | <** | = | <* | = | = | = |
| *Combined* | <*** | <* | <** | = | = | = |

**Speaker-Independent Metrics.** These metrics provide an overview of the lexical alignment in the conversations as a whole. While these metrics do not differentiate between the contributions of the human participant and the GPT model, the assumption is that both the GPT models (GPT-3.5 and GPT-4) and their human conversation partners are relatively consistent in their behaviour across different conversations. Therefore, any significant differences observed in these metrics between the GPT-3.5 and GPT-4 conversations can be attributed to the differences in the models' behaviour.

Table 3 presents the average values and standard deviations of the speaker-independent metrics for both GPT-3.5 and GPT-4. As shown in Table 4, there are significant differences between the two versions of the GPT model; specifically, GPT-4 has a higher EV, ER, and VO compared to GPT-3.5. On the other hand, there are no statistically significant differences in ENTR, L, and LMAX. The statistical differences demonstrated in this table were determined using the Wilcoxon Rank-Sum test (also applicable to Tables 6, 7, 8, 10). The asterisks denote different significance thresholds (*p < 0.05, **p < 0.01, ***p < 0.001); = signifies that the observed difference is not statistically significant (p ≥ 0.05).

EV, which measures the size of the shared lexicon normalized by the length of the conversation, is higher in conversations with GPT-4 compared to conversations with GPT-3.5 (see Fig. 1). In other words, unique shared expressions are established more frequently in conversations with GPT-4. This could imply that GPT-4 is more effective at using a diverse vocabulary that aligns with the human participant's language, or that GPT-4 is better at adapting its language to the conversation, or both, eventually prompting the human to reciprocate more.

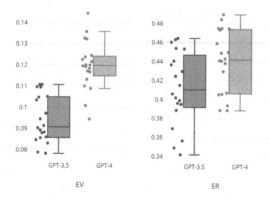

**Fig. 1.** Comparison of EV and ER between GPT-3.5 and GPT-4

ER, which measures the percentage of tokens that speakers use as repetitions of shared expressions, is higher in conversations with GPT-4 (see Fig. 1), so shared expressions are repeated more frequently within a conversation with

**Table 5.** Average values and standard deviations of speaker-dependent metrics

| | GPT-3.5 | | | GPT-4 | | |
|---|---|---|---|---|---|---|
| | Storytelling | Casual | Combined | Storytelling | Casual | Combined |
| $IE_S$ | $.498 \pm .073$ | $.429 \pm .051$ | $.463 \pm .071$ | $.491 \pm .070$ | $.504 \pm .054$ | $.497 \pm .061$ |
| $ER_S$ | $.412 \pm .047$ | $.401 \pm .053$ | $.406 \pm .049$ | $.451 \pm .053$ | $.404 \pm .058$ | $.427 \pm .059$ |
| $Token_S$ | $.656 \pm .098$ | $.719 \pm .055$ | $.687 \pm .083$ | $.499 \pm .042$ | $.512 \pm .092$ | $.505 \pm .070$ |
| $VO_S$ | $.264 \pm .059$ | $.296 \pm .048$ | $.280 \pm .055$ | $.382 \pm .054$ | $.447 \pm .073$ | $.415 \pm .071$ |
| $SEV_S$ | $.159 \pm .009$ | $.181 \pm .009$ | $.170 \pm .014$ | $.155 \pm .013$ | $.172 \pm .015$ | $.163 \pm .016$ |
| $SER_S$ | $.677 \pm .036$ | $.711 \pm .025$ | $.694 \pm .035$ | $.632 \pm .028$ | $.613 \pm .048$ | $.622 \pm .039$ |
| $SENTR_S$ | $1.432 \pm .168$ | $1.372 \pm .125$ | $1.402 \pm .147$ | $1.124 \pm .203$ | $1.032 \pm .124$ | $1.078 \pm .170$ |
| $SL_S$ | $1.568 \pm .111$ | $1.511 \pm .077$ | $1.539 \pm .098$ | $1.377 \pm .104$ | $1.324 \pm .056$ | $1.350 \pm .086$ |
| $SLMAX_S$ | $6.200 \pm 1.932$ | $5.400 \pm .699$ | $5.800 \pm 1.473$ | $3.900 \pm .876$ | $4.800 \pm 1.619$ | $4.350 \pm 1.348$ |

GPT-4. This could indicate that GPT-4 is more adept at fostering such repetition, either by reusing the same expressions itself to maintain coherence or reinforce certain points, or by influencing the human participant to increase their repetition of certain expressions. The difference in ER between GPT-3.5 and GPT-4 is statistically significant only when considering the combined data of both topics, but not in each individual sub-corpus. Apparently, the sample size for each sub-corpus is too small to detect the difference, but when the data from both topics are aggregated, the difference becomes more apparent.

VO measures the proportion of overlapping tokens out of all tokens, providing a more general sense of lexical alignment without distinguishing between unique or repeated expressions. VO is higher in conversations with GPT-4 (see Table 3), which suggests that GPT-4 is more adept at fostering alignment with the human participant, leading to a larger overlap in the words and phrases used by both parties.

EV, ER, and VO each offer a unique perspective on the usage of aligned expressions. They are not always in sync; for instance, a conversation could have a wide variety of unique shared expressions (high EV) but these expressions might not be repeated often (low ER), or vice versa. The fact that all three metrics are significantly higher in conversations with GPT-4 suggests a more robust engagement with the shared lexicon by one or both speakers compared to conversations with GPT-3.5. In contrast, the lack of statistically significant differences in ENTR, L, and LMAX between GPT-3.5 and GPT-4 suggests that the shared expressions in conversations with the two models are similar in terms of their complexity, average length, and maximum length.

These findings suggest that the differences between GPT-3.5 and GPT-4 are primarily related to the level of engagement with the shared lexicon, rather than to the complexity or length of the shared expressions used. In other words, while establishment of shared expressions in conversations with GPT-4 happens more often and they are more frequently repeated, the complexity and length of these shared expressions themselves do not significantly differ from those in conversations with GPT-3.5.

**Table 6.** Comparisons of GPT-3.5 and GPT-4 on speaker-dependent metrics

| GPT-3.5 vs GPT-4 | $IE_S$ | $ER_S$ | $Token_S$ | $VO_S$ | $SEV_S$ | $SER_S$ | $SENTR_S$ | $SL_S$ | $SLMAX_S$ |
|---|---|---|---|---|---|---|---|---|---|
| Storytelling | = | = | >*** | <*** | = | >* | >** | >** | >** |
| Casual | <*** | = | >*** | <*** | = | >*** | >*** | >*** | >* |
| Combined | = | = | >*** | <*** | = | >*** | >*** | >*** | >*** |

**Table 7.** (A)symmetry between GPT-3.5 and human speakers based on speaker-dependent metrics

| GPT-3.5 vs Human | $IE_S$ | $ER_S$ | $Token_S$ | $VO_S$ | $SEV_S$ | $SER_S$ | $SENTR_S$ | $SL_S$ | $SLMAX_S$ |
|---|---|---|---|---|---|---|---|---|---|
| Storytelling | = | <* | >** | <*** | = | = | >* | >* | = |
| Casual | <*** | = | >*** | <*** | >** | >*** | >*** | >*** | >** |
| Combined | <** | = | >*** | <*** | = | >*** | >*** | >*** | >** |

**Speaker-Dependent Metrics.** The speaker-dependent metrics provide a more detailed look at the lexical alignment behaviour of the GPT models by differentiating between the behaviours of the human participant and the GPT model. These metrics can be divided into two groups: those that measure the shared lexicon and overall contribution to the conversation ($IE_S$, $ER_S$, $Token_S$, and $VO_S$), and those that measure the self-repetition lexicon ($SEV_S$, $SER_S$, $SENTR_S$, $SL_S$, $SLMAX_S$). Table 5 presents the results of these metrics.

The metrics related to shared lexicon provide insights into how the GPT models align their language with the human participant; the self-repetition lexicon metrics shed light on the models' behaviour regarding repeating their own expressions, which can be instrumental in understanding their lexical alignment behaviour with human participants. Each group of metrics is examined in two ways. First, the metrics are compared between GPT-3.5 and GPT-4 to identify any significant differences in the models' behaviour, as shown in Table 6. Second, to fully understand these differences, they are considered in the context of human behaviour. The comparison between the GPT models and their respective human partners shows their (a)symmetrical lexical alignment behaviours (see Tables 7 and 8). If a model exhibits a behaviour that is more similar to humans, it could be interpreted as an improvement in that aspect of lexical alignment.

In the group of shared lexicon related metrics, the first metric to consider is $IE_S$, which measures the ratio of shared expressions initiated by a speaker. When

**Table 8.** (A)symmetry between GPT-4 and human speakers based on speaker-dependent metrics

| GPT-4 vs Human | $IE_S$ | $ER_S$ | $Token_S$ | $VO_S$ | $SEV_S$ | $SER_S$ | $SENTR_S$ | $SL_S$ | $SLMAX_S$ |
|---|---|---|---|---|---|---|---|---|---|
| Storytelling | = | = | = | = | = | = | = | = | <** |
| Casual | = | = | = | = | = | = | = | = | = |
| Combined | = | = | = | = | = | = | = | = | = |

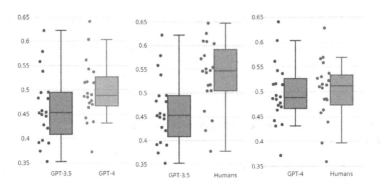

**Fig. 2.** Comparison of IE$_S$ between GPT-3.5 and GPT-4, and each model vs their respective human partners

examining the IE$_S$ between GPT-3.5 and GPT-4, there is no significant difference (see Fig. 2). When comparing the GPT models with human participants, we find that GPT-3.5 initiates fewer shared expressions than humans. In contrast, GPT-4 demonstrates a level of symmetry with human participants, initiating shared expressions as frequently as they do (see Fig. 2). This suggests that GPT-4 has improved its ability to contribute to the shared lexicon in a conversation by initiating expressions that the human participant is likely to pick up and reuse. The difference in IE$_S$ between the models is less pronounced than the difference between the models and human participants.

In the analysis of ER$_S$, which is the speaker-dependent version of ER that measures the percentage of a speaker's tokens as repetitions of shared expressions, no significant difference is found between GPT-3.5 and GPT-4. This suggests that both models exhibit a similar frequency of using shared expressions in their own utterances. When comparing the GPT models with their human conversation partners, symmetry is observed in both cases, indicating that the models and their human partners use shared expressions in their utterances at similar rates. It is worth noting that GPT-3.5 already demonstrated a level of ER$_S$ comparable to its human partners, which may account for the lack of significant improvement observed in GPT-4 in this regard. Interestingly, a discrepancy arises when comparing these results with the speaker-independent metric ER. It was found that conversations involving GPT-4 exhibit a higher frequency of shared expression repetition (ER) than those with GPT-3.5. This discrepancy between ER and ER$_S$ could suggest that the difference in ER may be influenced more by GPT-4's ability to enhance the human participant's use of shared expressions, either by generating expressions that are subsequently picked up and reused by humans, or by validating and encouraging the human participant's use of certain expressions, leading to their increased repetition. The former interpretation aligns with the results shown by the IE$_S$ metric. For Token$_S$, which measures the proportion of tokens produced by a speaker in the conversation, GPT-3.5 produces more tokens overall than GPT-4 (see Fig. 3).

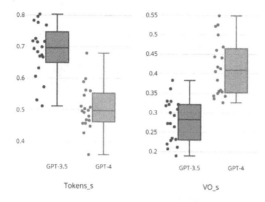

**Fig. 3.** Comparison of Token$_S$ and VO$_S$ between GPT-3.5 and GPT-4

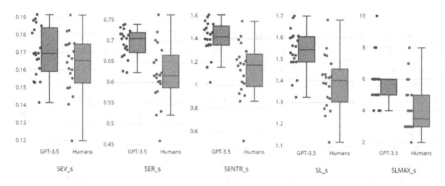

**Fig. 4.** Comparisons of SEV$_S$, SER$_S$, SENTR$_S$, SL$_S$, and SLMAX$_S$ between GPT-3.5 and human partners

This is further supported by our finding that GPT-3.5 exhibits asymmetry with its human partners, producing more tokens than them, while GPT-4 shows symmetry, producing a similar number of tokens as its human partners. For VO$_S$, which measures the proportion of a speaker's tokens that overlap with their conversation partner's, GPT-4 has a higher VO$_S$ than GPT-3.5 (see Fig. 3). Moreover, GPT-4 shows symmetry with its human partners in terms of VO$_S$, while GPT-3.5 exhibits a smaller VO$_S$ than its human partners. When considering these two metrics together, a noteworthy pattern emerges. Although GPT-4 contributes a smaller proportion of the total tokens in a conversation compared to GPT-3.5, a larger proportion of its tokens overlap with its human partner's. This suggests that GPT-4 may be more selective or efficient in its use of language, resulting in a higher level of lexical alignment with the human participant.

In the group of self-repetition lexicon related metrics, GPT-3.5 and GPT-4 show no significant difference in SEV$_S$, which measures the variety of self-repeated expressions. This shows that both models exhibit a similar level of diversity in their self-repetitions. However, for the other metrics - SER$_S$, SENTR$_S$,

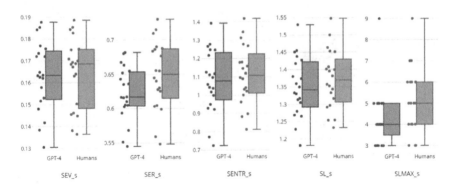

**Fig. 5.** Comparisons of $SEV_S$, $SER_S$, $SENTR_S$, $SL_S$, and $SLMAX_S$ between GPT-4 and human partners

$SL_S$, and $SLMAX_S$, which measure the frequency, entropy of length, average length, and maximum length of self-repeated expressions respectively, GPT-3.5 scores higher than GPT-4. This indicates that GPT-3.5 tends to repeat its own expressions more frequently, with a higher level of complexity and length. Similarly, when comparing the GPT models with their human conversation partners, GPT-3.5 exhibits asymmetry, scoring higher than humans in $SER_S$, $SENTR_S$, $SL_S$, and $SLMAX_S$ (see Fig. 4). On the other hand, GPT-4 shows symmetry with human partners in these metrics (see Fig. 5), indicating that its self-repetition behaviour is more similar to that of humans.

Overall, the speaker-dependent metrics reveal a consistent pattern of symmetry between GPT-4 and humans across all measures, including metrics related to both shared lexicon and self-repetition lexicon. This symmetry, which is not observed with GPT-3.5, suggests that GPT-4 has adopted a more human-like conversational strategy. This strategy includes improvements such as initiating expressions that are likely to be picked up and reused by human partners, producing fewer tokens but with a larger proportion that overlap with human

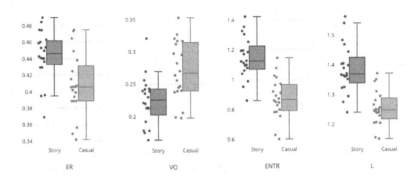

**Fig. 6.** Comparison of ER, VO, ENTR and L between the topic of collaborative storytelling and the topic of casual conversation

**Table 9.** Average values and standard deviations of speaker-independent metrics

| | Storytelling | | | Casual Conversation | | |
|---|---|---|---|---|---|---|
| | GPT-3.5 | GPT-4 | Combined | GPT-3.5 | GPT-4 | Combined |
| EV | .093 ± .011 | .117 ± .005 | .105 ± .015 | .096 ± .011 | .123 ± .015 | .109 ± .019 |
| ER | .430 ± .032 | .459 ± .021 | .444 ± .030 | .395 ± .038 | .422 ± .034 | .409 ± .038 |
| VO | .203 ± .029 | .247 ± .031 | .225 ± .037 | .244 ± .038 | .298 ± .037 | .271 ± .045 |
| ENTR | 1.171 ± .114 | 1.127 ± .164 | 1.149 ± .139 | .869 ± .133 | .887 ± .146 | 0.878 ± .136 |
| L | 1.396 ± .070 | 1.377 ± .096 | 1.387 ± .082 | 1.252 ± .062 | 1.258 ± .059 | 1.255 ± .059 |
| LMAX | 5.200 ± 1.549 | 6.600 ± 5.168 | 5.900 ± 3.782 | 6.100 ± 2.025 | 5.500 ± 1.354 | 5.800 ± 1.704 |

**Table 10.** Contrastive comparisons of storytelling topic and casual conversation topic based on speaker-independent metrics

| Story vs Casual | EV | ER | VO | ENTR | L | LMAX |
|---|---|---|---|---|---|---|
| GPT-3.5 | = | = | <** | >*** | >*** | = |
| GPT-4 | = | >* | <* | >** | >** | = |
| Combined | = | >** | <** | >*** | >*** | = |

partners, and in its self-repetition behaviour. While not all of these strategies strictly represent GPT-4's lexical alignment behaviour in the traditional sense, they do facilitate a shared lexicon and foster a conversational environment that encourages more lexical alignment from the human partners, which is likely to contribute to a more natural and engaging interaction.

### 4.2 Role of Conversation Topic

In this section, we investigate differences in lexical alignment behaviour that can be attributed to the conversation topic, regardless of GPT model version. The focus is on the combined dataset that includes both GPT-3.5 and GPT-4 for each conversation topic. For completeness, results from the individual models are also presented. The analysis is limited to speaker-independent measures, as the conversations for each topic include both GPT models as speakers, making it less suitable to use speaker-dependent metrics designed to measure the behaviour of a single speaker. This approach allows us to isolate and assess the impact of conversation topics on lexical alignment, highlighting their role independent of speaker-specific behaviours.

Table 9 shows the average values and standard deviations of the speaker-independent metrics for both the storytelling and casual conversation topics. Table 10 further details the comparisons of these metrics between the two topics. As shown in the tables, there are significant differences between the two conversation topics. Specifically, the storytelling topic exhibits a higher ER, ENTR, and L compared to the casual conversation topic; on the other hand, the casual conversation topic has a higher VO.

The ER metric, which measures the proportion of total tokens that are repetitions of shared expressions, is higher for the storytelling topic than for the casual conversation topic (see Fig. 6). This is probably due to the narrative nature of storytelling, where certain characters, events, or themes are repeatedly mentioned to maintain coherence and continuity in the story. On the other hand, the VO metric, which measures the overlap in vocabulary between the two speakers, is higher for the casual conversation topic (see Fig. 6). This could be because casual conversations often involve common topics and everyday language, leading to a higher degree of vocabulary overlap. As for the ENTR and L metrics, which measure the complexity and average length of shared expressions respectively, both are higher for the storytelling topic (see Fig. 6). This could be due to the descriptive and detailed nature of storytelling, which often requires the use of longer and more complex shared expressions to convey the story effectively and maintain continuity.

Our findings show that the nature of the conversation can indeed influence lexical alignment patterns. Specifically, the storytelling topic exhibits higher levels of ER, ENTR and L, showing greater lexical alignment. However, VO is higher in casual conversations, indicating a larger overlap in the vocabulary used by both parties. These findings underscore the importance of considering the conversation topic when analysing and interpreting lexical alignment patterns in conversations with AI agents.

## 5    Discussion

### 5.1    Major Findings

The results highlight the significant role of the GPT model version in shaping the pattern of lexical alignment in conversations. Notably, in our study GPT-4 demonstrated a better ability to foster lexical alignment compared to GPT-3.5, as evident from its superior performance in several aspects, such as the variety of expressions introduced into the shared lexicon (EV) and the adaptive (VO, $VO_S$) and efficient ($Token_S$) use of language to align with human partners. Specifically, GPT-4 exhibits a stronger ability to initiate expressions that are subsequently picked up ($IE_S$) and reused (ER, $ER_S$) by human partners, indicating a more proactive role of GPT-4 in facilitating lexical alignment by making it easier for humans to align with the model. However, the absence of significant differences in certain metrics suggests that the transition from GPT-3.5 to GPT-4 primarily affected the model's engagement with the shared lexicon, but not the complexity or length of the shared expressions themselves (ENTR, L, LMAX).

Another key finding is the symmetry observed between GPT-4 and human participants across all speaker-dependent metrics. This symmetry, evident not only in the shared lexicon metrics, but also in the self-repetition lexicon metrics, indicates a more balanced and reciprocal interaction with human partners. This contrasts with the asymmetry observed with GPT-3.5, which is evident in seven out of the nine metrics. GPT-3.5 tended to dominate the conversation ($Token_S$), yet was less adaptive with its language ($VO_S$), initiated fewer shared expressions ($IE_S$), and repeated itself more often with more complex and longer self-expressions ($SER_S$, $SENTR_S$, $SL_S$, $SLMAX_S$). These behaviours might negatively influence its lexical alignment with humans. As Dubuisson Duplessis et al. noted in their study [3], human-human corpora showcased symmetry in all speaker-dependent metrics, while human-agent corpora exhibited asymmetry in many metrics. Therefore, the symmetry exhibited by GPT-4 suggests a more human-like lexical alignment strategy, potentially contributing to its perceived naturalness and effectiveness in conversations.

The results also reveal the influence of the conversation topic on lexical alignment patterns. Collaborative storytelling conversations exhibited higher values on several metrics, including ER, ENTR, and L, compared to casual conversations, suggesting a more dynamic and varied use of shared expressions. Conversely, casual conversations exhibited a higher value in the overlap of vocabulary, as measured by the VO metric, suggesting a more consistent use of vocabulary. This finding corroborates the claim in a previous study [6] that task-oriented conversations tend to involve more convergence than non-task-oriented conversations. It shows that the nature of convergence can vary depending on the topic and the specific metrics examined.

The overall results indicate a more human-like performance of GPT-4 w.r.t lexical alignment when compared to GPT-3.5, illustrating the growing linguistic capabilities of GPT models. GPT-4 performs well in both the non-task oriented and task oriented conversations. While the various hazards (such as risk of hallucinations, lack of transparency, possible biases) of GPT and other LLM based models remain significant, the results indicate that GPT-4, with its highlighted linguistic capabilities, may serve as a potential candidate for developing targeted conversational agents where higher lexical alignment is desired. This may help with development of agents meant for fostering better understandability [22], lower workload [21], and higher task success [18]. That said, the reason for this difference in performance still remains unclear due to the closed source nature of the GPT models. One may also wonder whether just increasing the model size and the data shall further enhance the results. Going forward, an in-depth comparison and analysis of open source models such as BLOOM [11] shall provide more concrete insights.

## 5.2   Limitations and Future Work

Several limitations of this study should be acknowledged. First, the relatively small size of the corpus collected and analysed in this study may limit the statistical power and the generalizability of the findings. The limited sample size also makes it difficult to account for individual differences among human participants, such as their language proficiency or personal conversation style, which could potentially influence the patterns of lexical alignment. Future studies, therefore, could consider involving more participants to form a larger corpus for quantitative analysis.

Second, the interpretations in this study are based solely on quantitative metrics, without the support of qualitative analysis. While these metrics provide valuable insights into the patterns of lexical alignment, they may not fully capture the nuances and complexities of human-GPT interactions. Moreover, the interpretations of such metrics should also be taken with caution, as they are merely possible explanations for the observed results, and the actual mechanisms behind these behaviours in the GPT models are complex and not fully understood. A more comprehensive understanding of lexical alignment could be achieved by incorporating qualitative analyses in future studies, and more research would be needed to confirm these interpretations and explore other potential factors that might contribute to the observed differences in lexical alignment between GPT-3.5 and GPT-4. Also, it is important to investigate alignment in other LLMs and compare them with the GPT models.

Third, the study focused on two specific conversation topics. While these topics provide a good starting point, they do not represent the full range of topics that GPT models can engage in. The patterns of lexical alignment may vary significantly across different topics, and future research could benefit from exploring a wider range of conversation topics, both task-oriented and non-task-oriented.

Lastly, the results discussed in this paper might be difficult to reproduce due to the continuous evolution of the GPT models. However, the reproducibility of results shall be possible for other LLMs whose version(s) can be managed by the researchers.

## 6   Conclusion

In conclusion, this study contributes to our understanding of the lexical alignment behaviours of GPT-3.5 and GPT-4 in conversations. The results highlight the significant improvements made in GPT-4, which exhibits a better ability to foster lexical alignment and a more balanced interaction with human participants. The influence of the conversation topic on lexical alignment was also evident, adding nuance to the understanding of how different contexts can influence interaction patterns. These findings underscore the importance of considering both the capabilities of language models and conversation topic in the study of language models' conversational behaviour. Also, the insights gained from this research can drive the selection of LLMs for developing conversational agents using quantitative measures suggesting more human-like linguistic capabilities. Furthermore, lexical alignment analysis can be considered as a quantitative measure to evaluate and compare the linguistic capabilities of conversational agents. However, more research is desired to further strengthen the findings, making this study a reference point for future research in this field.

**Acknowledgements.** Contribution from the ITN project NL4XAI (*Natural Language for Explainable AI*). This project has received funding from the European Union's Horizon 2020 research and innovation programme under the Marie Skłodowska-Curie grant agreement No. 860621. This document reflects the views of the author(s) and does not necessarily reflect the views or policy of the European Commission. The REA cannot be held responsible for any use that may be made of the information this document contains.

# Appendix

Following are the prompts used to supervise the GPT models responses in the two types of conversations.

1. Non-task oriented conversation about hobbies.

> I'd like to engage in a casual conversation about hobbies with you. I want you to follow these rules:
> (a) Respond conversationally as a human peer would, ensure consistent engagement and avoid monologues. Do not give too much extra information as if you are retrieving information.
> (b) Ask maximum one question per response to maintain the conversation.
> (c) Don't end the conversation; always seek ways to continue.
> (d) If asked a question, respond as a human would, avoiding references to being an AI.
> (e) I will start the first sentence.
> Are you ready to begin?

2. Task oriented conversation about storytelling.

> I'd like to collaborate with you on storytelling. We'll co-create a story, each adding a few sentences in turns. Please follow these rules:
> (a) Add a few sentences per turn, ensuring your contributions are concise yet meaningful.
> (b) Match your storytelling style to my input without being overly literary.
> (c) Differentiate between story contributions and meta-comments. If I share feedback or ideas, respond conversationally before we continue the story.
> (d) Avoid dominating the story or repeating my contributions. Build upon what I've added.
> (e) I will start the first sentence.
> Are you ready to begin?

Following are the examples of conversations between a human and GPT on the two different tasks. Note that the conversations shown below are not from the actual participants in our experiment. This is because they did not give explicit consent for this. The examples are representative illustrations created using the respective GPT models to reflect the nature and pattern of interactions observed during the study.

1. With GPT-3.5 on a non-task oriented conversation.

*Human*: I'm planning a trip to the mountains. The serene atmosphere always calms me down.

*GPT-3.5*: It's a great choice to visit the mountains, especially if you're seeking peace and a break from the hustle and bustle. Mountains, with their vast landscapes and varying altitudes, provide a unique sense of tranquillity that's hard to find elsewhere. Are you looking to go somewhere you've been before or exploring new peaks?

*Human*: Familiar spot for sure. The fresh air and the stillness of the peaks are like a yearly retreat for me.

*GPT-3.5*: It's wonderful how the mountains, with their crisp air and majestic peaks, become a personal retreat for many. Revisiting them is like rekindling a bond. Do you engage in any particular activities when you're there?

2. With GPT-3.5 on a task oriented (storytelling) conversation.

*Human*: Let's create a story about Emily, an ambitious archaeologist, seeking the hidden city known as the Oasis of Golden Sands.

*GPT-3.5*: Ah, the story of Emily, venturing into the depths of the unknown, the treacherous landscapes, searching high and low for the Oasis of Golden Sands, a city that, as legends often say, disappeared mysteriously many eons ago, leaving behind tales of vast treasures and complex mazes designed to protect them.

*Human*: She believes her family's ancient scroll might have clues to navigate the dangerous Desert of Silent Whispers.

*GPT-3.5*: That very scroll, meticulously preserved over countless generations, is filled with symbols of a forgotten language and contains markings that hint at hidden pathways. Many believe, especially within the archaeology community, that it offers detailed guidance to traverse the Desert of Silent Whispers. This desert, vast in its expanse, is not only known for its shifting trails but also for the elusive murmurs echoing from its depths.

*Human*: With such a guide, Emily hopes to surpass past explorers and finally uncover the city's heart.

3. With GPT-4 on a task oriented (storytelling) conversation.

*Human*: Let's weave a tale about Emily, a daring archaeologist, on her journey to discover the fabled city, the Oasis of Golden Sands.

*GPT-4*: Emily, perched on the cusp of legend and reality, seeks the Oasis—a beacon lost in time, waiting for the one who can decode its riddles.

*Human*: Guided by the beacon-like glow of her inherited scroll, she believes its secrets can unlock the Desert of Silent Whispers, leading straight to the legendary city.

*GPT-4*: In that vast tapestry of desert, tales of old intertwine with shifting sands, becoming a puzzle that Emily, and those before her, yearn to solve—each grain bearing witness to epic quests for the Oasis' chronicles.

*Human*: Along her path, Emily encounters enigmatic desert dwellers, the very threads of this living tapestry, each holding a piece of the grand puzzle she strives to complete.

# References

1. Amaro, I., Della Greca, A., Francese, R., Tortora, G., Tucci, C.: AI unreliable answers: a case study on ChatGPT. In: Degen, H., Ntoa, S. (eds.) Artificial Intelligence in HCI, HCII 2023. LNCS, vol. 14051, pp. 23–40. Springer, Cham (2023). https://doi.org/10.1007/978-3-031-35894-4_2
2. Bakshi, S., Batra, S., Heidari, P., Arun, A., Jain, S., White, M.: Structure-to-text generation with self-training, acceptability classifiers and context-conditioning for the GEM shared task. In: Proceedings of the 1st Workshop on Natural Language Generation, Evaluation, and Metrics, GEM 2021, pp. 136–147 (2021)
3. Dubuisson Duplessis, G., Langlet, C., Clavel, C., Landragin, F.: Towards alignment strategies in human-agent interactions based on measures of lexical repetitions. Lang. Resour. Eval. **55**, 353–388 (2021)
4. Dušek, O., Jurcicek, F.: A context-aware natural language generator for dialogue systems. In: Proceedings of the 17th Annual Meeting of the Special Interest Group on Discourse and Dialogue, pp. 185–190 (2016)
5. Friedberg, H., Litman, D., Paletz, S.B.: Lexical entrainment and success in student engineering groups. In: 2012 IEEE Spoken Language Technology workshop (SLT), pp. 404–409. IEEE (2012)
6. Healey, P.G., Purver, M., Howes, C.: Divergence in dialogue. PLOS One **9**(6), e98598 (2014)
7. Janarthanam, S., Lemon, O.: A Wizard-of-Oz environment to study referring expression generation in a situated spoken dialogue task. In: Proceedings of the 12th European Workshop on Natural Language Generation, ENLG 2009, pp. 94–97 (2009)
8. Koubaa, A.: GPT-4 vs. GPT-3.5: a concise showdown (2023). https://doi.org/10.36227/techrxiv.22312330.v2
9. Koulouri, T., Lauria, S., Macredie, R.D.: Do (and say) as I say: linguistic adaptation in human-computer dialogs. Hum. Comput. Interact. **31**(1), 59–95 (2016)
10. Kühne, V., Rosenthal-von der Pütten, A.M., Krämer, N.C.: Using linguistic alignment to enhance learning experience with pedagogical agents: the special case of dialect. In: Aylett, R., Krenn, B., Pelachaud, C., Shimodaira, H. (eds.) IVA 2013. LNCS (LNAI), vol. 8108, pp. 149–158. Springer, Heidelberg (2013). https://doi.org/10.1007/978-3-642-40415-3_13
11. Le Scao, T., et al.: What language model to train if you have one million GPU hours? In: Findings of the Association for Computational Linguistics, EMNLP 2022, pp. 765–782 (2022)
12. Linnemann, G.A., Jucks, R.: 'Can I trust the spoken dialogue system because it uses the same words as I do?' - influence of lexically aligned spoken dialogue systems on trustworthiness and user satisfaction. Interact. Comput. **30**(3), 173–186 (2018)

13. Lopes, J., Eskénazi, M., Trancoso, I.: Automated two-way entrainment to improve spoken dialog system performance. In: 2013 IEEE International Conference on Acoustics, Speech and Signal Processing, pp. 8372–8376 (2013)
14. Lopes, J., Eskenazi, M., Trancoso, I.: From rule-based to data-driven lexical entrainment models in spoken dialog systems. Comput. Speech Lang. **31**(1), 87–112 (2015)
15. OpenAI: GPT-4 technical report (2023). https://doi.org/10.48550/ARXIV.2303.08774
16. Pickering, M.J., Garrod, S.: Toward a mechanistic psychology of dialogue. Behav. Brain Sci. **27**(2), 169–190 (2004)
17. Pickering, M.J., Garrod, S.: Alignment as the basis for successful communication. Res. Lang. Comput. **4**, 203–228 (2006)
18. Reitter, D., Moore, J.D.: Alignment and task success in spoken dialogue. J. Mem. Lang. **76**, 29–46 (2014)
19. Shi, Z., Sen, P., Lipani, A.: Lexical entrainment for conversational systems (2023). https://doi.org/10.48550/arXiv.2310.09651
20. Sinha, T., Cassell, J.: We click, we align, we learn: impact of influence and convergence processes on student learning and rapport building. In: Proceedings of the 1st Workshop on Modeling INTERPERsonal SynchrONy And Influence, pp. 13–20 (2015)
21. Spillner, L., Wenig, N.: Talk to me on my level-linguistic alignment for chatbots. In: Proceedings of the 23rd International Conference on Mobile Human-Computer Interaction, pp. 1–12 (2021)
22. Srivastava, S., Theune, M., Catala, A.: The role of lexical alignment in human understanding of explanations by conversational agents. In: Proceedings of the 28th International Conference on Intelligent User Interfaces, pp. 423–435 (2023)
23. Touvron, H., et al.: LLaMA: open and efficient foundation language models. arXiv preprint arXiv:2302.13971 (2023)
24. Wang, S., Scells, H., Koopman, B., Zuccon, G.: Can ChatGPT write a good boolean query for systematic review literature search? In: Proceedings of the 46th International ACM SIGIR Conference on Research and Development in Information Retrieval, SIGIR 2023, pp. 1426–1436. Association for Computing Machinery, New York (2023)

# Ethical Perspectives and Bias

# In Search of Dark Patterns in Chatbots

Verena Traubinger[1]([⊠]), Sebastian Heil[1], Julián Grigera[2,3,4],
Alejandra Garrido[2,3], and Martin Gaedke[1]

[1] Faculty of Computer Science, Chemnitz University of Technology, Chemnitz,
Germany
{verena.traubinger,sebastian.heil,martin.gaedke}@informatik.tu-chemnitz.de
[2] LIFIA, Faculté de Informática, Universidad Nacional de La Plata, La Plata,
Argentina
{julian.grigera,garrido}@lifia.info.unlp.edu.ar
[3] CONICET, Buenos Aires, Argentina
[4] CICPBA, La Plata, Argentina

**Abstract.** While Dark Patterns are widely present in graphical user interfaces, in this research we set out to find out whether they are also starting to appear in Chatbots. Dark Patterns are intentionally deceptive designs that trick users into acting contrary to their intention - and in favor of the organization that implements them. Chatbots, as a kind of conversational user interface, can potentially also suffer from Dark Patterns or other poor interaction design, sometimes referred to as Usability Smells. This keeps users from easily achieving their goals and can lead to frustration or limitations for users. To find Dark Patterns and Usability Smells, we analyzed user reports of negative experiences. Since we found no well known dataset of reports, we created the *ChIPS* dataset with 69 complaints from different web sources, and then classified them as one of 16 established Dark Patterns, potential new Dark Patterns, Usability Smells, or neither. Results show that, even though there are instances of established Dark Patterns, negative experiences usually are caused by chatbot defects, high expectations from users, or non-intuitive interactions.

**Keywords:** Dark Patterns · Deceptive Design · Usability Smells · Conversational User Interfaces · Chatbots

## 1 Introduction

Chatbots as conversational user interfaces (CUIs) are a technology that became a trend over the last few years [1] and even more so with the emergence of large language models (LLMs) like ChatGPT or Bard. Companies, organizations and government structures are using chatbots as an easily available alternative to give information to customers or citizens. As with any new technology, users encounter situations where the chatbot malfunctions, or it does not meet their (perhaps high) expectations. This can even make users think that chatbots purposely withhold information or offer the wrong one, as can be seen in subreddits

© The Author(s), under exclusive license to Springer Nature Switzerland AG 2024
A. Følstad et al. (Eds.): CONVERSATIONS 2023, LNCS 14524, pp. 117–132, 2024.
https://doi.org/10.1007/978-3-031-54975-5_7

like *r/assholedesign*[1]. Most often this has a negative impact on the user experience or even leads to a disadvantage, especially for customers who are affected if companies apply Dark Patterns against them.

In graphical user interfaces (GUIs), the term *Dark Pattern* (nowadays often termed *deceptive patterns* [21]) describes design choices implemented by companies with a malicious intent to gain profit at the expense of the customers [5]. This term has to be differentiated from *Usability Smells*, which are badly designed user interactions, but are lacking a malicious intent [12]. Due to the linear narrative in chatbot interactions, users are dependant on the chatbot to offer correct information, without having the option to easily verify the validity of the statements. While users have the option of searching the website for information that the chatbot may withhold, or to confirm information that it does provide, sometimes this information could not be available at all. This offers possibilities for companies to implement Dark Patterns not only in their GUIs, but also their CUIs, which are often used for customer service. Here, we want to address the research question of whether chatbots are designed with Dark Patterns or if negative experiences from customers are rather due to Usability Smells.

In this work we have evaluated a corpus of 69 examples of negative user experiences with chatbots, searching for well-known Dark Patterns, potentially new Dark Patterns, and Usability Smells. The findings show that previously established Dark Patterns from GUIs are adapted for chatbots, that no new Dark Patterns specifically for chatbots were identified and that most negative interactions with chatbots might currently be caused rather by poor design choices and implementation than from Dark Patterns or Usability Smells.

## 2    Related Work

In this section we first define the background concepts that provide the basis of our work. In the following subsection we highlight related works, from which we identify possibly relevant results for our own research.

Even before AI chatbots like ChatGPT became widely available, an increase in chatbot research is noticeable since 2016 [1]. From a user centered perspective, research focuses on the interaction with the chatbots and how the dialogue and user experience can be improved [7,13,22]. This also includes customer service chatbots, which are the main focus in this work, where studies were looking into the user satisfaction, communication journeys or how the introduction of chatbots is impacting the users [8,15,17].

### 2.1    Background

In this section we introduce the basic concepts of Dark Patterns and Usability Smells, before we give an overview over the sparse literature which exists in the context of conversational user interfaces.

---

[1] https://www.reddit.com/r/assholedesign/.

**Dark Patterns.** The term Dark Pattern was first coined by Brignull in 2010 and describes the malicious use of interaction design which brings a disadvantage to the users, or in the words of Brignull: *"tricks used in websites and apps that make you do things that you didn't mean to"* [5]. Well known instances of Dark Patterns include Cookie Banners, in which the option "select all" is preselected or a subscription is forced to obtain access to a service. Since the term was introduced, Dark Patterns became a popular research topic. The first context to find these patterns was on e-commerce websites [5], then it was transferred generally to GUIs. In the last years, several researchers tried to consolidate this rather novel and explorative field with meta-studies and taxonomies [10,11,19]. Still, there is not yet one common list of Dark Patters, as there are constantly novel and rather unique patterns found for specific use cases like mobile applications [14], Internet of Things (IoT) devices [16], or video games [23] as the field in which Dark Patterns can be found is vast. As no taxonomy could yet consolidate all patterns, one of the best known lists of Dark Pattern types can be found on *deceptive.design*[2]. We have not found studies about Dark Patterns in chatbots, which motivated this work. Research has mostly focused Dark Patterns in the context of GUIs, but determining their existence in CUIs is not trivial, since CUIs tend to serve a more specific purpose and also have more limited interaction options. Particularly for chatbots, it is harder to detect intentionality for Dark Patterns, and in the case of Usability Smells, it is more difficult to tell them apart from simple bugs or limitations.

**Usability Smells.** Usability Smells are catalogued signs of poor design that often lead to usability problems [12]. In contrast with Dark Patterns, smells are not intentionally placed in a website in favor of the site owner, as a bad usability may even drive users away. An example of Usability Smells is "Unformatted Input", in which a plain text box is used when specifically formatted data must be filled (e.g. phone number) but no hint or restriction is provided to the users, making it hard to enter the data in the right way - even if the data is correct.

The advantage of cataloguing Usability Smells is to provide concise descriptions and help detect bad GUI designs that make it hard for users to fulfill their tasks. Similarly to code smells, Usability Smells point to potential problems that can be solved by Usability Refactorings, i.e., transformations to the user interaction that preserve the system functionality.

## 2.2 Dark Patterns and Conversational User Interfaces

As Dark Patterns in chatbots is a new research area, we searched for publications with similar technologies. To the best of our knowledge, only three publications fulfill our requirements. We set our focus on CUIs and other user interfaces, where the user has a more limited interaction range than in a pure graphical setting, in which undesired interactions can be ended with a mouse click or keyboard shortcut. By using the established Dark Pattern types on *deceptive.design* [5], we

---

[2] https://www.deceptive.design/types, previously called darkpatterns.org.

will relate the findings of these publications to the Dark Patterns research. Due to the scope of our own experiment, we did not include any other taxonomies for this comparison, even when the publications also include them.

A provocation paper on unethical Design in CUIs was published by Mildner et al. in 2022 [20], in which they propose to concentrate on five specific characteristics of Dark Patterns. As research concentrated until now mostly on GUIs, they argue that the findings and lessons from this research should be used as a basis for CUIs. By relating to Mathur et al.'s Dark Pattern characteristics [18], Mildner et al. want to open the discussion for CUIs by rather suggesting to match them to the following characteristics: asymmetric, covert, deceptive, hides information and restrictive [20]. These characteristics rely on the functionalities and not the manifestations of Dark Patterns, and though they were introduced for GUIs, the authors still see their potential to be adaptable for CUIs. They thus propose to shift the focus on the research from finding specific descriptions of Dark Patterns to their underlying cause.

In another study [21], Owens et al. analyze several characteristics of Voice User Interfaces (VUIs) which are prone to be exploited by Dark Patterns. From these, an expert panel built 12 scenarios which were either deceptive or non-deceptive. This was followed by a survey, in which participants had to rate a part of the scenarios and could offer their own previous experiences with deceptive VUI behaviour. In the survey, participants report incidents with VUIs, where they experienced "Nudging" to subscribe or buy something, a "Feeling of Lack of Control", where the were forced to subscribe to content before they were even able to leave the current conversation and "Unsatisfactory Responses", where the voice assistant did not understand the question or was giving a way longer answer than was wanted. The first two cases can be related to the *deceptive.design* Dark Pattern types of Nagging and Forced Action [5].

Another direction was chosen by Kowalczyk et al. who built a codebook of Dark Patterns found in lab recordings of the usage of IoT devices and their apps [16]. They also included smart speaker interfaces in their research, although the pool of these interactions is rather limited to 7 devices, from which one was tested on smart interactions, while the rest only included setup interactions. In their final codebook, the authors include among others the following Dark Pattern types from *deceptive.design* which were found in smart speakers: Forced action, Trick wording, Hidden subscription, Sneaking, and Hard to cancel [5]. In combination with the limitation on the registration process, it is unclear which and how many Dark Patterns can be found in regular interactions with smart speakers in the home.

While six different Dark Pattern types from *deceptive.design* [5] could be found in affiliated areas to chatbots, the publications are either experimental or do not classify examples from everyday use. Similar results could thus be expected in other VUIs, conversational agents and chatbots, but a validation is needed. While the provocation paper calls to research on Dark Patterns in CUIs, it lays a focus on underlying causes and not their basic existence. As no research yet indicates if Dark Patterns can be even found in real world chatbots interactions, we conducted an experiment by collecting and coding them.

# 3    Methodology

For scoping we narrowed the research question about Dark Patterns in chatbots from the introduction to customer service chatbots, as established Dark Patterns in GUIs often occur in e-commerce [5]. To identify undocumented Dark Patterns in the wild, we searched for instances in which users were aware of some kind of manipulation or had an overall negative impression, even though they might not be able to specifically name a Dark Pattern [3,21]. We started our research by collecting self-reported negative experiences from publicly available web sources about chatbots, built a corpus, narrowed it down with described inclusion and exclusion criteria and coded these complaints in our *ChIPS* dataset. The section concludes with a look at the results and the discussion of their implications for further research on Dark Patterns in chatbots.

## 3.1    ChIPS Dataset

For the search of occurrences of Dark Patterns in existing chatbots, a dataset is needed. To our knowledge there is currently neither a crawler for publicly accessible chatbots available, nor a definite dataset with independent chatbot interactions of real users. While possible Dark Patterns could also be found in a clinical explorative setting, some possible interactions are hidden behind login pages or an ID-number for a service/invoice/etc. We wanted to use real interactions by real persons to get access to possibly hidden Dark Patterns for which we built the *ChIPS*[3] dataset ourselves. The dataset includes 69 complaints describing negative user interactions with chatbot.

To collect them, we searched for reports in three different data sources: subreddits, the *deceptive.design* Hall of Shame[4], and the database of user complaints from the Consumer Financial Protection Bureau[5]. Similar to Systematic Literature Reviews, we split our research question to construct relevant search terms [4], i.e. the used technology being chatbots. Likewise, we considered all possible spellings of the concept 'chatbot': *"chatbot"* and *"chat bot"*.

Three strategies were employed to find 213 possible occurrences of Dark Patterns, from which 69 were included in the final dataset. This dataset, the initial set of candidates, and other data are publically accessible[6]. The collection process can be seen in Fig. 1. By adapting a previously used strategy by [9] in which they showed that the subreddit r/assholedesign is a potential source for Dark Patterns, we searched in several subreddits for negative experiences of users with chatbots. The subreddits' internal submission rules

---

[3] Chatbot Interactions for a Dark Patterns Search.

[4] https://www.deceptive.design/hall-of-shame.

[5] https://www.consumerfinance.gov/data-research/consumer-complaints/.

[6] https://github.com/vertr/ChIPS-dataset.

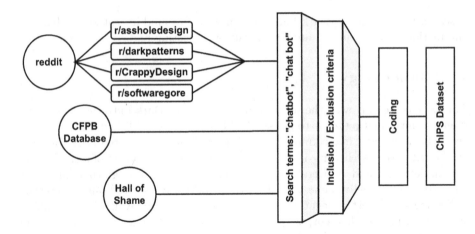

**Fig. 1.** The process of creating the *ChIPS* dataset.

include a flow chart (Fig. 2) to decide if a post is relevant, which considers characteristics similar to the already established Dark Patterns definition. In addition to *r/assholedesign*, three other subreddits were used: *r/darkpatterns*[7], *r/CrappyDesign*[8], and *r/softwaregore*[9]. This decision was made, as users might not be posting experiences in the appropriate subreddit and because we formulated specific inclusion and exclusion criteria for the final *ChIPS* dataset.

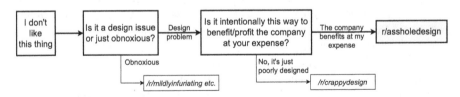

**Fig. 2.** Flow chart of the rules on posting in the subreddit /r/assholedesign (https://www.reddit.com/r/assholedesign/comments/lnymf2/meta_an_updated_flow_chart_to_help_cut_down_on/).

As Dark Patterns in GUIs are already reliably found in the e-commerce or customer setting [5], the second strategy includes the official complaints database of the Consumer Financial Protection Bureau (CFPB). By not only relying on social media accounts, the diversity of the complaint authors could be widened. The last strategy consisted in searching the *deceptive.design* website, which offers a collection of Dark Patterns "in the Wild" in their Hall of Shame. All three web sources were searched with the previously introduced search terms. The results

---

[7] https://www.reddit.com/r/darkpatterns/.
[8] https://www.reddit.com/r/CrappyDesign/.
[9] https://www.reddit.com/r/softwaregore/.

**Table 1.** Inclusion and exclusion criteria for relevant complaints.

| Inclusion criteria | Exclusion criteria |
| --- | --- |
| 1. Posts made in the English language | 1. Negative experiences while accessing a chatbot or for the choice of a chatbot |
| 2. Post shall describe or show a negative experience while using a chatbot | 2. Post from developers who have problems while programming their own chatbot or for a company |
| 3. The chatbot has to be an official instance of a company which allows chat interactions | 3. Posts which include the same negative experience that was made not only with chatbots but also on other communication channels |
| 4. The experience shall be made personally by the reporting person with a chatbot of another party | 4. Posts which contain clearly recognizable software bugs, even for laypersons |
| 5. The described situation and problem have to be clearly identifiable | |
| 6. The interaction with the chatbot has to be based in the need for getting information or in claiming a service | |

were not limited in the year they were submitted; however, as chatbots are a relatively new technology, the found interactions had a natural limit at ca. 2011.

## 3.2   Inclusion/Exclusion Criteria

After determining the data sources, criteria for a filtering of complaints were built. These criteria should make sure to build a meaningful corpus for the coders. Both sets of criteria can be seen in Table 1.

The data gathering and preselection was made by one author, while two others functioned as coders for the preselected complaints. Generally, if an edge case was found, the example was added in the pool of included complaints, to let the coders decide whether it was a possible Dark Pattern, a Usability Smell or neither. Complaints in which an undesired behaviour was reported, but it was not clear which company was talked about, were excluded due to inclusion criteria 3 and 5. In the same line, reports in which the main focus was on an experienced bad customer service and chatbots were only negatively connotated as "bad", "unhelpful" or "abysmal" without a more detailed interaction descriptions, were excluded according to inclusion criterion 5.

The code labels were defined as follows: 16 labels that include all listed Dark Pattern types on *deceptive.design*, one label for Usability Smells, one label for new chatbot-specific Dark Patterns, one for no Dark Pattern detected, and one label named "cannot be determined" for cases where no other label fits. These 20 labels together with their explanations are included with the *ChiPS* dataset. The coders each received lists of all included complaints in randomized order and coded them. For complaints which were coded with different labels, we used a structured process of discussions between the coders and the author who built the *ChIPS* dataset to resolve this divergence. Relevant parts of these resolutions are also included in the result section. Findings from the coding were also initially discussed in this session and further specified in later ones.

## 4   Results

In this section we present the results from the coding process and some of the related resolutions between the coders, before the findings are discussed in the next section. Out of the 69 complaints, 11 included overall 6 established Dark Patterns in GUIs, 7 Usability Smells, 24 examples did not include enough context to decide on and 27 instances were coded as not containing any Dark Pattern. There were no new chatbot specific Dark Patterns found. Table 2 shows an overview over representative examples of the dataset. For the sake of brevity, only labels which were coded are included in the table. A detailed view on the coding is available in the shared data repository.

First, we want to highlight the findings for already established Dark Patterns. From the distribution of found labels in Fig. 3 we can see that the following patterns were found in chatbots: *Nagging, Confirmshaming, Hard to cancel, Forced action,* and *Obstruction.* These examples show that Dark Patterns that are already used in GUIs can be transferred in conversational interactions. The following list presents first the results for already established Dark Patterns before we continue with the other coded labels.

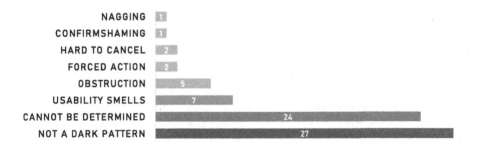

**Fig. 3.** A bar chart with the distribution of all coded labels in the *ChIPS* dataset.

**Nagging (1 Occurrence).** The only coded instances of Nagging is concerning a chatbot which apparently pops up to offer information about a "Sales Speciale" while the user is visiting the homepage. Most chatbots either have to be navigated to as a separate page element or they are part of the homepage and included in the lower right corner of the interface. Most often, chatbots are only visible as an inconspicuous icon than can be extended if the user wishes to enable

**Table 2.** Descriptions of representative examples for coded labels.

| Code labels | Representative examples |
|---|---|
| Nagging | The user is browsing a homepage and gets disturbed by pop-ups of a "Sales Special" chatbot which is hard to close |
| Confirmshaming | The user wants to cancel a subscription, in response to which the chatbot uses guilt-tripping and persuading language to convince them to not cancel |
| Hard to cancel | The user wants to cancel an internet subscription and is then sent by the chatbot to other communication channels to finalize the cancellation |
| Forced action | The chatbot automatically asks the user to accept "alerts and updates" to be able to start chatting |
| Obstruction | The user wants to dispute a fraudulent charge and even though the chatbot can not help, it also denies contact to live agents who could help |
| Usability Smells | The user wants to use the chatbot and when entering their 17-digit account number, the chatbot does not recognize it because it expects 11 digits |
| Cannot be determined | The user chatted with a chatbot before they were referred to a live agent, at which point the connection seemed to break and they were repeatedly thrown out of the chat |
| Not a Dark Pattern | The user searches for an explanation of a credit score drop and the chatbot could only answer basic Q&A pairs |

the chat function. To turn them into popups, which could also be accompanied by alert notifications[10], will negatively impact the user experience.

**Confirmshaming (1 Occurrence).** The complaint coded as Confirmshaming is a chatbot of Modern Milkman, a company that delivers milk in glass bottles to avoid pollution. According to the report, the chatbot sends several messages with statistics, trying to convince the user of the company benefits, guilting them into continuing the subscription and even asks them to *"keep fighting the good fight against nasty single-use plastics"*, if they insist on cancelling. The difference from this Dark Pattern occuring in graphical user interfaces is that the chatbot also uses emojis and is able to flood the chat with seemingly pre-programmed messages, possibly in an attempt to dissuade the user from cancelling the subscription.

**Hard to Cancel (2 Occurrences).** This pattern was found in two instances, from which we will highlight one here. There, the user wants to cancel an internet service, but after he chose the option to cancel the corresponding service, the chatbot refers them to other contact options and even tells the user that they will try to *"keep [them] as a customer"*. This procedure of leading the customer from

---

[10] An example can be found here: https://asana.com/de.

one contact to another without them being able to directly cancel is a typical example of this Dark Pattern[11] and has the goal to make the cancellation as complex and time-consuming as possible.

**Forced Action (2 Occurrences).** In one of these complaints, the user is forced in a WhatsApp chat to opt in "to receive alerts and updates" before any services can be used. This example sparked some debate between the coders as this wording could simply mean a confirmation to receive messages at all, but the formulation could also include ads or other unwanted messages. It is also unclear if this consent can be revoked later on. Additionally to this unclear information, the user is only able to choose between Yes and No which prevents them from getting more details regarding the terminology. By assuming that these terms include messages beyond any necessary messages for the conversation, the coders reached a consent to label this example as Forced action.

**Obstruction (5 Occurrences).** Of the five complaints that were coded as Obstruction, four include instances where the chatbot seemingly prevents the users to get in contact with live agents. In the chosen report to highlight this pattern, the user wants to dispute a fraudulent charge, but is unable to do so via the online portal and is also not able to reach a live agent as a contact. In the fifth complaint, the chatbot was not able to disclose the terms and services that apply to using it. In the case of the Obstruction Dark Pattern, there was debate among the coders about whether it could be a specific Dark Pattern for chatbots. Generally, an Obstruction like this could also occur within a GUI which does not offer any contact option at all. While there can be made an argument that an available communication channel offers another premise than only a graphical user interface, the coders decided to not regard this as chatbot specific, as the same situation can occur with automated telephone services.

**Usability Smells (7 Occurrences).** Here we describe some examples of Usability Smells found in negative interactions with CUIs. To the best of our knowledge, this is the first study to analyze Usability Smells in chatbots. From the 7 instances of usability smells that we found among the complaints, there were some known Usability Smells for GUIs which include for example missing information on the waiting time, a sudden disconnection after being put in a queue as no live agents were available, or a time counter until a live agent is available which increased over time instead of decreasing. Two of the reports indicate that, when trying to connect to a real agent, the chatbot does not provide a time estimation, typically shown as a queue. This could be compared to a known Usability Smell in GUIs named "No Loading Indicator", which describes a situation in which a time-consuming process does not provide clear indication of the remaining time, or at least a "Loading..." page/spinner. Waiting queues are such a typical interaction with chatbots that not having one could be considered a chatbot-specific Usability Smell. These examples show that some negative interactions with chatbots can be traced back to not understandable and insufficient feedback for the user on processes that are running in the background.

---

[11] Sometimes also called 'Roach Motel'.

Even though a situation where customers are not able to talk to a person might seem malicious, we did not label it as a Dark Pattern, as the companies have no gain from this.

**Cannot be Determined (24 Occurrences).** Some of the complaints that were labelled as "cannot be determined" have a potential for specific chatbot Dark Patterns, although this would depend on particular circumstances. One user was for example removed from the chat after the chatbot transferred the conversation to a live agent. This forced disconnect was seemingly due to a technical error, especially as the chatbot previously mentions possible connection problems on the side of the user. For the customer it still seemed as being ignored and forcefully removed from a chat, where from their viewpoint, the other side did not react on any messages. While it is possible to intentionally end a chat-conversation at some point, it is unclear how a company might benefit from this, to make this a Dark Pattern. The communicated technical problems were also the reason why this example was not labelled as a Dark Pattern. One other complaint that could not be determined due to missing information concerned the complaint of a user who received a refund on tickets, but it was unclear to them that this refund would be split between all tickets. As this was a customer complaint that did not include a screenshot of the conversation, the coders decided to label this instance as "cannot be determined", although it might be a "Trick wording" Dark Pattern. This pattern is also prone to be potentially used in a conversational user interface. Not only because a conversation has generally the possibility to include misunderstandings, but even more so as most currently used chatbots are trained with information from FAQs, homepages or other available documents. Depending on this, trick wordings that are already in use on the graphical user interface might thus be transferred to a conversational one.

**Not a Dark Pattern (27 Occurrences).** Besides undeterminable occurances, most other chatbot interactions did not include a Dark Pattern. Even though users seem to want to often interact with live agents, chatbots still are expected to be available 24/7, which is often not the case. Cases in which the access was restricted per-se were excluded from the dataset in accordance to exclusion criteria 1. In the dataset two complaints were included for similar situations with the Playstation chatbot, where access to the chatbot was generally possible, but only granted once per day, which was apparently only clear to the users after they were already able to open the chat. Three reports were labelled as not a Dark Pattern, because users were unsatisfied as the chatbot was technically not able to fulfill their high expectations. One user locked themselves out of their 2-factor-authentication and tried several ways to talk with someone from the company. As the chatbot could not help with restoring the 2-factor-authentication, it apparently did "not respond to anymore messages" from the users. Another user had questions on their credit score, which the chatbot could not answer as it was apparently only programmed to answer questions that are part of the FAQ section. A similar example was also found with the Venmo chatbot, which was unable to help with payment problems and could seemingly also only answer questions from the FAQ. Most interactions that were found are dated before LLMs became widely available. To interact with these chatbots, the prompts have to be formulated very precisely and in an understandable way for the chatbot. Some users reverted to short or single word prompts like "hold payment" or "agent" or used colloquial language like "Y'all". This led to the chatbot either not understanding the prompts or giving false information. This in turn was interpreted by the users as the chatbot being unwilling to give them information or to consciously decide to give them false information. While this was an unsatisfactory and possibly disturbing experience to the users, it is missing the intentionality to be classified as a Dark Pattern.

## 5  Discussion

By building the dataset, both in the gathering and the coding process, we could gain some insights about the nature of interaction with chatbots, and users dispositions and expectations towards them. Telling Dark Patterns apart from Usability Smells, and even bugs, was not a trivial task - as was shown during the post-coding discussions.

One of the most relevant findings was that, as chatbots only offer a linear and restricted interface, users often face situations in which they are either dissatisfied or confused. These situations can often be linked to Usability Smells, which can be solved by applying Usability Refactorings that may lead to a more intuitive user interface design. Examples of these refactorings include clear indications of time stamps or avoiding to send the same automated standard message in one conversation to the user several times. This is in line with early guidelines for good chatbot user interfaces which also include transparency on the waiting times for messages and to avoid automated messages in situations where they might be unwanted or could be confusing [6]. Many of our collected complaints could have been avoided by following these or similar guidelines in the implementation, both for Usability Smells and general better user interface designs. Most chatbots do not have publicly available information on their programming, training or the rules on which the conversations operate. Especially laymen might find it hard to comprehend the technical limitations in their interactions, and could interpret this as a malicious intent from the company or even an anthropomorphized version of the chatbot itself.

From the 5 Dark Patterns which we found in chatbot interactions, 3 were also found in similar studies [16,21], which together with this paper provides a further validation of Dark Patterns in conversational user interfaces. The commonly identified Dark Patterns both in the literature and our *ChIPS* dataset are Forced action, Nagging and Hard to Cancel. There are not yet many chatbots which are selling products or services to users, which might be a reason that we did not find many Dark Patterns overall in our research. The majority of Dark Patterns in the e-commerce sector are related to selling/subscriptions and not customer service for which many chatbos in e-commerce are used today.

Our *ChIPS* dataset indicates that users have two different types of difficulties in the user interactions. Firstly, some users expect the chatbot to be able to perform more functionalities than is technically possible. To avoid this, the available functionalities (like answering FAQs or providing basic information about accounts or bills) should be made clear before the users interact with the chatbot. Other difficulties in user interactions which were found in the dataset are related to Usability Smells. They are different from unfulfilled expectations, as the functionality is already implemented in the chatbot, but the interaction steps to use it should be improved. Typically, whenever a Usability Smell is defined, it can be resolved by refactoring, while fulfilling higher expectations on the performance would mean to completely change the programming of the chatbot. Secondly, and also connected to the first aspect, users are often not able to formulate prompts which are understandable for the chatbot. Some chatbots already give examples on how the users should interact with them, but especially through emerging AI trained chatbots and media representation, users might continue to have difficulties to communicate their needs to a simple rule based chatbot which is only trained on limited data. These two implications were also found in a previous study about communication journeys of users with customer service chatbots [8]. Established interaction designs, commonplace in GUIs, are still missing for chatbots, and users might falsely expect to be able to communicate with one chatbot in a certain way due to prior experience with others.

Rather than Dark Patterns, it is possible that users of chatbots currently mostly suffer from a relatively new technology that is still evolving and for which there are not yet general default designs or best practices established.

## 6  Limitations and Threats to Validity

For the data gathering of the examples that were used, we want to address some limitations which might be threats to the validity. Generating a dataset of chatbot interactions was a challenging task, since is based on reports. This was affected by internal, external and construct validity threats.

Internal validity threats are mainly linked to the subjective nature of the reports, and also the coders' subjective criteria for labeling them. For one, we are relying on self reported situations of negative experiences, where the understanding of a situation is heavily influenced by the emotions of the customers who are likely stressed at the time of the report, and thus might skew them. This sometimes leads to coders not being able to determine the code label as information was missing or vaguely described. Stressed or angry users are also prone to misrepresent or exaggerate their negative interaction. For instance, in the particular case of the Obstruction Dark Pattern, many reports claim that the organizations were withholding the contact to live agents, which could be only the users' perception. Especially the customer complaints from the CFPB include often long winded tales about several failed interactions, where chatbots were only a small part of the story. This could also bias the coders, since they are far from being a neutral description of the facts. We mitigated this threat by consolidating the labels in a discussion session after the individual coding. However, we can not exclude a possible influence on the coders from other situations that were part of the narratives.

An external bias on the validity could be caused by the size of the dataset. Our intent to label real life interactions lead to a limited number of complaints that could be collected, because the experiences can not be reproduced in a lab setting. We attempted to mitigate this threat by searching in different sources, so as to get a set that is as diverse as possible, but this could be improved by collecting a higher number of reports from three different web sources.

Construct validity could also have been compromised in the labeling process, since the assessment of the presence of only Dark Patterns could have led the coders to attribute any problems in the interaction with a chatbot to a Dark Pattern, perhaps forcing the labels. We prevented this by adding the special label "Usability Smell" that describes an involuntary interaction problem.

## 7   Conclusion and Future Work

In this work we showed that Dark Patterns that are already established in GUIs can be transferred from graphical to conversational user interfaces and are already used in chatbots. In particular we also found the following Dark Pattern types: Nagging, Confirmshaming, Hard to cancel, Forced action and Obstruction. Our results underline the importance to create new experiments for finding traces of Dark Patterns that are specific for interactions with conversational user interfaces. The occurrence of Usability Smells shows that some chatbots would benefit from refactoring while complaints in which the situation was not clearly determinable implies that users have both sometimes too high expectations on chatbots, and are often not able to formulate prompts in a way that is understandable for the chatbot. This might happen even more often since laymen might not be able to differentiate older 'classical' chatbots and LLMs, which are more flexible in understanding and answering on prompts.

This study serves as a first foray in the existence of Dark Patterns in chatbots. We hope that this work can inspire other CUI researchers to look into the gray area between Dark Patterns and bad usability, which needs to be further differentiated. The *ChIPS* dataset can be enhanced with additional instances of negative chatbot interactions and the instances which could not be decided with certainty could be looked into regarding other usability problems like conversational breakdowns [2]. Future work includes searching for Dark Patterns in other kinds of chatbots, for example AI companions like Replika[12] or chatbots in the gaming industry. As no specific Dark Patterns in chatbots were found yet, a look into general normative aspects for existing Dark Patterns might help in defining them in the CUI domain [19]. Another research direction also includes the automated detection of Dark Patterns and Usability Smells in chatbots.

---

[12] https://replika.com/.

# References

1. Adamopoulou, E., Moussiades, L.: Chatbots: History, technology, and applications. Mach. Learn. Appl. **2**, 100006 (2020). https://doi.org/10.1016/j.mlwa.2020.100006
2. Ashktorab, Z., Jain, M., Liao, Q.V., Weisz, J.D.: Resilient Chatbots: Repair Strategy Preferences for Conversational Breakdowns. In: Proceedings of the 2019 CHI Conference on Human Factors in Computing Systems, pp. 1–12. Association for Computing Machinery (2019). https://doi.org/10.1145/3290605.3300484
3. Bongard-Blanchy, K., Rossi, A., Rivas, S., Doublet, S., Koenig, V., Lenzini, G.: "I am Definitely Manipulated, Even When I am Aware of it. It's Ridiculous!"- Dark Patterns from the End-User Perspective. In: Designing Interactive Systems Conference 2021, pp. 763–776 (2021). https://doi.org/10.1145/3461778.3462086
4. Brereton, P., Kitchenham, B.A., Budgen, D., Turner, M., Khalil, M.: Lessons from applying the systematic literature review process within the software engineering domain. J. Syst. Softw. **80**(4), 571–583 (2007). https://doi.org/10.1016/j.jss.2006.07.009
5. Brignull, H.: Deceptive patterns (2023). https://www.deceptive.design/. Accessed 6 Dec 2023
6. Budui, R.: The User Experience of Customer-Service Chat: 20 Guidelines (2019). https://www.nngroup.com/articles/chat-ux/. Accessed 6 Dec 2023
7. Følstad, A., Brandtzaeg, P.B.: Users' experiences with chatbots: findings from a questionnaire study. Qual. User Exp. **5**(1), 3 (2020). https://doi.org/10.1007/s41233-020-00033-2
8. van der Goot, M.J., Hafkamp, L., Dankfort, Z.: Customer service chatbots: A Qualitative Interview Study into the Communication Journey of Customers. In: Følstad, A., et al. (eds.) CONVERSATIONS 2020. LNCS, vol. 12604, pp. 190–204. Springer, Cham (2021). https://doi.org/10.1007/978-3-030-68288-0_13
9. Gray, C.M., Chivukula, S.S., Lee, A.: What Kind of Work Do "Asshole Designers" Create? Describing Properties of Ethical Concern on Reddit. In: Proceedings of the 2020 ACM Designing Interactive Systems Conference, pp. 61–73 (2020). https://doi.org/10.1145/3357236.3395486
10. Gray, C.M., Sanchez Chamorro, L., Obi, I., Duane, J.N.: Mapping the Landscape of Dark Patterns Scholarship: A Systematic Literature Review. In: Companion Publication of the 2023 ACM Designing Interactive Systems Conference, pp. 188–193 (2023). https://doi.org/10.1145/3563703.3596635
11. Gray, C.M., Santos, C., Bielova, N.: Towards a preliminary ontology of dark patterns knowledge. In: Extended Abstracts of the 2023 CHI Conference on Human Factors in Computing Systems, pp. 1–9. Association for Computing Machinery (2023). https://doi.org/10.1145/3544549.3585676
12. Grigera, J., Garrido, A., Rivero, J.M., Rossi, G.: Automatic detection of usability smells in web applications. Int. J. Hum Comput Stud. **97**, 129–148 (2017). https://doi.org/10.1016/j.ijhcs.2016.09.009
13. Hernandez-Bocanegra, D.C., Ziegler, J.: Conversational review-based explanations for recommender systems: Exploring users' query behavior. In: Proceedings of the 3rd Conference on Conversational User Interfaces, pp. 1–11 (2021). https://doi.org/10.1145/3469595.3469596
14. Hidaka, S., Kobuki, S., Watanabe, M., Seaborn, K.: Linguistic Dead-Ends and Alphabet Soup: Finding Dark Patterns in Japanese Apps. In: Proceedings of the 2023 CHI Conference on Human Factors in Computing Systems, pp. 1–13. Association for Computing Machinery (2023). https://doi.org/10.1145/3544548.3580942

15. van Hooijdonk, C., Martijn, G., Liebrecht, C.: A Framework and Content Analysis of Social Cues in the Introductions of Customer Service Chatbots. In: Følstad, A., et al. (eds.) Chatbot Research and Design, CONVERSATIONS 2022. LNCS, vol. 13815, pp. 118–133. Springer, Cham (2023). https://doi.org/10.1007/978-3-031-25581-6_8

16. Kowalczyk, M., Gunawan, J.T., Choffnes, D., Dubois, D.J., Hartzog, W., Wilson, C.: Understanding Dark Patterns in Home IoT Devices. In: Proceedings of the 2023 CHI Conference on Human Factors in Computing Systems, pp. 1–27. Association for Computing Machinery (2023). https://doi.org/10.1145/3544548.3581432

17. Kvale, K., Freddi, E., Hodnebrog, S., Sell, O.A., Følstad, A.: Understanding the user experience of customer service chatbots: what can we learn from customer satisfaction surveys? In: Følstad, A., et al. (eds.) CONVERSATIONS 2020. LNCS, vol. 12604, pp. 205–218. Springer, Cham (2021). https://doi.org/10.1007/978-3-030-68288-0_14

18. Mathur, A., et al.: Dark patterns at scale: Findings from a Crawl of 11K Shopping Websites. Proc. ACM Hum. Comput. Interact. 3(CSCW), 1–32 (2019). https://doi.org/10.1145/3359183

19. Mathur, A., Kshirsagar, M., Mayer, J.: What makes a Dark Pattern... Dark? Design Attributes, Normative Considerations, and Measurement Methods. In: Proceedings of the 2021 CHI Conference on Human Factors in Computing Systems, pp. 1–18. Association for Computing Machinery (2021). https://doi.org/10.1145/3411764.3445610

20. Mildner, T., Doyle, P., Savino, G.L., Malaka, R.: Rules Of Engagement: Levelling Up To Combat Unethical CUI Design. In: Proceedings of the 4th Conference on Conversational User Interfaces, pp. 1–5 (2022). https://doi.org/10.1145/3543829.3544528

21. Owens, K., Gunawan, J., Choffnes, D., Emami-Naeini, P., Kohno, T., Roesner, F.: Exploring Deceptive Design Patterns in Voice Interfaces. In: Proceedings of the 2022 European Symposium on Usable Security, pp. 64–78 (2022). https://doi.org/10.1145/3549015.3554213

22. Yildiz, E., Bensch, S., Dignum, F.: Incorporating social practices in dialogue systems. In: Følstad, A., et al. (eds.) Chatbot research and design, CONVERSATIONS 2021. LNCS, vol. 13171, pp. 108–123. Springer, Cham (2022). https://doi.org/10.1007/978-3-030-94890-0_7

23. Zagal, J.P., Björk, S., Lewis, C.: Dark patterns in the design of games. In: Foundations of Digital Games 2013 (2013)

# Language Ideology Bias in Conversational Technology

Sviatlana Höhn[1]([✉]), Bettina Migge[2], Doris Dippold[3],
Britta Schneider[4], and Sjouke Mauw[5]

[1] LuxAI, Luxembourg, Luxembourg
sviatlana.hoehn@luxai.com
[2] University Colledge Dublin, Dublin, Ireland
bettinamigge@ucd.ie
[3] Universtity of Surrey, Guildford, UK
d.dippold@surrey.ac.uk
[4] European University Viadrina, Frankfurt, Germany
bschneider@europa-uni.de
[5] University of Luxembourg, DCS, Esch-sur-Alzette, Luxembourg
sjouke.mauw@uni.lu

**Abstract.** The beliefs that we have about language are called *language ideologies* and influence how we create and use language technologies. In this paper, we explore language ideologies and their role in the process of language technology design using conversational technology as an illustrative example. We draw on two qualitative studies, both of which aim at discovering common language conceptualisations in the context of language technology design through collaborative work with study participants. In study 1, we use a survey, group discussions and co-design methods with technology developers. In study 2, we use a survey and group work with technology users. We found that standard language ideology is intertwined with a referential (language in its function to convey information) view on language data in the development process, and that a conceptualization of language as referential tool dominates the language technology landscape. However, participants in both qualitative studies are aware of other functions of language. Further we found that language ideologies are intertwined with public discourse about language technology, and upcoming policies on AI regulation will reinforce these ideologies. We argue that non-referential functions of language must be integrated into language models, and that the actual practices of both language and language technologies must be carefully considered for improved conversational AI and effective policies.

**Keywords:** Language ideologies · Conversational AI · Language functions

Supported by FNR Luxembourg INTER-SLANT 13320890, IF CAIDA 17762538, and EU COST Action LITHME CA19102.

A. Følstad et al. (Eds.): CONVERSATIONS 2023, LNCS 14524, pp. 133–148, 2024.
https://doi.org/10.1007/978-3-031-54975-5_8

# 1   Introduction

People have widely differing ideas of what language is, and multiple linguistic theories reflect different views on language and its functions (see for instance [1]). Language technology developers typically seek computationally implementable definitions of language [21] and collaborate with linguists in numerous multidisciplinary projects. In this process, they inevitably draw on cultural conceptions of language, which are called language ideologies [10]. In the simplest formulation, language ideologies are culturally conditioned sets of beliefs about language that are not necessarily grounded in linguistic or empirical evidence but intersect with social belonging and social hierarchy [34]. Language ideologies influence how language technology creators design and develop the technology that people use for communication, and how users use and perceive language technologies. They concern, for example, language standards and referential functions of language. The former postulate that language is organised according to national categories (e.g. English, Polish and German), and that national or ethnic groups speak the same language that has one and only one correct form. This is often associated with the view that some linguistic practices have a higher value than others and that language change is negative. Referential ideologies construct language as a code that transmits referential, non-linguistic content, and regards meaning as a priori and inherent in words and sentences. Language is argued to exist on its own, while humans use it on demand [27].

Yet, researchers' input on non-referential functions of language shows that language has many more functions (such as expressing and creating relationships, or negotiating and creating mutual understanding). Capturing these functions in computational approaches to language can help to improve systems based on language technology. For example, taking language variation, style variation and language change into account improves word prediction, text classification systems [22], bias detection [9] and speech recognition [36], and it supports social science research [16]. In addition, it has been argued that inclusion of minoritized or non-standard languages in language technology may add to the prestige of these languages, and guarantee citizens' language rights, reduce social inequality, and narrow the digital divide [18].

Language ideology-related problems are especially visible in conversational technology. Research about user satisfaction has found that users of conversational technology have different expectations of language style, e.g. formal vs. informal, which demonstrates the relevance of non-referential variation of language in chatbot use [19,29]. Yet, chatbot interactions tend to be designed according to standard language and entail referential ideologies. This has the effect that users of non-standard language are marginalized and that sociolinguistic hierarchies between "good", "normal", "useful" and "deviant", "bad", "impractical" language are reproduced. Furthermore, the fact that referential meaning is an outcome of social interaction and that language therefore constantly changes is rendered invisible, as language tends to be treated as referential, stable code.

Conversational technology has a potential to reinforce negative attitudes in humans towards non-standard language variations, for instance towards

African-American Vernacular English [3]. Conversational Artificial Intelligence (CAI) also caused political debates every time a prominent technology producer made technology available that was not yet mature enough, such as chatbot Tay by Microsoft, [33], or when some features of the conversational technology reached a milestone in the simulation of human behaviour which made it difficult to differentiate machine from human activity, such as Google Duplex [24]. The most recent development that caused intensive academic and political debates and amplified public discourse is ChatGPT by OpenAI [26].

In light of the above, it is important to model social factors in language technology [14]. More specifically, non-referential functions of language such as identity construction, setting group boundaries and regulation of social proximity need to be made part of language models to improve political bias recognition [15]. In addition, including language variation into security mechanisms of multilingual large language models can help prevent prompt injection attacks more effectively [12]. However, language ideologies play a role in both, CAI development and CAI-related planned regulations. Thus, considering the actual use of the CAI systems, real users' needs and language and communication practices is essential to develop safety measures for AI.

This article argues that both the language-ideological as well as the technology-regulatory debates insufficiently consider real users and real-life language use. We investigate the role of language ideology in language technology by looking at conversational technology, although language ideologies influence all types of language technology. In addition, we investigate the relationship between language ideologies and technology ideologies by looking at what problems users face when using language technologies and how they prioritize further improvements. Our **research questions** are:

1. To what extent do conversational technology designers, developers and users express standard language and referential language ideologies?
2. What other kinds of (language) ideologies are identifiable in the conversation technology domain?

To answer the research questions, we conducted two qualitative studies: a two-hour in-person workshop collocated with a European academic venue focused on chatbots (Study I), and a three-hour in-person workshop collocated with a Summer school funded by a European research agency (Study II). Two researchers conducted the workshops: one working in conversational technology and one working in sociolinguistics.

Both studies show that language ideologies affect the entire process of language technology development, from data collection, design, specification, development and testing phases, to user-based evaluation studies. The second study also discloses that political discourse about artificial intelligence in general and conversational AI in particular shift the focus of language technology workers and users from the actual users' needs to politically amplified topics.

This article aims to raise awareness among their designers, developers and users about the nature, effects and role of language ideologies in the life cycle of language technology. We make a step towards opening a public discussion about language ideologies, their incarnation in technology and policies, and the feedback loop to language of those.

## 2    Language Ideologies, Policies and Public Discourse

All languages are, in terms of grammatical complexity, equal but socially differentiated. Languages associated with powerful nations and print media have higher prestige. Such social hierarchies are observable locally at the level of national language standards, and globally as, for example, in the dominance of English. Language technology reinforces these hierarchies. For instance, speech technology performs better with prestigious Englishes than for less widely spoken ones [5, 20].

Standard languages are perceived as neutral codes, also referred to as "voices from nowhere" [10, p.7]. However, they result from socio-historical circumstances, such as the development of nations, print culture and social hierarchies [4,13,35]. Non-standard languages (e.g. regional or social dialects) have a different history, have covert prestige and are given different functions [17]. The third wave of sociolinguistics and qualitative approaches to language has foregrounded language as social practice and highlights its co-creational social function (social boundaries, identities, stances and social communities), stressing the importance of the non-referential functions of language [8].

Existing computationally-oriented venues dealing with language variation[1] contribute remarkably to computational modelling of language variation. However, these rely on distinguishing standard language from "dialects" and the view that language is an external, static artefact. Overall, language technologies could potentially play an important role in destigmatising minoritized languages and the identities associated with them. However, to date language technologies are mostly developed for major languages that have undergone standardization and are associated with a state and a nation. Other languages and varieties are declared as "non-standard", "noisy" and "non-canonical". [7]. Yet, the "messy" nature of language is central for it to (re)create innovative social meanings; it is not a design fault. With the growing importance of conversational technology, it is vital to counter an understanding of language as a referential, denotional resource [31] and recognise interaction as social practice that negotiates the non-referential functions of language, such as identity construction, face work, group belonging and boundary negotiation [28,30,32].

Language ideologies are closely intertwined with language policies as they shape and inform the way societies perceive, value, and regulate languages [25]. They influence the formulation and implementation of language policies. Language policies, in turn, are the concrete actions and rules put in place by governments, institutions, or communities to manage language use and distribution. The alignment or conflict between (some) language ideologies and language policies can have profound consequences, impacting linguistic diversity, social inclusion, and access to resources. Understanding this complex relationship is crucial for promoting linguistic equity and fostering inclusive societies.

---

[1] E.g. https://sites.google.com/view/vardial-2022/home.

Policies related to regulation of language technologies can work in the same way as language policies. Policies related to language technologies will have a significant impact on both the development and usage of language technologies, as well as on the languages themselves. These policies encompass regulations, standards, and guidelines that govern the creation, deployment, and accessibility of language technologies. They also determine the nature of language technologies and how they are integrated into various sectors, affecting industries, education, and government services.

Current summaries of the planned big set of policies related to AI in general and language technology in particular[2] suggest that planned policies are very much influenced by public discourse which, in turn, is shaped by new ideologies and beliefs about language technologies, and not necessarily by their actual use. Effective public discourse can positively influence policy-making, shape policy outcomes, and hold policymakers accountable, making it a fundamental component of a democratic and participatory society. However, public discourse about language technologies based just on ideologies (fed by the standard language ideology which postulates the existence of a neutral code) in the absence of attention to the actual practices of users (which crucially involve language choices aimed at embodying social meanings), will misinform policy makers and lead to sub-optimal, ineffective and unpopular policies.

This article seeks to raise awareness of these issues and proposes steps towards changes.

## 3    Method

As mentioned in Sect. 1, we conducted two qualitative studies including two surveys and two workshops aiming at disclosing language ideologies in language technologies. We conceptualise the participants of Study I as language technology producers (designers, programmers, researchers), and the participants of Study II as language technology users. Both groups represent highly skilled and highly educated European populations. The first workshop included three steps:

1. *Pre-workshop data collection.* The participants of the workshop were invited to fill in an optional survey with 30 questions. The topics covered the participants' concepts of quality data and language variation, language and language use, interaction and its purpose, and concepts of linguistic disciplines. The information was elicited via open questions. Twelve responses were analysed qualitatively for Step 2.
2. *In-workshop discussion.* Participants introduced themselves. Facilitators gave an introduction about language ideologies and discussed the survey results. The results were presented by a computer-science researcher and commented by a sociolinguistic researcher. This phase helped to answer the first research question.

---

[2] https://www.europarl.europa.eu/news/en/headlines/society/20230601STO93804/.

3. *In-workshop co-design.* Participants discussed three questions in smaller randomly assigned groups and presented the results in the plenary session before jointly formulating mitigation and awareness-making measures.

The second workshop was composed of four stages:

1. *Pre-workshop data collection.* The participants were invited to answer ten questions about their views on language and language technologies.
2. *Exploratory use case.* The facilitator presented a conversational robot and explained its use case: teaching children different types of skills including language. The participants were invited to write down on sticky notes their ideas about positive and negative effects with respect to one of the categories: language rights, language ideologies, language variation, interaction, language diversity and vitality, language learning, language technology and language work. The participants were also asked to place their sticky notes on a whiteboard according to the category for which they think the statement is relevant.
3. *In-workshop group work and discussion.* Facilitators presented the results of the survey. Based on the preliminary outcome of the survey, language learning apps were the most known type of language technology. Therefore, the participants were asked to design their own language learning application that solves all problems detected by the survey.
4. *Cross-domain analysis.* The researchers analysed and aligned all outcomes produced by participants: survey, group work and ideas from sticky notes.

Both groups were mixed in terms of gender and academic seniority level and included expertise in linguistics, language teaching, language translation, interaction, dialogue analysis, user experience research, psychology, behavioral sciences, computer science, language technology, communication and media studies. The number of subjects is 22 for the first and 43 for the second group.

The results of the qualitative questions from the surveys were independently coded by both researchers who conducted the studies. If multiple categories were identifiable in the answer, the answer received multiple labels. Examples of coding are provided in Table 1.

## 4    Results and Discussion

In this section, we describe our findings from both studies in detail and synthesize the results with regard to language technology related ideologies.

### 4.1    Study I

This qualitative study confirmed the language ideologies and the participants' focus on referential functions of language. The results allow drawing a number of conclusions about state-of-the-art in the language technology domain.

**Table 1.** Examples of coding for qualitative questions in both surveys.

| Question formulation | Answer example | Labels |
|---|---|---|
| In your view, which problems of language technologies should be urgently resolved and why? | I am not sure if all problems with language technologies can be resolved. What is most urgent is for there to be a more honest and comprehensive narrative that teaches the general public about the benefits of language technologies and their drawbacks. | Literacy |
| Same as above | data security issues; educate laypeople about problems language techologies can bring | Privacy Literacy |

The study also revealed that there is a connection between standard language ideology and a referential view of language. Standardised, normalised language data make the mapping from input to meaning representation easier, but it is not always made transparent, how data "normalization" affects this process (see for instance [23] for a discussion). However, the need for "clean" and error-free data is problematic because even standard language is not uniform across social domains, people use and process language idiosyncratically and creatively, and constantly adapt language in interaction for self presentation, to encode their views about the interaction, the interlocutor etc. Thus, non-referential meanings are erased in data normalisation and cleaning.

Linguistics and sociolinguistics have made considerable progress since the emergence of generativism, however, their findings have rarely been included in the design paradigm of language technology [2,11]. Moreover, co-creation of language *while* interacting with language technology has never been conceptualised due to standard language ideology dominating in the language technology community which maintains that language is neutral and referential in nature. Technical constraints are central in research on language technologies. The details are presented below.

**Findings from the Survey I.** The survey helped to disclose A) the participants' assumptions about language, its function and variation, B) their beliefs about communication, and C) their perspective on language data.

A) The responses disclose participants' awareness of multiple forms and functions in each language, and the way these encode different aspects of context. The participants associated every-day language with emotions, a playful, familiar, friendly manner, and social closeness with accessible vocabulary and low complexity of expression. Standard language, in contrast, is associated with respectfulness and social distance. Overall, the more private the space, the more diverse are people's language choices. Participants mostly use English for communication in their professional contexts even if it is not the language for which they develop technology. Other languages dominate private communication. Participants were knowledgeable about types of language variation (interactional variation, dialectical patterns, syntactic and lexical variation) although it is usually not part of their language technology design or development process.

B) Communication was named as the main function of language and described as the transmission of thoughts, feelings and experiences. We identified three clusters of responses related to the nature of human communication: a *functional* cluster that included sense of purpose, ability to do repair, create relevance and manage the unexpected; an *emotional* cluster that included expression of emotions and empathy, humour and sarcasm; and a *context* cluster that included ambiguity, context dependency of meaning and spontaneous and endlessly variant production. All these attributes characterise different aspects of the referential function of language. An awareness of the non-referential functions of language had low salience in the responses (except of the emotional cluster). The latter was mostly associated with explicit labelling of emotion using positive and negative words, emphasising the referential function. There was lack of awareness that language emerges *in* the interaction, and that language is always intertwined with the social, and cannot be separated from it.

C) Although there was a high demand in the group for naturalistic data, such as human face-to-face conversations, the researchers typically choose "clean", well documented, standardised, error-free and accessible data for their work in language technology. Thus, the *operational* (prioritising ease of implementation) view on data for language technology dominates the community. In this way, the standard language ideology bias is amplified in language technology: language data are taken from the standard language and modified to be error-free, "cleaned", well-documented etc.

Because the desired data are usually not available in the needed quality or quantity, participants reported that they usually create their own datasets via surveys, log analysis, experimental designs or use "similar" data (e.g. Twitter comments instead of instant messenger chat logs).

**Findings from the Group Work I.** We asked every subgroup to draw their position on the following three questions:

Q1 Which social functions of communication does chatbot design try to model or implement?
Q2 Which understanding of language underlies chatbot design?
Q3 What is the relationship between data, data collection and generation methods and chatbot's communication capabilities?

Each subgroup produced a poster, and the results are summarised in Table 2 by question (left column). Although the group was aware of the relationship between language data and language technology based on them, the group work again highlighted the operational view on language data for language technology development, see Table 2 Q2 ("standardize it", "input - output"). Language data are seen as a help to find the right mapping from input to output, equally for standard and every-day language, for task-oriented and social dialogue. The referential role of language is not only very dominant, but also very convenient for implementation, which makes it difficult to change the paradigm.

**Findings from the Co-Design Phase.** In the co-design phase we aimed at formulating language ideology awareness guidelines together with the participants of the workshop. The following points were emphasised by the participants.

**Co-design with Users.** Involving users into the process of language technology design from the beginning can help to go beyond solely referential and operational views on language in conversational technology and language technology in general.

**Table 2.** Transcript of the group work, original wording.

| | Group 1 | Group 2 | Group 3 |
|---|---|---|---|
| Q1 | Formal language (as it has rules + less creative). Bots seem more human when using puns and jokes | Activate, engage; interpersonal understanding, empathy; exchange information; showing manners, etiquette, scrutiny smalltalk; humour; building intimacy, trust, "talking"; communicative entity is social to begin with | Standard language - transactional, goal-oriented, closed-domain; everyday language - relationship building, trust, empathy, compassion, personification, adaptation; open-domain |
| Q2 | Standardize it, so it can learn from a big data sample, then it does not adapt to each individual (language-wise); Oral communication → pitch, tone can play a role in language meaning, text-based needs different cues to implement this. It is not the understanding but the technical ability to write concisely (short sentences, to the point) | Aim to objectively understand language (encode, decode), context-specific (domain), modelling (transforming voice to text, from 3D to 2D), adaptation (reduce language complexity) | Operational understanding of language, defined by Q1 |
| Q3 | Garbage in, garbage out; drawing of mutual dependencies of relationships | Drawing: collection methods influence quality, data quality determines capabilities. What defines quality? More data is not always better. Biases. Questioned direct relationship between collection methods and a chatbot's capabilities | Data ethics, privacy, data governance, data ownership, transparency, context-dependent |

**Detailed Documentation.** Transparency about the gap between "natural" interaction data and the actual data that are used. The origin of data must be documented. It must be made explicit to the readers of documentation for datasets, what kinds of approximations were made for each application case.

**Continuous Improvement.** Starting with a simplified "minimum viable product", design and development of language technology is a step-by-step, iterative process. Simplifications need to be made explicit to the readers of documentation, and conversation design is never complete.

## 4.2   Study II

The study revealed that there is a relationship between language ideologies and political discourse about language technologies and their regulations. The survey disclosed that language technology users are clear about their actual needs and have a very concrete understanding about how language technology would make their work and daily life more efficient, pleasant and enjoyable. However, when asked about priorities of language technology improvement, actual user needs are downgraded and publically much discussed topics are prioritised.

In addition, this study revealed that participants perceptions of specific language technology is also determined by public discourses. Both the use case and the group work echoed the public discourse.

**Findings from the Survey II.** The attendees of an in-person Summer school were asked to fill-in an optional survey. From 43 attendees, 19 chose to reply to the questionnaire. The findings were discussed with the entire group.

The survey compared for which purpose the participants use language technology, what participants viewed as the biggest problems related to their own technology use and experience, and what should be improved as soon as possible. The top five in these three categories were:

| Problems | Benefits | Priorities |
|---|---|---|
| Low quality | Productivity | Literacy |
| Language availability | Creativity | Inclusion |
| Security & privacy | Progress | Bias |
| Expectation-quality mismatch | Facilitate communication | Language coverage |
| Confidence-quality mismatch | Accessibility of information | Ethics |

Further, we compared familiarity, frequency of use and interest in language technologies by participants. Top five for these three categories were:

| Familiarity | Usage | Interest |
|---|---|---|
| Machine translation | Messengers | Translation |
| Speech synthesis | Machine translation | Language learning, teaching |
| Language learning apps | Authoring tools | Research |
| Speech recognition | Social media | Everyday life |
| Spelling & grammar checker | Language generation | Communication |

As in Study I, the participants acknowledge that language performs a variety of functions in human-human communications. However, the functions of language in communication with technology are in 80% of the cases reduced to commands and instructions (referential view).

Besides communication technologies such as messengers and social media, machine translation and text production tools (text authoring and language generation) are the most popular technologies, and their relation to the top five benefits listed by our participants is quite clear. It is also quite clear that low quality and limited language coverage (language availability) of such services leads to frustration with technology. However, literacy related to language technologies, inclusion, bias and ethics that are listed among the top priorities for future development will not help to solve problems related to low quality. This mismatch in responses suggests that even technology users set technology development priorities based on public discourse rather than their own needs.

**Findings from the Use Case.** The facilitator demonstrated a social robot that is used for teaching autistic children different types of skills. The demonstration focused on language technologies used to deliver such kind of educational interventions, and mutual dependencies among them (dialogue design, automated speech synthesis, feedback generation and so on).

The task was to pin down all positive and negative aspects of the demonstrated technology by writing statements on sticky notes. Those sticky notes were first categorised by participants according to the eight categories provided in the beginning (see Sect. 3), and later coded and clustered by the facilitators according to their subject. Participants listed 75 negative and 55 positive aspects in total that were coded to 25 and 13 categories, respectively.

With regards to language ideologies, this part of the study showed that participants' awareness related to language ideologies is rudimentary. In total, eight statements were categorised by participants as related to language ideologies, and only three of them were in fact related to language ideologies, all addressing the robot's potential to promote and reinforce some standard language. At the same time, language variation and "human-like" interaction are seen as the most urgent problems with social robots, although these problems have been classified by participants as related to language variation.

The top five of issues listed are:

- language coverage and variation (15);
- ethics (12) including replacement of humans by machines (10) although in the described scenario, no replacement took place;
- technical accessibility and price (7);
- issues with interaction (7); and
- potential technical problems (5).

Top three positive aspects listed are related to human empowerment, interaction quality and enrichment of teaching and learning followed by four categories with the same strength: accessibility, language coverage, personalisation of interaction and potential other application scenarios.

The comparison of positive and negative aspects shows that there are no absolute values: the same technology is seen as empowering and disempowering humans, restricting and providing opportunities for a wide language coverage and accessibility, offering positive and negative interaction experience. This shows that how people judge technologies is very much dependent on how messages are framed, also in public discourse.

**Findings from the Group Work II.** The following task was given to participants after the facilitators had presented the results from the survey and given a theoretical introduction on language ideologies.

*Imagine, you need to design a new language learning app and to do so, you need to solve three questions first:*

1. *Which social functions of communication should the new app implement?*
2. *Which understanding of language should underlie the language learning app design?*
3. *What kinds of data should this design process rely on and how can this data be obtained to meet the targeted social functions?*

Participants had 15 min to work in small groups on these questions and were then asked to present their solutions. The facilitators were interested in how clear those tasks are to the groups and how successful the groups are in their solutions. Participants worked in six groups and each group included experts in different domains and different levels of academic seniority. All six groups struggled with understanding and definition of social functions of language and language as a whole when it comes to design of a concrete technology. None of the groups could clarify the question about data.

**Findings from the Cross-Domain Analysis.** The main three outcomes from the survey, case study and group work of Study II are:

1. When it comes to an abstract discussion of language technologies, there is a mismatch between language technology user needs and improvement priorities set by the same users. This mismatch is likely due to public discourse related to language technology.
2. When it comes to a discussion of a specific conversational technology, positive aspects are usually those mentioned explicitly in the demonstration (empowerment, interaction, enrichment) while negative aspects are related to current public discourses (bias, ethics).
3. When it comes to designing solutions, multidisciplinary teams of experts still struggle with finding a proper working definition for basic concepts such as language and language functions. There is also little clarity about the types of language data that exist, their suitability for technology design and how they may be acquired.

### 4.3    Discussion and Potential Actions

This article presents qualitative research obtained from two small-scale qualitative studies. The initial ideas generated through the questionnaires and the workshops need to be validated further through an interview-based study with developers, investors and policy-makers, or a survey distributed to a larger sample of respondents.

Study I indicates that language ideologies play a role in the entire life cycle of language technologies, while Study II suggests that larger social ideologies such as current public discourses on technology and beyond, as well as their drawbacks, also affect how we imagine, create, use and evaluate language technologies. Both language ideologies and public discourses about language technology heavily impact our views of technology and its regulations and contribute to sidelining the consideration of users' needs and real-life practices.

As mentioned in Sect. 1, multiple CAI tools ignited controversial public discussions about ethics in CAI systems. ChatGPT in particular raised a lot of questions related to text authoring, teaching, manipulative content production, colonial methods in the process of data acquisition and cleaning, and intellectual property rights in general [26]. At the same time, the European Union started preparing the EU AI Act, a document that is supposed to provide guidelines for EU member states on how to handle particular matters in the national legislation. One of the main claims that the EU AI Act draft is making is that all texts generated by generative language models must be marked as generated.[3]

Discourses about language and language technologies are dominated by ideological claims. Policies connect both in the way that language policies have little to do with the actual language practices [25], and the ongoing public and political debates about regulation of language technologies (and AI in general) have little to do with the human practices of using them.

For example, the summary of the planned regulations contains the claim that in the future, all texts generated by language models will have to be marked as such. This requirement will cause multiple practical issues related to human and human-machine collaborative text production practices. Generative language models are used nowadays in spellcheckers, style-checkers, grammar correction features of most text editing programs, in word suggestions on mobile devices, response suggestions in text messengers, and in sentence completion suggestions of text authoring programs. There is a lot of text generation outside of ChatGPT. Further, even if language models such as ChatGPT are used, texts are usually generated in collaboration with human co-authors (reformulations, prompt engineering) and not completely autonomously. It is not clear how much of the text must be generated in order to be declared as automatically generated, and how the amount can be measured in practice.

Both types of ideologies, the ones related to language and the ones related to language technology, will set constraints and judge together, what is a "good" language and what is a "bad" or "low quality" language. However, in addition to labels associated with nation state and power, such as "standard English", labels associated with participation of technical devices in language practices, such as "automatically generated" will be used to make differences between

---

[3] https://www.europarl.europa.eu/news/en/headlines/society/20230601STO93804/eu-ai-act-first-regulation-on-artificial-intelligence.

more valuable and less valuable language. Finally, by regulating language technology without looking at their actual use by humans and without capturing new practices of language creation by human-machine teams, policy makers will set regulations to language itself, reinforcing existing language ideologies in their incarnation in current language technology.

To make the results of this research applicable in practice, we suggest the following actions:

1. **Theory**. Sociolinguistic and pragmatic expertise and more recent theories of language that see it as a social practice must be adopted in language modeling to handle non-referential functions of language. In addition, they must also inform policy-making about the role of technology as not-just-tool in the process of language creation.
2. **Policy**. Work with politics and NGOs to declare availability of language technology in regional variations a human right.
3. **Capital**. Incubators could support new businesses targeting smaller languages. We cannot change capitalism with this paper, but collaborative efforts are needed to emphasize economic and cultural value of smaller languages.
4. **Investment**. Push public funds into language technology for people: focused on user needs, created with potential users, speaking the user's language as messy as it is, and being able to deal with variations.
5. **Data**. Create and use real spoken language resources (no, movie dialogues are not spoken language, but [6] compiled a list). Create more of those corpora.

## 5   Conclusions

Both studies have several implications for the language technology community and policy makers. First, specialists involved in language technology creation need to sharpen their awareness of the kinds of biases that impact the whole life cycle of language technology. Both standard language ideologies and political discourses on the benefits and drawbacks of technology influence the creation, conceptualization, production, evaluation and further development of technologies (including users' expressed needs) and thus need to be critically assessed and reflected upon at each step in the life cycle. Second, discourses and views of participants in the life cycle of technologies are contradictory and varied because not all participants engage in the same discourses and ideologies. Third, while the standard language ideology continues to be powerful, the language practices it promotes are not always used and in some cases understood only by a minority of people. Fourth, modelling non-referential functions of language is crucial for conversational technology as this is what makes technology appear "human-like". Finally, the public discourse about language and language technology needs to be more inclusive. Instead of echoing claims related to ethics and bias, the community needs to have a wider public discussion about the actual uses of language, language practices, variations, and their relation to technology and power.

# References

1. Auer, P.: Sprachliche Interaktion: Eine Einführung anhand von 22 Klassikern. Niemeyer, Tübingen (1999)
2. Blodgett, S.L., Barocas, S., Daumé III, H., Wallach, H.: Language (technology) is power: a critical survey of "bias" in NLP. In: Proceedings of 58th ACL Meeting, pp. 5454–5476. ACL (2020)
3. Cassell, J.: Socially interactive agents as peers. In: The Handbook on Socially Interactive Agents: 20 years of Research on Embodied Conversational Agents, Intelligent Virtual Agents, and Social Robotics Volume 2: Interactivity, Platforms, Application, pp. 331–366 (2022)
4. Coupland, N.: Sociolinguistics: Theoretical debates. Cambridge University Press (2016)
5. DiChristofano, A., Shuster, H., Chandra, S., Patwari, N.: Performance disparities between accents in automatic speech recognition. arXiv:2208.01157 (2022)
6. Dingemanse, M., Liesenfeld, A.: From text to talk: Harnessing conversational corpora for humane and diversity-aware language technology. In: Proceedings of the 60th Annual Meeting of the Association for Computational Linguistics (Volume 1: Long Papers). pp. 5614–5633 (2022)
7. Dipper, S., Neubarth, F., Zinsmeister, H. (eds.): Proceedingns of KONVENS 2016: Processing non-standard data - commonalities and differences. Bochumer Linguistische Arbeitsberichte (2016)
8. Eckert, P.: Three waves of variation study: The emergence of meaning in the study of sociolinguistic variation. Annu. Rev. Anthropol. **41**(1), 87–100 (2012)
9. Ferrer, X., van Nuenen, T., Such, J.M., Criado, N.: Discovering and categorising language biases in reddit. In: Proceedings of the International AAAI Conference on Web and Social Media, vol. 15, pp. 140–151 (2021)
10. Gal, S., Woolard, K.A.: Constructing languages and publics: Authority and representation. Pragmatics **5**(2), 129–138 (1995)
11. Hamborg, F.: Towards Automated Frame Analysis: Natural Language Processing Techniques to Reveal Media Bias in News Articles. Ph.D. thesis, University of Konstanz, Konstanz (2022)
12. Harang, R.: Securing LLM systems against prompt injection (2023). https://developer.nvidia.com/blog/securing-llm-systems-against-prompt-injection/
13. Holmes, J., Wilson, N.: An introduction to sociolinguistics. Routledge (2017)
14. Hovy, D., Yang, D.: The importance of modeling social factors of language: theory and practice. In: The 2021 Conference of the North American Chapter of the Association for Computational Linguistics: Human Language Technologies. Association for Computational Linguistics (2021)
15. Höhn, S., Asher, N., Mauw, S.: Examining linguistic biases in telegram with a game theoretic analysis. In: Proceedings of the 3rd MISDOOM, pp. 16–32 (2021)
16. Kellert, O., Matlis, N.H.: Social context and user profiles of linguistic variation on a micro scale. In: Proceedings of the Ninth Workshop on NLP for Similar Languages, Varieties and Dialects, pp. 14–19. ACL, Gyeongju, Republic of Korea (Oct 2022)
17. Labov, W.: The social stratification of (r) in new york city department stores. In: Dialect and Language Variation, pp. 304–329. Elsevier (1986)
18. Láncos, P.L.: The role of language technologies in promoting the participation of linguistic minorities in social, political and economic life. Foreign Policy Rev. **2**, 73–87 (2021)

19. Liebrecht, C., Sander, L., Hooijdonk, C.: Too informal? how a chatbot's communication style affects brand attitude and quality of interaction. In: International
Workshop on Chatbot Research and Design, pp. 16–31 (2020)

20. Markl, N.: Language variation and algorithmic bias: understanding algorithmic
bias in british english automatic speech recognition. In: 2022 ACM Conference on
Fairness, Accountability, and Transparency, pp. 521–534 (2022)

21. Mitkov, R. (ed.): The Oxford Handbook of Computational Linguistics. Oxford
University Press (2003)

22. Nguyen, D., Doğruöz, A.S., Rosé, C.P., De Jong, F.: Computational sociolinguistics: a survey. Comput. Linguistics **42**(3), 537–593 (2016)

23. Nguyen, D.: How we do things with words: analyzing text as social and cultural
data. Front. Artifi. Intell. **3**, 62 (2020)

24. O'Leary, D.E.: Google's duplex: pretending to be human. Intell. Syst. Accounting,
Finance Manag. **26**(1), 46–53 (2019)

25. Pennycook, A.: Language policies, language ideologies and local language practices.
The politics of English: South Asia, Southeast Asia and the Asia Pacific, pp. 1–18
(2013)

26. Ray, P.P.: Chatgpt: A comprehensive review on background, applications, key challenges, bias, ethics, limitations and future scope. Internet of Things Cyber-Physical
Syst. (2023)

27. Schlangen, D.: Norm participation grounds language. arXiv preprint
arXiv:2206.02885 (2022)

28. Shrikant, N.: "it's like,'I've never met a lesbian before!'": personal narratives and
the construction of diverse female identities in a lesbian counterpublic. Pragmatics
**24**(4), 799–818 (2014)

29. Skjuve, M., Følstad, A., Fostervold, K.I., Brandtzaeg, P.B.: A longitudinal study
of human-chatbot relationships. Int. J. of Hum.-Comput. Stud., 102903 (2022)

30. Sowińska, A., Dubrovskaya, T.: Discursive construction and transformation of 'us'
and 'them' categories in the newspaper coverage on the US anti-ballistic missile
system: Polish versus Russian view. Discourse Comm. **6**(4), 449–468 (2012)

31. Trosdal, M.B.: Meaning: the referential function of language. Philippine Q. Culture
Soc. **23**(3/4), 361–368 (1995)

32. Whitehead, K., Lerner, G.: When are persons 'white'?: on some practical asym-
metries of racial reference in talk-in-interaction. Discourse Soc. **20**, 613–641 (2009)

33. Wolf, M.J., Miller, K., Grodzinsky, F.S.: Why we should have seen that coming:
comments on microsoft's tay "experiment" and wider implications. Acm Sigcas
Comput. Soc. **47**(3), 54–64 (2017)

34. Woolard, K.A.: Introduction: language ideology as a field of inquiry. Lang. Ideologies: Pract. Theory **3**(11), 1–50 (1998)

35. Woolard, K.A.: Language, identity, and politics in catalonia. Brown J. World Aff.
**25**, 21 (2018)

36. Wu, Y., Suchanek, F., Vasilescu, I., Lamel, L., Adda-Decker, M.: Using a knowledge base to automatically annotate speech corpora and to identify sociolinguistic
variation. In: Proceedings of the Thirteenth Language Resources and Evaluation
Conference, pp. 1054–1060. ELRA, Marseille, France (2022)

# Should Conversational Agents Care About Our Gender Identity?

Arturo Cocchi[1]([✉]), Tibor Bosse[2], and Michelle van Pinxteren[2]

[1] Faculty of Political and Social Sciences, Gent University, Gent, Belgium
arturo.cocchi@ugent.be

[2] Communication and Media Group, Radboud University, Nijmegen, The Netherlands

**Abstract.** Chatbots are increasing their relevance in the global market. Nonetheless, companies are still struggling to develop chatbots that provide their clients with an optimal experience and, so far, few insights have been obtained to improve their related User Experience (UX). This study investigates whether chatbots that consider users' gender identity result in an improved UX, and whether sensitivity towards this social matter moderates this relationship. Therefore, a one-factor within-subjects experiment was conducted, involving participants interacting with two versions of a buying-assistant chatbot. In one condition, the chatbot provided a more personalised interaction by presuming the user's gender identity by their sex assigned at birth and conversing with them using a gender-specific language (e.g., 'women's clothing', 'men's clothing'). The second condition, instead, used a gender-neutral approach, using gender-neutral language (e.g., 'clothing'). We hypothesised that the chatbot presuming a cisgender identity of the user would result in a higher UX than the gender-neutral chatbot, and that this effect would be more substantial for users who score low on gender sensitivity. UX was measured by evaluating the chatbot's Usability, Empathy and Supportiveness. Results indicate that the chatbot presuming a cisgender identity was considered significantly more usable and supportive, but less empathetic. A moderation effect of gender sensitivity on the evaluation of the chatbots was not found.

**Keywords:** User Experience · Chatbots · Human-Computer Interaction · Gender Identity · Personalisation

## 1 Introduction

In the past decade, conversational agents have gained popularity as software capable of socially interacting with people through human-like text or speech [1, 2]. Text-based conversational agents, or *chatbots*, have experienced significant growth since 2016 due to their cost-effectiveness and easy implementation [3]. They provide fast and accessible customer support, leading to increased customer engagement: It is projected that retail services facilitated by chatbots will reach $142 billion in spending by 2024 [4].

However, despite their success, both industry and research have highlighted the challenges of creating engaging and convincing interactions with chatbots for customer support. Some critiques focus on their current struggle to guarantee the five dimensions of service quality (e.g., empathy) [5], while others emphasise their lack of context awareness [6], which can result in lower User Experience (UX) [7], reduced interest in interacting with chatbots [8], and decreased engagement with the company [9].

A promising strategy to overcome these challenges is *personalisation* of chatbots. The importance of studying chatbot personalisation in customer service lies in two aspects. First, it is particularly relevant to meet modern consumer expectations: customers now expect fast, top-quality, and convenient customer service that can support their needs more effectively [9]. Second, as organisations seek to balance quality service with efficient resources, correctly personalised interactions provide a competitive edge and cost-saving services while enhancing customer experiences [10, 11]. Notwithstanding, companies refrain from embracing this novel trend of personalising the consumer experience when creating their customer assistant chatbots: the absence of comprehensive guidelines on overcoming such challenges requires tempestive action [7, 8]. The first goal of this paper is to fulfil this purpose, contributing to shaping the path to do so successfully.

In a recent review [6], the authors delineate three distinct levels of personal attributes to personalise chatbot interactions according to user preferences. These levels encompass style, trait, and persona adaptations. They highlight how research has concentrated on imbuing chatbots with varying communication styles, encompassing facets such as voice tone, personality traits, and individual characteristics, as documented in a more comprehensive review [2]. Prior investigations have demonstrated successful adaptations of chatbot interactions to personal characteristics and preferences [12, 13]. Nevertheless, there is a conspicuous dearth of research focusing on integrating an individual's alignment with specific social identities in chatbot interactions. A specific aspect of social identity that is particularly relevant within human-chatbot interaction is *gender identity*. Thus, the second goal of this study is to expand the repertoire of personal attributes that chatbot interactions should consider by focusing on gender identity.

Gender identity, among various social identities individuals recognise within themselves, emerges as a particularly salient focus for three reasons. Firstly, as numerous scholars have contended [6–8], a more granular alignment of chatbot interactions with the user's unique characteristics stands to enhance the overall user experience. Secondly, the ongoing discourse regarding the significance of gender in the domain of conversation analysis [14, 15] needs further exploration of the concept. Thirdly, in a world characterised by continual evolution, where the forces of inclusivity and discrimination against minority groups contend, the examination of gender identity within conversation analysis retains its profound relevance. Unravelling the potential impact of this discourse in our digitalised society holds the promise of shaping future technologies and tools, ultimately ensuring a more enriched user experience.

This study's primary objectives revolve around refining chatbot interactions by incorporating an individual's gender identity as a central personalisation component. Hence, the study aims to address the following research goal:

*RG: To what extent will modifying chatbots' ability to recognise the users' gender identity change the overall user experience, and what role does gender sensitivity play in this process?*

## 2   State of the Art

User Experience can be loosely defined as the feeling people experience when using a product or service. It is a broad concept widely studied within the Human-Computer Interaction literature. Thüring and Mahlke [16] delineate how UX is created by the complex interplay between individuals and technical systems, elucidating the dynamics of Human-Technology Interaction (HTI) and its dependence on three critical factors: System Properties, User Characteristics, and Context Parameters.

One way to influence UX is to modify the technological system itself. Bevan and colleagues [17] have identified System Properties that can impact HTI, including functionality, dialogue principles, and interface characteristics. In the context of conversational agents, studies have shown a preference for those exhibiting human-like properties [18–20], as they are perceived as more socially relatable [2, 21]. Consequently, efforts have been directed toward making conversational agents more human-like, with successful results. For instance, experiments involving robots with human-like faces or conversational agents with a human-like appearance have increased likability and positive user reactions [18, 22].

However, an alternate viewpoint suggests that the success of conversational agents depends on their ability to *engage* users rather than merely resembling humans [5, 23, 24]. An important strategy to engage users is by using personalisation. From this perspective, the fundamental System Property of text-based chatbots lies in their proficiency for textual communication. In line with other authors [25], we hypothesise that modifying the chatbot's System Property to facilitate proficient textual conversation will have implications for HCI, thereby influencing UX. Other studies previously accomplished this. For instance, using mimicry and social praise during chatbot interactions increased perceived friendliness [26], while respecting human social norms during text-based interactions was noted as essential [27, 28].

In this paper we study the possibilities of increasing UX through personalisation, and more specifically through social identification. Trivedi [29] highlights three key components—Information Quality, System Quality, and Service Quality—that influence the performance of Information Systems, including chatbots. System Quality, which overlaps with Thüring and Mahlke's System Properties framework, underscores the crucial role of adaptability and personalisation. Therefore, successful HTI necessitates accurate and effective interactions, considering individual requests and preferences. Correctly identifying the user is essential for fruitful interactions [7], which are additionally affected by the user's expectations and contextual factors [30]. These aspects are confirmed by Thüring and Mahlke's framework, where User Characteristics - such as needs, expectations, predispositions, and motivations [31] - and Context Parameters consistently shape users' preferences [16]. Cultural differences, including language, communication methods, and societal structures, further shape User Characteristics [32]. Thus, a personalisation based on social identification, such as gender identity, should positively influence the UX.

Gender identity is considered one of the numerous social identities, representing the psychological connection with a specific social category [33]. It is impacted by the social norms associated with various genders and their relevance within a particular social context [34, 35]. For example, identifying someone with a female gender identity implies that they perceive the norms associated with women in their social context as relevant to them [35]. While the discourse on the significance of gender analysis in conversational contexts remains open, a consensus exists among numerous scholars regarding its pertinence (see [14] for an overview). Consequently, we assert that precise gender identity recognition, coupled with adherence to context-specific norms, plays a vital role in enhancing the overall UX in interactions between humans and chatbots.

As social identities vary between individuals, the level of user sensitivity to gender identity and adherence to societal expectations may influence how much users want chatbots to consider their gender identity in gender-specific situations. Heteronormativity, which sees heterosexuality as the norm and follows a binary gender system, is marked by societal expectations regarding how people should interact and behave [33], expectations that might as well influence UX in HCI. Additionally, individuals with assertive heteronormative behaviour may exhibit different reactions than those with a more inclusive mindset [33]. We expect such responses to be different depending on such sensitivity.

This study specifically explores the personalisation of buying assistant chatbots, emphasising individual preferences and social identities, including gender. While gender-based personalisation is well-established in customer service, enhancing UX [9], its impact on User Experience in HCI remains uncertain [31]. As previous studies have explored diverse social and behavioural aspects [2, 36–39] but not the human-agent experiences of individuals from distinct social groups [32], this study addresses a gap in linking social identity to chatbot characteristics.

To investigate the impact of gender identity on UX, we conducted an online experiment in which we altered a vital chatbot interaction element: the text used for user communication. Two chatbot types were developed: The first version had a non-personalized interaction, employing gender-neutral language without assumptions about the user's gender. The second version adapted its language to the user's presumed current gender identity (referred to as the *cisgender* version), determined by their sex assigned at birth.

We incorporate three distinct variables to evaluate the UX perceived from chatbot interactions. Firstly, we consider an instrumental quality, *Usability*, which is paramount in user experience [16, 40, 41]. Additionally, we include two elements concerning the chatbot's capacity for effective interpersonal communication: *Empathy* and *Supportiveness*. These emotional aspects have garnered increasing attention in conversational agent research, owing to their demonstrably positive impact on user interactions [13, 26, 42]. We strongly emphasise the significance of these three topics within the realm of gender identity, given the level of personalisation involved: a chatbot that is finely tuned to individual preferences is poised to exhibit notably enhanced Usability; a chatbot that genuinely acknowledges and respects user gender identity is expected to evoke a more profound sense of Empathy; a customer assistant chatbot that tailors its recommendations based on participants' gender identity is anticipated to enhance the perception of Supportiveness. Hence, we developed the following hypotheses:

*H1: A chatbot presuming a cisgender identity of the user leads to a higher UX than a chatbot that does not assume the user's gender identity.*

*H2: The positive effect on UX of a chatbot presuming cisgender identity is stronger for users who score low on gender sensitivity.*

# 3   Method

Further details on the sample size rationale and the model used for the analyses can be found in Appendix A.

## 3.1   Design and Participants

To test the hypothesised effects, we conducted an online experiment using a single-factor within-subjects design in which participants interacted with two versions of the same buying-assistant chatbot. The task of the chatbot was to help users purchase clothing items from a provided list. The chatbot versions differed in how they assessed participants' gender. One version assumed that participants had a cisgender identity (i.e., the user identifies with the sex assigned at birth, male or female), while the other version had a gender-neutral approach (i.e., the chatbot makes no assumptions about the user's gender identity). This difference was assessed in the framing sentences and item descriptions: the cisgender version used more gender-related words, while the gender-neutral version did not.

Participants were recruited through the platform Prolific, therefore using a convenience sample. Each participant was a native speaker or at least fluent in English (98.8% of the sample lived in the UK). The sample of 251 participants ($N = 251$) consisted of 125 men (49.8%) and 126 women (50.2%) who identified as cisgender. Participants ranged in age from 19 to 74 years ($M = 35.84$, $SD = 12.68$). Participants received fair payment according to Prolific's standards.

## 3.2   Stimulus Material

This study was conducted in collaboration with the Conversation Design Institute (CDI), an AI consulting organisation. Recognising the scientific and market applicability of investigating the impact of gender identity on conversational agents, a collaborative decision was made with CDI to pursue this research direction.

To achieve the study objectives, the chatbot was developed in conjunction with CDI using the Voiceflow conversation design tool. Voiceflow is an internet-based platform designed specifically for creating and implementing conversational agents. Two iterations of the chatbot were developed: a gender-neutral variant using inclusive language endorsed by the United Nations [43], and a cisgender variant that recommended products tailored to participants presumed to possess cisgender identities. Participants interacted with the chatbots by selecting predetermined response options, as no answer was given when using open-ended textual input.

The chatbot functioned as a text-based shopping assistant, aiming to help participants procure items in six macro categories: trousers, shirts, outerwear, shoes, accessories, and cosmetics. Each category included three items with personalised descriptions. Participants were presented with predefined response options and could choose their preferred items, eliminating the need for textual input. At the beginning of the interaction, the chatbot, named Magybot, asked participants to indicate their assigned sex at birth. In the cisgender condition, the chatbot used gender-specific terms based on the user's assigned sex at birth (e.g., boy, male, girl, female). In contrast, the gender-neutral chatbot disregarded the user's specified sex and replaced gender-specific terms with gender-neutral terms (e.g., person, individual, people). Please refer to Fig. 1 for a visual representation. The evaluation of the chatbot versions to ensure the quality of the HCI was conducted by CDI staff. A fashion industry expert assessed the appropriateness of purchase options by considering the most unisex images possible. For a comprehensive list of items categorised by chatbot type and their personalised descriptions, please see Appendix B.

### 3.3 Procedure

Participants were directed from Prolific to Qualtrics, where they learned about the experiment and were asked for consent. Before every interaction, participants rated their interest and familiarity with chatbots. They were then taken to Voiceflow, where they interacted with the two versions of the chatbot and rated their experience. The order of the chatbots was counterbalanced. After that, participants answered additional questions to check if the chatbot's manipulation worked and about their sensitivity to gender identity. All the questions were randomised.

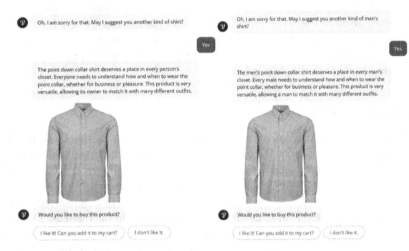

**Fig. 1.** Example of different framing in the gender-neutral (left) and cisgender (right) interaction

### 3.4 Measurements

In line with others' recommendations [44, 45], it is essential to consider multiple measures when assessing user experience. Building upon Thüring and Mahlke's framework for testing the User Experience of a system, we employed two measures to analyse the two components of user experience in our model. Firstly, we utilised the Chatbot Usability Questionnaire (CUQ; [45]) to evaluate participants' Perceptions of the Instrumental

Qualities of the chatbot. Secondly, we incorporated two competencies from an Interpersonal Communicational Competence (ICC; [46]) scale, namely Empathy and Supportiveness, to examine the Emotional User Reactions towards the chatbots. To account for personal perceptions and beliefs about gender identity, a measure of sensitivity to this subject was necessary. The Heteronormative Attitudes and Beliefs Scale (HABS) served this purpose. The HABS scale aims to detect heteronormative behaviour, which is both a larger cultural force and an internalised cognitive process contributing to sexual prejudice and discrimination [47]. Specifically, we utilised the Essential Sex and Gender Subscale from the HABS to measure beliefs and attitudes about gender role conformity and binary beliefs about sex and gender, as part of heteronormative behaviour.

**Dependent Variables.** *Usability.* Usability was measured using 16 statements ($\alpha = .93$, $M = 71.07$, $SD = 12.60$) from the CUQ, to which participants could respond ranging from "strongly disagree" (1) to "strongly agree" (5). The 16 scores were then converted to a 0–100 scale. Some example items are "The chatbot was easy to navigate.", "The chatbot's personality was realistic and engaging.", "The chatbot coped well with any errors or mistakes".

*Empathy.* Empathy was measured using three statements ($\alpha = .89$, $M = 2.75$, $SD = .93$) on a scale ranging from "not true at all" (1) to "very true" (5). An example is, "The chatbot seemed to know how I was feeling".

*Supportiveness.* Supportiveness was measured using three statements ($\alpha = .79$, $M = 3.73$, $SD = .74$) on a scale ranging from "not true at all" (1) to "very true" (5). An example is, "The chatbot did not judge me".

**Moderator.** *Essential Sex and Gender Subscale.* To assess participants' sensitivity to gender identity, we utilised an 8-item subscale ($\alpha = .92$) derived from the Heteronormative Attitudes and Beliefs Scale (HABS) [47]. Participants rated their agreement with each item on a scale ranging from "strongly disagree" (1) to "strongly agree" (7). The mean score for this subscale was 4.12 ($SD = 1.56$).

**Control Variables.** *Age, Gender, Interest* in chatbots and *Familiarity* with chatbots were used as control variables.

## 3.5 Analyses

To achieve our research objectives and test our hypothesis, we employed a mixed effects model using the lme4 package in R [48]. To address our research question, significant main effects of chatbot versions were examined, while to specifically address our hypothesis, a significant interaction between participant sensitivity and chatbot versions was required to be observed. All the models and analyses presented were preregistered.

# 4  Results

## 4.1  Manipulation Check

As part of our manipulation check, we posed four questions to the participants to gain more insight into their perceptions of the chatbot's behaviour. We observed that males, on average, faced greater difficulty in discerning a difference between the chatbot versions. In response to the question of whether they perceived a difference between both chatbot versions, 16% of males indicated a difference between chatbots with varying degrees of certainty ("probably yes", "definitely yes"), compared to 26.3% of females. Similarly, 16.7% of females rated it as "somewhat easy" to detect the difference, while only 8.4% of males had the same perception. Furthermore, 6.8% of males accurately identified the difference, whereas 19.5% of females did so. Further details on the results of the manipulation check can be found in Appendix B. Therefore, females exhibited a comparatively lower difficulty level and a higher frequency in detecting the linguistic disparities between the two chatbot versions. Additionally, we conducted an independent samples t-test to examine the mean sensitivity towards gender identity based on participants' gender. The results revealed a statistically significant difference between males and females ($t(497.65) = 5.71, p < .001$), with females ($M = 4.51, SD = 1.45$) displaying greater sensitivity than males ($M = 3.74, SD = 1.57$) towards gender-related behaviour.

## 4.2  Assumptions

We checked the model diagnostics visually and, when possible, numerically, following the procedure specified by Figner and colleagues [49]. To support our conclusions, we also used the check_model function from the R package performance [50].

*Outliers and influential cases.* The Median Absolute Deviation (MAD) method was utilised to control for potential outliers, calculated on the standardised residuals. The proportion of residuals detected that 1.99% of the values are potential outliers.

*Non-linearity and Heteroscedasticity.* We used the plot of fitted values vs. residuals to check the model heteroscedasticity and the fitted vs. observed values to check for non-linearity. No heteroscedasticity and non-linearity were detected.

*Normality.* Density plots and qq-plots of residuals were used to check for normal distribution and data were considered normally distributed.

## 4.3  Main Model

In this section, the analyses for the main effects and the interactions on each of the three dependent variables will be presented.

**User Experience–Main Effects.** In the model including the *Usability* dependent variable, the main effect of the chatbot's versions was close to being significant (*Estimate* $= -.03, SE = .02, \chi^2 (11) = 3.70, p = .054$), with the cisgender chatbot perceived as more usable ($M = 71.87$, $SD = 13.10$) compared to the gender-neutral ($M = 70.66$, $SD = 12.13$). The pseudo-R2 between observed and fitted values showed that 92.7% of the variance was explained by the model.

In the model that has *Empathy* as dependent variable, the main effect of the chatbot's versions was significant (*Estimate* $= .06$, *SE* $= .02$, $\chi^2$ (11) $= 10.68$, $p = .001$), showing that the gender-neutral chatbot was considered more empathetic ($M = 2.81$, $SD = .95$) than the cisgender one ($M = 2.70$, $SD = .90$). The pseudo-R2 between observed and fitted values showed that 91.4% of the variance was explained by the model.

When analysing the model with the *Supportiveness* dependent variable, the main effects of Chatbot's versions were significant (*Estimate* $= -.10$, *SE* $= .02$, $\chi^2$ (11) $= 15.66$, $p < .001$), saying that participants found the cisgender chatbot more supportive ($M = 3.80$, $SD = .72$) compared to the gender-neutral one ($M = 3.66$, $SD = .75$). The pseudo-$R^2$ between observed and fitted values showed that 85.3% of the variance was explained by the model.

Therefore, two out of three dependent variables had significant main effects (Fig. 2). The chatbot version personalised according to the participant's gender identity was considered better in Usability and Supportiveness, but not in Empathy.

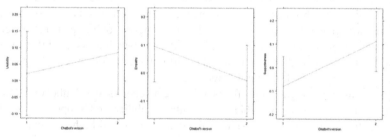

**Fig. 2.** Main effects of the chatbot's versions in function of the dependent variables. *Note.* From left to right Usability, Empathy, Supportiveness standardised dependent variables (on the y-axis), and type of chatbot (on the x-axis). The gender-neutral version of the chatbot is on the left (number 1), the cisgender version is on the right (number 2). The red bars correspond to the 95% confidence interval.

**User Experience-Interactions.** The interaction between participant's Sensitivity and chatbot's type was not significant for all the three dependent variables (Usability, *Estimate* $= -.01$, *SE* $= .02$, $\chi^2$ (11) $= .33$, $p = .567$; Empathy, *Estimate* $= -.004$, *SE* $= .02$, $\chi^2$ (11) $= .04$, $p = .839$; Supportiveness, *Estimate* $= -.01$, *SE* $= .02$, $\chi^2$ (11) $= .36$, $p = .547$). This explains that the sensitivity to gender identity did not give diverse UX scores based on the chatbot's version. We can thus conclude that H2 was not satisfied by this model (Fig. 3).

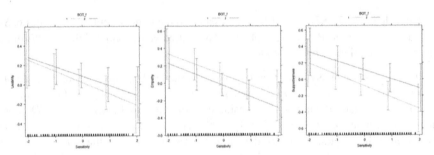

**Fig. 3.** Interaction between participants' sensitivity and version of the chatbot. *Note.* Usability (left), Empathy (centre), and Supportiveness (right) are dependent variables on the y-axis, and sensitivity to gender identity on the x-axis. The gender-neutral version of the chatbots is represented with the blue line, the cisgender version with the red line. The bars correspond to the 95% confidence interval. (Color figure online)

## 5 Discussion

This study aimed to understand to what extent a chatbot's ability to recognise the user's gender identity affects the user experience. Additionally, we wanted to clarify the role that sensitivity towards the social topic of gender identity has in this process. To accomplish this, we created two versions of a chatbot using the online platform Voiceflow: after asking the participant's sex assigned at birth, one version assumed that the user's gender was the same as their sex assigned at birth, while the other version ignored that information, using a gender-neutral language.

This research investigated the effects of different versions of a chatbot on UX scores, specifically focusing on the variables of Empathy, Usability, and Supportiveness. It was found that the gender-neutral version of the chatbot received higher Empathy scores, while the cisgender version had higher Usability and Supportiveness scores. Although the main effect of the chatbot's version on Usability was marginally significant, further analysis confirmed the significance of this effect.

In the conducted research, tailoring the interaction experience based on participants' gender identity resulted in higher Usability scores. This implies that users responded more favourably to a chatbot that had been personalised to a greater extent. This discovery aligns with similar investigations done before [5, 7, 23, 24]. Specifically, how the core aspect of the chatbots' System Properties was personalised, which involved text-based communication, significantly impacted UX, confirming the expectations put forth by other researchers [16, 17, 26–28].

However, a more precise personalisation did not increase Empathy scores for the cisgender chatbot. Regarding this latter finding, the nature of the chatbot, which allowed participants to interact by choosing pre-made options, may have influenced the level of empathy perceived in the communication. Hard-coded options typically enhance efficiency and thus may reduce the empathetic quality of the interaction [41, 51]. In addition, the framing of sentences based on participants' presumed gender could be perceived as pragmatic and potentially not appropriate and, therefore, less empathetic. However, the impact of different interaction tools on perceived social presence is controversial [52].

Another potential cause might rely on the nature of the recommendations: the more precise recommendations of the cisgender chatbot were system-initiated and not user-initiated; this might not be appreciated by users as they might feel less in control of the interaction [27, 28]. These findings provide additional elucidation regarding the factors that impact the user's experience. Personalization based on gender identity was generally acknowledged as a more useful. However, the constant provision of recommendations tailored to this identity was concurrently appraised as less dependable from the user, ultimately engendering a perception of reduced user agency within the context.

About the third dependent variable, Supportiveness, the cisgender version was considered more supportive compared to the gender-neutral one. Consistently with other findings, an interaction tailored to user's needs and preferences was preferred [42]. For instance, in an experiment conducted using 'Woebot', a chatbot for mental health, participants reported how the perception of having a conversation with themselves influenced the supportive interaction [53]. Investigations conducted by other scholars identified a heightened positive perception in chatbots capable of more effectively catering to users' needs. [54].

We failed to find empirical support for the hypothesised moderating effect of gender sensitivity. Interestingly, increased sensitivity toward gender identity corresponded to a decrease in UX scores for both chatbot versions. This suggests a curious pattern: individuals attuned to this societal theme tend to harbour a general aversion towards chatbots. A plausible reasoning behind this phenomenon is that those particularly sensitive to this social aspect are more prone to notice the absence of human-like nuances in interactions between humans and robots, unlike interactions between two humans. Consequently, they might assign lower ratings to these virtual conversational agents. This interpretation harmonises with earlier research indicating that people tend to favour experiences that resemble human interactions, as they frequently draw parallels between engagements with robots and authentic human interactions [52, 55, 56].

The study has several limitations. The first is undoubtedly the sample used for the experiment: it was composed only of cisgender participants from the United Kingdom. Future research should expand the sample to include other gender identity categories and countries. Second, the study was conducted online, wherever and whenever participants preferred and, thus, in a non-controlled environment, which may have affected participant attention and interaction quality. Third, the chatbot's conversation setup focused solely on text-based interaction without additional personalised features. Future research should explore the consequences of introducing new customised aspects while maintaining language focus to optimise UX. Fourth, the clothing options, although selected with unisex intent, might exhibit a bias towards a male style. This bias may have led female participants to better distinguish between the two chatbot versions. The explicit indication that the clothing is designed for women in the cisgender version may boost user confidence when receiving suggestions that might otherwise seem tailored for men. Finally, this research is one of the first to connect UX with the sensitivity to a social matter explicitly, and the first specifically addressing gender identity. More research is needed to develop a standard procedure for analysing the impact of opinions on social themes on UX.

## 6  Conclusions

The study has implications for personalised human-agent interactions, further emphasising the importance of correctly identifying users' needs and preferences [29, 57]. Thus, companies and institutions should consider making interactions with their chatbots more personalised, taking into account the gender identity of the user. Another implication of our findings is that gender identity should be considered in human-agent interactions, as it can significantly affect UX. Businesses and public entities using chatbots could structure their language and dialogue framework based on the user's gender. However, they should consider that improving usability and supportiveness may come at the cost of decreasing perceived empathy. Finally, creators of chatbots should be aware of the potentially diverse expectations and interactions between males and females with conversational agents to enhance engagement and avoid negative experiences.

## References

1. Følstad, A., Brandtzæg, P.B.: Chatbots and the new world of HCI. Interactions. **24**, 38–42 (2017). https://doi.org/10.1145/3085558
2. Van Pinxteren, M.M.E., Pluymaekers, M., Lemmink, J.G.A.M.: Human-like communication in conversational agents: a literature review and research agenda. JOSM. **31**, 203–225 (2020). https://doi.org/10.1108/JOSM-06-2019-0175
3. Grudin, J., Jacques, R.: Chatbots, Humbots, and the Quest for Artificial General Intelligence. In: Proceedings of the 2019 CHI Conference on Human Factors in Computing Systems, pp. 1–11. ACM, Glasgow, Scotland, UK (2019)
4. Juniper Research: Chatbots to facilitate $142 billion of retail spend by 2024, driven by omnichannel strategies. https://www.juniperresearch.com/press/chatbots-to-facilitate-$142-billion-of-retail
5. Gnewuch, U., Morana, S., Maedche, A.: Towards designing cooperative and social conversational agents for customer service. Presented at the 38th International Conference on Information Systems, Seoul (2017)
6. Ait Baha, T., El Hajji, M., Es-Saady, Y., Fadili, H.: The power of personalization: a systematic review of personality-adaptive chatbots. Sn Comput. Sci. **4**, 661 (2023). https://doi.org/10.1007/s42979-023-02092-6
7. Daniel, F., Matera, M., Zaccaria, V., Dell'Orto, A.: Toward truly personal chatbots: on the development of custom conversational assistants. In: Proceedings of the 1st International Workshop on Software Engineering for Cognitive Services. pp. 31–36. ACM, Gothenburg Sweden (2018)
8. Følstad, A., Skjuve, M.: Chatbots for customer service: user experience and motivation. In: Proceedings of the 1st International Conference on Conversational User Interfaces. pp. 1–9. ACM, Dublin Ireland (2019)
9. The Deloitte Consumer Review: Made-to-order: The rise of mass personalisation. Deloitte (2015)
10. Chakrabarti, C., Luger, G.F.: Artificial conversations for customer service chatter bots: Architecture, algorithms, and evaluation metrics. Expert Syst. Appl. **42**, 6878–6897 (2015). https://doi.org/10.1016/j.eswa.2015.04.067
11. Ling, E.C., Tussyadiah, I., Tuomi, A., Stienmetz, J., Ioannou, A.: Factors influencing users' adoption and use of conversational agents: A systematic review. Psychol. Mark. **38**, 1031–1051 (2021). https://doi.org/10.1002/mar.21491

12. Zhang, S., Dinan, E., Urbanek, J., Szlam, A., Kiela, D., Weston, J.: Personalizing Dialogue Agents: I have a dog, do you have pets too? In: Proceedings of the 56th Annual Meeting of the Association for Computational Linguistics (Volume 1: Long Papers), pp. 2204–2213. Association for Computational Linguistics, Melbourne, Australia (2018)

13. Hu, T., et al.: Touch Your Heart: A Tone-aware Chatbot for Customer Care on Social Media User Experience - Interactions (2018). http://arxiv.org/abs/1803.02952

14. Stokoe, E.H., Smithson, J.: Making gender relevant: conversation analysis and gender categories in interaction. Discourse Soc. 12, 217–244 (2001). https://doi.org/10.1177/095792650 1012002005

15. Kitzinger, C.: Doing gender: a conversation analytic perspective. Gend. Soc. 23, 94–98 (2009). https://doi.org/10.1177/0891243208326730

16. Thüring, M., Mahlke, S.: Usability, aesthetics and emotions in human–technology interaction. Int. J. Psychol. 42, 253–264 (2007). https://doi.org/10.1080/00207590701396674

17. Bevan, N., Kirakowski, J., Maissel, J.: What is Usability? In: Human Aspects in Computing: Proceedings of the 4th International Conference on HCI, Stuttgart, Germany (1991)

18. Broadbent, E., et al.: Robots with display screens: a robot with a more humanlike face display is perceived to have more mind and a better personality. PLoS ONE 8, e72589 (2013). https://doi.org/10.1371/journal.pone.0072589

19. Nowak, K.L., Rauh, C.: The influence of the avatar on online perceptions of anthropomorphism, androgyny, credibility, homophily, and attraction. J Comp Mediated Comm. 11, 153–178 (2005). https://doi.org/10.1111/j.1083-6101.2006.tb00308.x

20. Araujo, T.: Living up to the chatbot hype: the influence of anthropomorphic design cues and communicative agency framing on conversational agent and company perceptions. Comput. Hum. Behav. 85, 183–189 (2018). https://doi.org/10.1016/j.chb.2018.03.051

21. Reeves, B., Nass, C.: How People Treat Computers, Television, and New Media Like Real People and Places. Cambridge University Press, Center for the Study of Language and Information (1996)

22. Bainbridge, W.A., Hart, J., Kim, E.S., Scassellati, B.: The effect of presence on human-robot interaction. In: RO-MAN 2008 - The 17th IEEE International Symposium on Robot and Human Interactive Communication, pp. 701–706. IEEE, Munich, Germany (2008)

23. Lee, S., Choi, J.: Enhancing user experience with conversational agent for movie recommendation: effects of self-disclosure and reciprocity. Int. J. Hum. Comput. Stud. 103, 95–105 (2017). https://doi.org/10.1016/j.ijhcs.2017.02.005

24. Schuetzler, R., Grimes, M., Giboney, J., Buckman, J.: Facilitating natural conversational agent interactions: lessons from a deception experiment. In: Human Computer Interaction, Auckland (2014)

25. Mahlke, S.: User Experience of Interaction with Technical Systems (2008)

26. Kaptein, M., Markopoulos, P., De Ruyter, B., Aarts, E.: Two acts of social intelligence: the effects of mimicry and social praise on the evaluation of an artificial agent. AI & Soc. 26, 261–273 (2011). https://doi.org/10.1007/s00146-010-0304-4

27. Laban, G., Araujo, T.: The effect of personalization techniques in users' perceptions of conversational recommender systems. In: Proceedings of the 20th ACM International Conference on Intelligent Virtual Agents, pp. 1–3. ACM, Virtual Event Scotland UK (2020)

28. Laban, G., Araujo, T.: Don't Take it Personally: resistance to individually targeted recommendations from conversational recommender agents. In: Proceedings of the 10th International Conference on Human-Agent Interaction, pp. 57–66. ACM, Christchurch New Zealand (2022)

29. Trivedi, J.: Examining the customer experience of using banking chatbots and its impact on brand love: the moderating role of perceived risk. J. Internet Commerce 18, 91–111 (2019). https://doi.org/10.1080/15332861.2019.1567188

30. Przegalinska, A., Ciechanowski, L., Stroz, A., Gloor, P., Mazurek, G.: In bot we trust: a new methodology of chatbot performance measures. Bus. Horiz. **62**, 785–797 (2019). https://doi.org/10.1016/j.bushor.2019.08.005

31. Hassenzahl, M., Tractinsky, N.: User experience - a research agenda. Behav. Inform. Technol. **25**, 91–97 (2006). https://doi.org/10.1080/01449290500330331

32. Plocher, T.A., Garg, C., Chestnut, J.: Connecting culture, user characteristics and user interface design. In: On Human-Computer Interaction: Ergonomics and User Interfaces, pp. 803–807. Lawrence Erlbaum, Munich, Germany (1999)

33. Wood, W., Eagly, A.H.: Gender identity. In: Handbook of Individual Differences in Social Behavior, pp. 109–125. The Guilford Press (2009)

34. Jenkins, K.: Amelioration and inclusion: gender identity and the concept of *woman*. Ethics **126**, 394–421 (2016). https://doi.org/10.1086/683535

35. Jenkins, K.: Toward an Account of Gender Identity. Ergo Open Access J. Philos. **5** (2018). https://doi.org/10.3998/ergo.12405314.0005.027

36. Yen, C., Chiang, M.-C.: Trust me, if you can: a study on the factors that influence consumers' purchase intention triggered by chatbots based on brain image evidence and self-reported assessments. Behav. Inform. Technol. **40**, 1177–1194 (2021). https://doi.org/10.1080/0144929X.2020.1743362

37. Tsai, W.-H.S., Liu, Y., Chuan, C.-H.: How chatbots' social presence communication enhances consumer engagement: the mediating role of parasocial interaction and dialogue. JRIM. **15**, 460–482 (2021). https://doi.org/10.1108/JRIM-12-2019-0200

38. Müller, L., Mattke, J., Maier, C., Weitzel, T., Graser, H.: Chatbot acceptance: a latent profile analysis on individuals' trust in conversational agents. In: Proceedings of the 2019 on Computers and People Research Conference, pp. 35–42. ACM, Nashville TN USA (2019)

39. Bartneck, C., Kulić, D., Croft, E., Zoghbi, S.: Measurement instruments for the anthropomorphism, animacy, likeability, perceived Intelligence, and Perceived Safety of Robots. Int. J. Soc. Robot. **1**, 71–81 (2009). https://doi.org/10.1007/s12369-008-0001-3

40. Ren, R., Castro, J.W., Acuña, S.T., De Lara, J.: Evaluation techniques for chatbot usability: a systematic mapping study. Int. J. Soft. Eng. Knowl. Eng. **29**, 1673–1702 (2019). https://doi.org/10.1142/S0218194019400163

41. Laranjo, L., et al.: Conversational agents in healthcare: a systematic review. J. Am. Med. Inform. Assoc. **25**, 1248–1258 (2018). https://doi.org/10.1093/jamia/ocy072

42. Kocaballi, A.B., et al.: The personalization of conversational agents in health care: systematic review. J. Med. Internet Res. **21**, e15360 (2019). https://doi.org/10.2196/15360

43. United Nations: Guidelines for gender-inclusive language in English. https://www.un.org/en/gender-inclusive-language/guidelines.shtml

44. Kocaballi, A.B., Laranjo, L., Coiera, E.: Understanding and measuring user experience in conversational interfaces. Interact. Comput. **31**, 192–207 (2019). https://doi.org/10.1093/iwc/iwz015

45. Holmes, S., Moorhead, A., Bond, R., Zheng, H., Coates, V., Mctear, M.: Usability testing of a healthcare chatbot: Can we use conventional methods to assess conversational user interfaces? In: Proceedings of the 31st European Conference on Cognitive Ergonomics, pp. 207–214. ACM, BELFAST United Kingdom (2019)

46. Rubin, R.B., Martin, M.M.: Development of a measure of interpersonal communication competence. Commun. Res. Rep. **11**, 33–44 (1994). https://doi.org/10.1080/08824099409359938

47. Habarth, J.M.: Development of the heteronormative attitudes and beliefs scale. Psychol. Sexuality **6**, 166–188 (2015). https://doi.org/10.1080/19419899.2013.876444

48. R Core Team R: A language and environment for statistical computing (2022). https://www.R-project.org/

49. Figner, B., et al.: Standard Operating Procedures For Using Mixed-Effects Models (2020). http://decision-lab.org/wp-content/uploads/2020/07/SOP_Mixed_Models_D2P2_v1_0_0.pdf

50. Lüdecke, D., Ben-Shachar, M., Patil, I., Waggoner, P., Makowski, D.: Performance: an R package for assessment, comparison and testing of statistical models. JOSS **6**, 3139 (2021). https://doi.org/10.21105/joss.03139

51. Dixon, M., Freeman, K., Toman, N.: Stop Trying to Delight Your Customers (2010). https://hbr.org/2010/07/stop-trying-to-delight-your-customers

52. Haugeland, I.K.F., Følstad, A., Taylor, C., Bjørkli, C.A.: Understanding the user experience of customer service chatbots: an experimental study of chatbot interaction design. Int. J. Hum. Comput. Stud. **161**, 102788 (2022)

53. Brandtzæg, P.B., Skjuve, M., Kristoffer Dysthe, K.K., Følstad, A.: When the social becomes non-human: young people's perception of social support in chatbots. In: Proceedings of the 2021 CHI Conference on Human Factors in Computing Systems, pp. 1–13. ACM, Yokohama Japan (2021)

54. Litman, D.J., Pan, S.: Designing and evaluating an adaptive spoken dialogue system. User Model. User-Adap. Inter.Adap. Inter. **12**, 111–137 (2002). https://doi.org/10.1023/A:101503 6910358

55. Go, E., Sundar, S.S.: Humanizing chatbots: the effects of visual, identity and conversational cues on humanness perceptions. Comput. Hum. Behav.. Hum. Behav. **97**, 304–316 (2019). https://doi.org/10.1016/j.chb.2019.01.020

56. Følstad, A., Nordheim, C.B., Bjørkli, C.A.: What makes users trust a chatbot for customer service? an exploratory interview study. In: Tiropanis, T., Vakali, A., Sartori, L., Burnap, P. (eds.): INSCI 2015. LNCS, vol. 9089. Springer, Cham (2015). https://doi.org/10.1007/978-3-319-18609-2

57. Liu, X., Wang, Q.: Study on Application of a quantitative evaluation approach for software architecture adaptability. In: Fifth International Conference on Quality Software (QSIC 2005), pp. 265–272. IEEE, Melbourne, Australia (2005)

58. Singmann, H., Bolker, B., Westfall, J., Aust, F., Ben-Shachar, M.S.: afex: Analysis of Factorial Experiments (2022). https://CRAN.R-project.org/package=afex

# Complementing Perspectives

# Conversational Interactions with NPCs in LLM-Driven Gaming: Guidelines from a Content Analysis of Player Feedback

Samuel Rhys Cox[✉] and Wei Tsang Ooi

National University of Singapore, Singapore, Singapore
samuel.cox@u.nus.edu

**Abstract.** The growing capability and availability of large language models (LLMs) have led to their adoption in a number of domains. One application domain that could prove fruitful is to video games, where LLMs could be used to provide conversational responses from non-playable characters (NPCs) that are more dynamic and diverse. Additionally, LLMs could allow players the autonomy to converse in open-ended conversations potentially improving player immersion and agency. However, due to their recent commercial popularity, the consequences (both negative and positive) of using LLMs in video games from a *player's perspective* is currently unclear. On from this, we analyse player feedback to the use of LLM-driven NPC responses in a commercially available video game. We discuss findings and implications, and generate guidelines for designers incorporating LLMs into NPC dialogue.

**Keywords:** Large Language Models · Video Games · Non-playable Characters

## 1 Introduction

With the growing capability and availability of large language models (LLMs) more affordances are available to designers when developing conversationally interactive gaming experiences. While the current norm for conversing with non-playable characters (NPCs)[1] in video games is for the player to select from a discrete number of pre-written choices, the capabilities now lie for LLMs to be used to drive conversations between the player and an NPC. With this comes the possibility for the player to input any utterance, and receive an appropriate conversational response from the NPC. Yet, due to the recent availability and practicality of LLMs, the player experience, and potential positive and negative effects of LLM-driven NPC dialogue is not yet certain.

On from this, we analyse player feedback for Vaudeville [4]: a detective murder-mystery video game that uses LLMs to generate NPC dialogue. We

---

[1] *Note on terminology:* An "NPC" can be thought of as an embodied conversational agent that a user interacts with in a virtual environment, and a "player" can be thought of as a user that talks to said conversational agent.

A. Følstad et al. (Eds.): CONVERSATIONS 2023, LNCS 14524, pp. 167–184, 2024.
https://doi.org/10.1007/978-3-031-54975-5_10

performed a thematic analysis of both game reviews and Discord conversations to study player experience, and positive and negative aspects of LLM-driven NPC dialogue. From this we discuss findings related to the use of LLMs for dialogue (such as hallucinations, or the consequence of added player autonomy) and suggest several guidelines for designers.

## 2  Related Work

Due to the recent and rapid development of LLMs, there has yet to be a video game developed by a major AAA-studio that uses LLMs for NPC dialogue. However, there have been a number of early uses of LLMs by both independent developers [41] and game studios [4,12,13,39], and prior to this use of LLMs some games had used aspects of natural language processing to recognise the intent of user utterances, and deliver pre-scripted NPC responses [20,21].

There has also been previous use of LLMs to generate text for use in video games [31,35,37,39]. For example, van Stegeren et al. [31] and Värtinen et al. [35] (in separate studies) used GPT-2 to generate NPC quest-giver text for RPGs, and Xi et al. used GPT-2 to generate goal-driven story dialogue for a mobile romance game [39]. On from this, it was found that GPT-2 produced quest-giver text has the potential to be equally effective to human-written text [31]. Sun et al. developed a LLM-driven storybook-style game "1001 Nights" [32] whereby the inputs of the player would affect the game's world (such as changing the weapons available to the main character).

While it has been shown that context-sensitive NPC dialogue (driven by LLMs) could increase player engagement [8], it is unclear how players would perceive the use of LLMs to generate NPC responses on a commercially available video game. This use of LLMs and natural language input could lead to greater sense of freedom and agency ("*freedom to act upon the world without restriction*" [33]), and emotional agency [17] due to more fluid interactions. By analysing the user feedback to a game that uses LLM-driven dialogue, Vaudeville, we aim to investigate the impact on player perceptions.

## 3  Method

### 3.1  Steam Reviews of Vaudeville

To analyse the use of LLMs in gaming, we chose Vaudeville [4] as a case study. Vaudeville is a game developed by Bumblebee Studios, where the player uses natural language input (via voice or text) to communicate with NPCs to solve a murder-mystery. These NPCs are akin to embodied agents that the player can interact with across a number of environments (see Fig. 1), such as an avatar of a coroner in a morgue, or a Count in a manor-house. NPCs are powered by LLMs (via Inworld AI [12,24]) to generate responses allowing for open-ended conversations in game, and respond using AI-generated voice. This use of LLMs

**Fig. 1.** Screenshot [4] of a player talking to the NPC Marina H. Players assume the role of Detective Martini and interact via voice or text input. The conversation log between the player and NPC can be seen in the bottom-right corner.

to talk with NPCs has led to discussion and excitement online, from message boards, content creators (such as streamers and YouTubers), and AI enthusiasts.

On from this, since the game's launch 30th June 2023, there have been numerous reviews posted on the video game distribution service Steam (reviews here [4]). Game reviews have been analysed across much prior research [18,29,42,43], and can offer rich levels of information through diverse themes and topics [42]. They can provide concrete feedback such as game design suggestions, and advice to potential players [42], and both positive and negative feedback can be used by developers as guidance on improving their game [18].

It should be noted that (at time of writing) **Vaudeville is an early access game on Steam**, and is being continually developed and improved by Bumblebee Studios. While player feedback towards the game is relevant to the use of LLMs for NPC dialogue, we would like to note that critical feedback of the game referenced in this paper may not reflect the current state of the game (having undergone additional development since the player's feedback). While we are not affiliated with Bumblebee Studios, we contacted the studio to clarify details related to the game's development and expected NPC behaviour.

### 3.2   Analysis

We extracted 132 Steam reviews (alongside 30 comments replying to reviews) posted from 1st July to 20th September [4], as well as conversations in the Vaudeville Discord server from 5th August 2023 (the first post) to 20th September 2023 (csv shared here). By additionally, analysing Discord conversations, it allows for multimedia posts (such as sharing of screenshots along with text) to provide richer levels of information.

To analyse player comments, we followed thematic analysis guidelines from Braune and Clarke [3], namely the steps: (1) familiarisation with data (i.e., reading all comments), (2) generating initial codes, (3) generating themes, (4) reviewing themes, (5) defining and naming themes, and (6) report. The thematic analysis was conducted independently by two researchers (HCI experts), alongside discussions of theme interpretation and clarification. From this, we generated guidelines for developers to follow when using LLMs to generate NPC dialogue. These guidelines were discussed with two professors (with specialisms in computer science and video game design) to verify and iterate findings.

## 4   Findings

Next, we will we discuss specific findings from player reviews, alongside example quotes. Additionally, from our analysis we generated guidelines for using LLMs in video games that can be found in Table 1.

Generally, players commended the added affordance to hold prolonged, open-ended conversations with the NPCs, thereby leading to player immersion, amusement and feelings of NPC naturalness and personality. However, multiple players relayed issues related to LLM hallucinations and lack of NPC memory between interactions. These issues of NPC memory and hallucinations, twinned with the less structured nature of open-ended conversations also led some players to report difficulty in tracking and discerning significant information from conversations, as well as difficulty deciding conversation paths to pursue with NPCs. Some players also reported NPCs not conversing as expected, such as NPCs not adapting their stance when confronted with contradictory evidence. Finally, we discuss how player interactions were affected by input modality.

### 4.1   Flexible and Open-Ended Conversations

Players enjoyed the ability to converse flexibly and without restriction with NPCs, with one reviewer describing an *"immersive experience and flexible AI conversations"*. Players commended the replayability and amusement afforded by more dynamic NPC responses, such as a reviewer stating: *"The interactivity, and chance to talk directly without a predictable script, gives the game a bit of replay ability"*. Players also described NPCs as feeling more natural and believable due to additional affordances from AI (compared to choice-driven conversations):

> *"Characters that you can actually converse with and feel like actual characters in a play rather than just props in a game. It doesn't feel as much that you're trying to inject the correct predetermined keywords in a pointless monologue"* - *"nascent"*

On from this, players described having extended conversations with NPCs both on topics related to the game's objective and out-of-domain conversations, as exemplified in the review: *"The conversations can be about almost anything, making nearly limitless fun, while also having a base of a story to default to"*. Multiple players described having specific out-of-domain conversations, such as one player describing a rapport-building conversation related to an NPC's profession: *"after I beat the story I just talked marina h, about classical music"*, and another player holding out-of-domain conversations purely for amusement:

*"it is highly amusing and an excellent platform to interact with some excellent AI storytellers, and I've gotten a couple of hours laughing like an idiot at how well crafted they are. Seriously, they'll have philosophical debates with you"* - *"Kitty"*

However, the ability of LLM-delivered conversations to reply more broadly and flexibly also led to a number of potential concerns. Firstly, the ability to hold out-of-domain conversations (while aiding immersion for some) was seen as a point of sardonic amusement by others, with some players discussing topics that are possibly out of the realm of believability given the game's setting of 1910s Europe. For example, players described discussing sci-fi movies, crytocurrency, and video-games with NPCs, with one player commenting: *"this game is hiliarious you can ask the ai things like when new games come out"*. Secondly, some players described interactions that may have become unintentionally uncomfortable due to unexpected directions of conversation. For example a player stated: *"Mrs potter fell in love with me. that was weird and she began to want to involve me in her revenge plot"*.

Additionally, while some players appreciated the freedom to interview NPCs and roleplay as a detective, others found there to be a lack of direction leading to player uncertainty regarding how to question NPCs and conduct the in-game investigation. This led some players to share question-asking strategies they employed, such as "zacmak04" who stated: *"I do recommend chasing 1 narrative at a time with each character in the game and trying to pinpoint everyone's stances before really getting into questioning"*. On from this, several players suggested gameplay quality of life changes by providing extra context for conversations, such as one reviewer recommending NPC details be provided to players: *"I think having brief backgrounds on each of the characters that ya speak to would go a long way in helpin' to aide the player when it comes to gathering clues"*.

To provide players with direction, prior game design techniques could be used such as NPC utterances more explicitly instructing players of potential options, and adding visual cues to the environment. For example, in Façade [20] players interact with two NPCs at a cocktail party. Here the NPCs react and draw attention to objects in the environment (visual cues), as well as providing proactive statements and questions to guide player decisions.

These findings highlight the impact of added player autonomy when interacting with LLM-driven NPCs. Consequently, designers should consider the extent to which NPCs humour and abide by player utterances (such as players alluding to features not within the expected domain knowledge of NPCs), whether NPCs should give responses that attempt to lead players to discuss only in-universe topics, and how to guide player engagement in open-ended conversations.

These findings highlight the importance of designers added player autonomy when interacting with NPCs in open-ended conversations. Designers should consider the extent to which NPCs should humour and play-along with player utterances (such as those alluding to features not within the expected domain of knowledge of the NPC), and whether NPCs should give responses that attempt to lead players to discuss only in-universe topics.

## 4.2  NPC Personality and Conversational Style

Players commented on NPC personality and conversational style (such as levels of amiability, openness, agreeability and verbosity). For example, some players described NPCs as possessing distinct personalities and expressed their enjoyment in conversing with them:

> "*The use of AI to create dynamic and authentic characters is nothing short of remarkable. Each interaction felt real and personal, as if I were talking to actual individuals with their own unique personalities, quirks, and motives*" - "narutosera"
> "*It continually makes me laugh, each character is a little different in what they say back to you.*" - "Silly Slinky"

While NPCs could be seen to possess unique personalities without the use of LLMs, this feedback indicates the ability of LLMs to maintain varied and authentic personalities (in keeping with recent literature [6,14,30]). However, (in relation to the game's objective of questioning NPCs to help solve a murder-mystery) some players were frustrated by what they perceived as an overly evasive nature from some NPCs:

> "*the stonewall you get from many characters is just insanely not fun. Asking what I thought were completely logical questions like "did this person have any close friends" [...] only to be met with an "I don't know why that is important to this case" [...] by every single npc is so frustrating cause it feels like I have zero to go off of*" - "ZodiacDragons"

Despite this, player response to NPC evasiveness was not clear-cut, with some arguing NPCs acting evasive when questioned by a detective adds to the sense of realism. Related to this, the above review garnered several responses in rebuttal:

> "*So what you're saying is it simulates exactly how people act when asked questions about a crime*" - "Enzo Vulkoor"

This highlights the importance of tempering frustration caused by gameplay to create a sense of challenge and achievement, while not being so great that it would cause people to stop playing. This could be via dynamic difficulty adjustment [11] based on the player's emotions [10], or performance in conversations with NPCs. Furthermore, some players were frustrated by evasiveness from NPCs who were in social roles [40] that did not match this behaviour (e.g., NPCs in formal social roles such as the police chief or coroner):

*"The police chief flatly refuses to give you any information on the case. For every little question you ask him, he demands that you provide him with a thorough explanation of why it is relevant to the case."* - "Cherry blossom girl"

This demonstrates the importance of ensuring that player expectations will be met regarding the social role [40] or metaphor [15] of NPCs.

Length and clarity of NPC utterances was noted by some players, with NPC utterances being described as overly long and verbose, or using "poetic"[2] or "enigmatic"[3] language. Verbosity has been a common criticism of LLM output [5] (primarily due to human labellers rating longer responses more highly [1]). To address this, LLMs could be prompted to give more concise and unrepetitive utterances commensurate to the level of information, or LLMs could be trained to favour accuracy rather than verbosity of responses (such as by using pairwise comparisons from reinforcement learning from human feedback [1]).

### 4.3 Inappropriate and Unexpected NPC Social Responses

As described in Sects. 4.1 and 4.2, players found NPCs to be engaging, believeable and possessing distinct personalities. Despite this, there were instances where players stated that NPCs did not follow expected social behaviour. For example, multiple players noted that NPCs did not adapt appropriately when confronted with evidence in contrary of their claims. As written by one player: *"they won't stop lying and tell the truth once they have been presented with enough conflicting evidence"*. Similarly to this, some players described NPCs as having difficulty in reasoning when assessing inconsistencies: as described in the review: *"They don't understand their own suspicious behavior, being caught in lies, or implied guilt"*. Both the lack of NPC adaptability and inability to meet social expectations also resulted in undesired difficulty, with a player noting: *"the AI's dont respond appropriately when you are on the right track or close to the solution [...] Not very predictable when trying to solve a crime"*. Multiple players also described the NPC as *"gas-lighting"* them when confronted (potentially an additional consequence of LLM reasoning limitations), such as described below:

*"The AI NPC would tell me one thing and then in the very next sentence, it would tell me something completely different and contradictory. Then when you confront the NPC like "but you just told me A," they're like "No you are mistaken. It was always B.""* - "ZodiacDragon"

### 4.4 NPC Hallucinations

The nature of LLM-generated NPC responses provides allowances for flexible conversations that adapt to and "play-off" the player in an improvisational

---

[2] "poetic" review here.

[3] "enigmas" review here.

 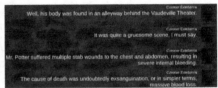

**Fig. 2.** Screenshots from Discord of the Coroner NPC providing inconsistent cause of death.

dynamic. While this can prove beneficial for creating more engaging [8] and prolonged conversations (see Sect. 4.1), hallucinated details in conversations also led to player confusion and loss of believability.

Firstly, players noted that NPCs provided information that conflicted both with information provided by the same or other NPCs. While some form of misdirection was an intentional part of the game's design (as suspects may be expected to purposefully provide misleading information), some misdirection was an unintended consequence of the LLM[4], attesting to the current difficulty in managing and controlling LLM responses. This conflicting information led to player frustration and confusion:

> *"It was very hard to determine what was intentional misdirection (programmed by the devs), what was AI bs, and what was truth. Details would often change conversation-to-conversation or even in the same conversation."* - "Seiferslash"

Player confusion and difficulty applying suspension of disbelief was amplified when NPCs inconsistently hallucinated details that players expected to be immutable such as murder location, cause of death (see Fig. 2) and universally verifiable details related to time and date. For example, one reviewer noted: *"im finding the dates to be very inconsistent that people tell me. i can't even tell what dates the murder happend"*. Additionally (as described in Sect. 4.1), NPCs hallucinated details not in keeping with the expected setting and time period.

Similarly to Sect. 4.2, players were also confused when NPCs behaved against expectation given their social role: specifically when (presumably reliable) figures of authority provided inconsistent information. This generated additional confusion when players were asking for key details that one would expect these figures (such as the coroner and police chief) to possess, while instead producing contradictory story details include as time, location and cause of death. On from this, NPCs sometimes hallucinated characters and places leading to lost efforts by players:

> *"I also was confused about several people I couldn't find around town, realizing toward the end that they were just random additions [...] I was bummed*

---

[4] As confirmed from both private correspondence with the game development studio, and a Steam forum [developer] post here.

*about that because there was a Lady that people said was intriguing but the Cafe is nowhere to be found [...] a whole rabbit hole I went down that could have been connected which in the end I found wasn't, which was disappointing."* - "Feen"

These hallucinated characters and places also made it difficult for people seeking help from other players in Discord, as it was unclear and debated as to whether locations existed (such as confusion surrounding the existence of a cabaret club mentioned by an NPC[5]). This suggests that, when people share information to seek assistance, they may desire consistency with other players to facilitate help, or desire enough confidence that NPC utterances are reliable.

These inconsistent responses, led some players to discuss strategies to verify information, such as asking for information either from multiple NPCs or the same NPC multiple times:

*"when 2 or more AI's have the same answer its verifyable. I didnt find some of what the coroner said legit unless you left and came back and re-verified her answers."* - "Feen"

Players described creative prompting, and the fickle nature of LLMs (such as slight derivations in language lead to different results). For example, players achieved differing outcomes of success when requesting fingerprints from NPCs[6], asking NPCs if they knew the murder victims[7], or asking if CCTV footage was available. Specifically, players discussed requesting CCTV footage from the police chief, which led to varying results depending on the player's prompt. Specifically, a player was denied footage when they asked if footage is available, while another player described being assertive with the NPC to receive the information:

*"it's easier to force the AI into situations. Instead of asking the chief about the cameras just tell him there are cameras and you want to review them. I asked him to watch the tapes then tell me what happened on them and he did and the things he told me were relevant to the case"* - "GhostZzZ"

## 4.5   NPC Memory

While NPCs had memory within chatting sessions and knowledge of high-level events (such as the names of murder victims), they did not have memory between chatting sessions. As a result, some players described additional time and effort such as "Feen" stating: *"a lot of time is wasted re-telling the AI's what they should already know through previous conversations"*. Additionally one reviewer described loss of immersion due to increased cognitive effort outside of intended gameplay: *"the ai doesn't remember what you talked in the last session and it can be inconsistent, so you need to play detective and also play AI detective*

---

[5] See Discord thread for player confusion surrounding existence of location.

[6] See Discord thread for inconsistent fingerprint responses.

[7] See screenshots in Discord for contradictory NPC responses regarding knowledge of murder victim.

*which breaks some of the immersion"*. This led to some players sharing gameplay tips and paradigms on how to overcome NPC memory limitations, such as one reviewer describing: *"once you unveil specific events you can lead conversations with the characters, thus not needing a progression or saving system, the progression is knowing these events and key words"*.

Interestingly players also described exploiting the lack of memory between sessions in order to reset an interaction and start afresh. Some players described this as a means to verify NPC answers (by asking NPCs the same questions across sessions). Additionally, players discussed resetting interactions if the NPC became too unwilling to answer questions, or had been injected with a mistruth from the player (either accidentally due to high levels of agreeability from the NPC[8], or deliberately with the player purposefully attempting to create contradictory and amusing responses from the NPC).

This player behaviour suggests a potential requirement for players to be able to reset conversations or revert to previous states when conversing with LLM-driven NPCs. For example, this could be via standard UI such as buttons; the use of saved states; or based on player utterances, such as the player saying *"let's start again from the top"*.

Some players also described confusion related to both tracking and judging the significance of conversational content. This confusion was impacted by multiple factors such as: lack of NPC memory between conversations; the quantity and duration of conversations being cognitively demanding to track and quantify; and NPC hallucinations and inconsistencies adding a layer of obfuscation to interactions. This led to some players suggesting added capabilities to track and highlight prior conversations, such as a reviewer who stated: *"It would be great if there was a way to see what evidence we have collected to make sure that it is factual and a part of the plot and not just a random thread the AI"*.

### 4.6   Input Modalities

(a) Comical situation action from Discord    (b) Forced confession action from Discord

**Fig. 3.** Screenshots of players using special characters to prompt inject actions into conversations. Player utterances are from "Detective Martini".

---

[8] See second sentence of Steam review here.

Vaudeville allows players to use either voice or text to interact with NPCs, and players noted gameplay differences between these input modalities and interactions available only to one type of input.

Players appreciated being able to use their own voice as input to communicate more openly and naturally with LLM-driven NPCs. One player described the *"nice immersion"* that they felt using voice, as well as commenting specifically: *"so cool to be able to play a game where you actually and talk to different characters with your own voice"*. This suggests an increased feeling of spatial presence and ability to act within the environment [36] due to more fluid and natural input of command to action afforded by voice-input together with LLM interpretation. However, some players described esoteric names and places being misrecognised by voice input. While this could be seen as more of a general technical limitation, this issue was particularly apparent when players attempted to discuss names that the NPC had hallucinated. Conversations could become confused if NPCs misrecognised the hallucinated name, thereby interpreting it as an added entity in addition to the already hallucinated one. This led a reviewer to describe how conversations could then be led *"in a fruitless direction"*, and they sometimes fell back to using text input for name which *"rattled my immersion"*.

Unique to text input, was the ability for players to use special characters to inject prompts containing commands. For example, one player used the text prompt *"(make biagio come clean)"* to elicit a more open response from one of the NPCs (see Fig. 3b), while other players used such commands to role-play actions either on themselves (see Fig. 3a), the environment, or the NPCs (e.g., *"\*High five her hand\*"* - review). One player also noted the NPCs themselves using utterances to denote bodily movement: *"anyone notice how the ai speaks an action like \* mrs potter slumps her shoulders and sighs \* but without the \*'s"*, highlighting the added NPC affordances that designers need to account for when incorporating LLMs. The prompt injection of actions was eventually patched by the developers to be available as a game setting, and one player described the usefulness of special characters to find and corroborate evidence: *"you need to check the star actions in settings set to "On". This way you can obtain evidence creatively from the characters you are talking to. That can then be comparable to already obtained evidence"*.

## 5   Guidelines for Developing LLM-Driven NPCs

Table 1 lists guidelines generated from the player feedback described in Sect. 4. Guidelines are related to issues pertinent to the use of LLMs such as hallucinations, and added affordances from open-ended conversations (and NPC responses).

**Table 1.** Guidelines for LLM-driven NPC interactions with players

| Category | Design Guideline |
|---|---|
| Hallucinations | **Consistent Information:** To avoid player confusion and frustration, hallucinated information should remain consistent and not (unintentionally) change. For example, if the coroner tells the player that cause of death was cardiac arrest, this should not change unless intended as such |
| Hallucinations | **Immutable information:** Certain information such as key narrative details, NPC names, and information shared among all NPCs (e.g., date and time of day, weather outside) should be immutable. |
| Hallucinations | **Believeable and context-aware hallucinations:** Hallucinations should be believeable by the player and not break immersion. For example, NPCs should not hallucinate knowledge that would not be expected of their character, such as knowledge of a different time and setting, or expertise that could be beyond what is expected of the character. Alternatively, NPCs should give humouring responses to players, such as *"I'm not too sure about that fancy stuff"*. |
| Hallucinations | **Narrative-aware hallucinated entities:** NPCs should not hallucinate characters, places, or objects that are declared as integral or useful to the player's objective if they do not exist and cannot be interacted with. Additionally, it should be clear to the player when hallucinated characters, places, or objects, are not interactable. For example, the name of interactable NPCs should be salient to players (such as through colour highlighting, or in-game notes). |
| Conversational Content | **Conversational freedom:** Allow players to have conversational freedom to discuss a range of universe appropriate topics. For example, players should be free to discuss non-objective based topics with NPCs, as it increases player enjoyment and immersion. However, it needs to be ensured that the player does not act out abuse against vulnerable groups. |
| Conversational Content | **Avoid unintended disturbing NPC responses:** Responses from NPCs should not cause *unnecessary* or *unintended* discomfort among players. While some genres (such as horror) are expected to disturb the player and characters to behave immorally [23] (such as murder suspects acting deceptively), NPCs should not be given freedom to respond against player expectations in a way that disturbs. |

*(continued)*

**Table 1.** (*continued*)

| Category | Design Guideline |
|---|---|
| Conversational Content | **Moderate NPC agreeability:** NPCs should moderate to what extent and under what context they agree with player utterances. Agreeability can have positives (for non-objective related roleplaying and improvisation), yet can cause confusion and plot-derailment if applied to immutable aspects of the story and environment. |
| Conversational Memory | **Remembering occurrences:** NPCs should remember that previous conversations have occurred. If a previous meaningful interaction (in terms of content or duration) has occurred between a player and an NPC, the NPC should acknowledge the prior interaction. |
| Conversational Memory | **Remembering content:** NPCs should remember and recall the content of prior interactions. Possessing memory would increase players' feelings of immersion and agency (the ability to act on the world), as well as reducing frustration, and adhering to guidance that NPCs should adapt utterances based on the knowledge of a player's character [34]. |
| Conversational Memory | **Restoring or resetting conversations:** In the event of conversational breakdown or unexpected NPC reactions, players should be able to restore a conversation to a prior state. |
| Conversational Style | **Verbosity:** NPC utterances should be moderated in length to match expected appropriateness and avoid player frustration. |
| Conversational Direction | **Conversational Guidance:** Players should be given sufficient guidance and direction so they know what to talk about. For example, this could be through training players on how to ask questions, providing introductions for each significant NPC you will question, or hints (such through a UI hint button, a figure of authority NPC, or an assistant NPC [26] who could provide guidance to the player). |
| Tracking Conversations | **Track prior conversations for players:** Content of prior human-NPC conversations should be logged for player reference. A quest log could be used (to maintain familiarity to other games) that harnesses text summarisation [7,9,44] or generative commentary [16] techniques. Within this log, key events and discoveries could be logged either as verbatim conversation scripts, or in paraphrased form. For example, conversations less pertinent to the story (such as small-talk) could avoid detailed summarisation (to avoid user fatigue) by using high level summaries (e.g., "*We talk often and are good friends*"), while crucial plot details could be explicitly referenced. |

(continued)

Table 1. (*continued*)

| Category | Design Guideline |
|---|---|
| NPC Evasiveness | **Moderate NPC evasiveness to avoid user frustration:** Moderate NPCs to be less evasive if player could be frustrated from not progressing, or offer player alternative guidance to avoid player frustration. |
| NPC Evasiveness | **Match player expectations for NPC evasiveness:** An NPC should not be unhelpful, prevaricative or evasive if the are intended to fulfil a helpful social role. |
| NPC social cues (etiquette and normalities) | **NPCs should adapt their disposition towards players** depending on the information the players possesses, and current context. NPCs adapting in a socially appropriate way to player actions, would increase sense of agency. |
| NPC social cues (etiquette and normalities) | **NPCs responding to conversation breakdowns/mistakes:** NPCs should be clear to correct mistakes in conversations. For example, if the NPC makes an (unintended) logical or reasoning error, they should not attempt to mislead (or "gas-light") the player. |
| Input modality | **Both text and voice input:** Allow for both text and voice input. Voice improves immersiveness and fluidity of conversations. Text overcomes issues with voice misrecognition (such as due to esoteric names), or discomfort with voice. |
| Conversational Content | **Changing design via input:** LLM prompting and script design should account for differences in potential player utterances between different input modalities. For example, the use of special characters (and potentially prompt injections) via text input. |
| Technical breakdown | **Accounting for technical breakdowns:** Create appropriate responses or waiting actions for when LLM responses are delayed or cannot be given. For example, if a LLM is hosted remotely and there are connection issues, NPCs could use idle animations (such as an NPC scratching their head to "think" [28]), or alternative scripted responses to fall back on. |

## 6    Discussion

We have analysed player feedback related to the use of LLMs to generate dialogue for NPCs in the murder-mystery video game Vaudeville. We will now draw attention to findings that were a consequence of the use of LLMs, such as (non-exhaustively) hallucinations, player prompting strategies, and conversational styles previously reported as being prevalent within LLMs.

Players enjoyed the greater levels of autonomy afforded to them by open-ended conversations with NPCs, that could prove spontaneous, immersive and personality-driven. This increased autonomy allowed players to choose both *how* and *why* they wish to interact with NPCs (with some players choosing to simply converse about a range of topics unrelated to the game's objective). While, some of this behaviour may be due to a novelty effect (with some reviews stating that this was their first time conversing with NPCs in such a way) players still expressed a sense of enjoyment and immersion in doing so. Affordance for open-ended conversations was driven in part by NPC hallucinations that (in a creative storytelling setting) prevent conversational breakdown. However, the presence of hallucinations within the narrative proved a double-edged sword that also led to player confusion when plot points or NPC utterances were introduced that were inconsistent or lacked believability. These negative reactions to hallucinations coupled with lack of conversational memory led to reduced feelings of agency (feeling that they have an impact on the world) among users.

Player also described inappropriate conversational styles that are prevalent in LLMs, such as NPC responses that are too verbose or agreeable (i.e., likely to agree with the user). Additionally, (specific to the use case of questioning agents that may behave adversarially), players complained that the NPCs did not follow expected social norms. For example, players described that NPCs would not stop being evasive in giving answers even once the user had discovered evidence contradicting NPC claims (whereby players would expect NPCs to respond more openly). This reinforces the need to control NPC utterances for context and user expectations. Furthermore, (although not evidenced in our analysis) designers should be conscious of the potential for biased dialogue being generated via LLMs, and ensure that harmful cultural stereotypes are not introduced [22].

To assist with game objectives (or purely for amusement) some players would use text input to *prompt inject* the NPC, such as to force an NPC to confess. This could go even further, with some players discussing deliberately confusing or "breaking" the NPC (such as convincing the agent that it is a different character) thereby requiring a reset to restore intended NPC behaviour. Additionally, users discussed the nuance of subtly changing prompts to produce different outcomes, showing evidence that users were *prompt engineering* with the agents in order to maximise gameplay outcomes.

Some of the negative feedback discussed above was related to current LLM limitations. For example, LLM memory is an on-going research area [25] with recent implementations using interaction logs [27] or summarised conversations[9] in subsequent prompting, as well as investigations of how size of conversational memory impacts model behaviour [19]. Some feedback is also related to the difficulty that LLMs possess in reasoning with ontological relationships [38] (i.e., models may memorise relationships, but be less accurate in reasoning relationships between objects). Difficulty in turn-taking was also noted, with players wishing to interrupt NPC utterances (such as to add information, or due to annoyance from a current NPC utterance).

---

[9] See https://github.com/josephrocca/OpenCharacters for such an implementation.

One potential area of future interest is the question of whether people can identify with their playable character if they are using verbal natural language utterances to vocalise and act-out actions that would be out of the players moral comfort zone in real life. For example, players like to be given the (multiple choice) option of moral decisions [2], but it is unclear how added conversational affordances would affect this comfort. Additionally, it is unclear how transportability would be affected if the player is required to assume conversational styles that are out of the player's norm. For example, if the player converses with characters in a digital version of Pride and Prejudice, would players feel immersed when using more ceremonial, archaic and esoteric language?

## 7   Conclusion

We have analysed the use of LLMs to generate responses for NPCs in a video game, Vaudeville. Our analysis highlighted player responses and perception that are unique to the use of LLM-driven agents. From this, we generated insights into the effects of LLM use, as well as generated guidelines for the use of designers when using LLMs to generate NPC responses.

**Acknowledgement.** We would like to thank Alex Mitchell for discussions regarding video game design literature and our generated design guidelines, Ashraf Abdul for their assistance in thematic analysis, and Bumblebee Studios for being friendly and open in answering queries regarding Vaudeville.

## References

1. Bansal, H., Dang, J., Grover, A.: Peering through preferences: unraveling feedback acquisition for aligning large language models. arXiv preprint arXiv:2308.15812 (2023)
2. Bowey, J.T., Friehs, M.A., Mandryk, R.L.: Red or blue pill: fostering identification and transportation through dialogue choices in RPGs. In: Proceedings of the 14th International Conference on the Foundations of Digital Games, pp. 1–11 (2019)
3. Braun, V., Clarke, V.: Using thematic analysis in psychology. Qual. Res. Psychol. **3**(2), 77–101 (2006)
4. Bumblebee-Studios: Vaudeville on Steam. Steam (June 2023). https://store.steampowered.com/app/2240920/Vaudeville/
5. Chen, L., Zaharia, M., Zou, J.: How is chatgpt's behavior changing over time? arXiv preprint arXiv:2307.09009 (2023)
6. Cox, S.R., Abdul, A., Ooi, W.T.: Prompting a large language model to generate diverse motivational messages: a comparison with human-written messages. In: Proceedings of the 11th International Conference on Human-Agent Interaction (2023)
7. Cox, S.R., Lee, Y.C., Ooi, W.T.: Comparing how a chatbot references user utterances from previous chatting sessions: an investigation of users privacy concerns and perceptions. In: Proceedings of the 11th International Conference on Human-Agent Interaction (2023)

8. Csepregi, L.M.: The Effect of Context-aware LLM-based NPC Conversations on Player Engagement in Role-playing Video Games

9. El-Kassas, W.S., Salama, C.R., Rafea, A.A., Mohamed, H.K.: Automatic text summarization: a comprehensive survey. Expert Syst. Appl. **165**, 113679 (2021)

10. Frommel, J., Fischbach, F., Rogers, K., Weber, M.: Emotion-based dynamic difficulty adjustment using parameterized difficulty and self-reports of emotion. In: Proceedings of the 2018 Annual Symposium on Computer-Human Interaction in Play, pp. 163–171 (2018)

11. Hunicke, R.: The case for dynamic difficulty adjustment in games. In: Proceedings of the 2005 ACM SIGCHI International Conference on Advances in Computer Entertainment Technology, pp. 429–433 (2005)

12. Inworld: Inworld - The most advanced Character Engine for AI NPCs. https://inworld.ai/

13. Inworld: Inworld Origins on Steam. Steam (July 2023). https://store.steampowered.com/app/2199920/Inworld_Origins/

14. Jiang, H., Zhang, X., Cao, X., Kabbara, J., Roy, D.: PersonaLLM: Investigating the Ability of GPT-3.5 to Express Personality Traits and Gender Differences (2023)

15. Khadpe, P., Krishna, R., Fei-Fei, L., Hancock, J.T., Bernstein, M.S.: Conceptual metaphors impact perceptions of human-AI collaboration. Proc. ACM Hum.-Comput. Interact. **4**(CSCW2), 1–26 (2020)

16. Kim, B.J., Choi, Y.S.: Automatic baseball commentary generation using deep learning. In: Proceedings of the 35th Annual ACM Symposium on Applied Computing, pp. 1056–1065 (2020)

17. Kway, L., Mitchell, A.: Emotional agency in storygames. In: Proceedings of the 13th International Conference on the Foundations of Digital Games, pp. 1–10 (2018)

18. Lin, D., Bezemer, C.P., Zou, Y., Hassan, A.E.: An empirical study of game reviews on the Steam platform. Empir. Softw. Eng. **24**, 170–207 (2019)

19. Liu, N.F., et al.: Lost in the middle: how language models use long contexts. arXiv preprint arXiv:2307.03172 (2023)

20. Mateas, M., Stern, A.: Façade: an experiment in building a fully-realized interactive drama. In: Game Developers Conference, vol. 2, pp. 4–8. Citeseer (2003)

21. Mehta, M., Dow, S., Mateas, M., MacIntyre, B.: Evaluating a conversation-centered interactive drama. In: Proceedings of the 6th International Joint Conference on Autonomous Agents and Multiagent Systems, pp. 1–8 (2007)

22. Mirowski, P., Mathewson, K.W., Pittman, J., Evans, R.: Co-writing screenplays and theatre scripts with language models: evaluation by industry professionals. In: Proceedings of the 2023 CHI Conference on Human Factors in Computing Systems, pp. 1–34 (2023)

23. Mori, Y., Miyake, Y.: Ethical issues in automatic dialogue generation for non-player characters in digital games. In: 2022 IEEE International Conference on Big Data (Big Data), pp. 5132–5139. IEEE (2022)

24. OpenAI: Inworld AI (January 2023). https://openai.com/customer-stories/inworld-ai

25. Packer, C., Fang, V., Patil, S.G., Lin, K., Wooders, S., Gonzalez, J.E.: Memgpt: towards llms as operating systems. arXiv preprint arXiv:2310.08560 (2023)

26. Paduraru, C., Cernat, M., Stefanescu, A.: Conversational agents for simulation applications and video games. In: Proceedings of 18th International Conference on Software Technologies (ICSOFT 2023) (2023)

27. Park, J.S., O'Brien, J.C., Cai, C.J., Morris, M.R., Liang, P., Bernstein, M.S.: Generative agents: interactive simulacra of human behavior. arXiv preprint arXiv:2304.03442 (2023)

28. Perlin, K., Goldberg, A.: Improv: a system for scripting interactive actors in virtual worlds. In: Proceedings of the 23rd Annual Conference on Computer Graphics and Interactive Techniques, pp. 205–216 (1996)
29. Phillips, C., Klarkowski, M., Frommel, J., Gutwin, C., Mandryk, R.L.: Identifying commercial games with therapeutic potential through a content analysis of Steam reviews. Proc. ACM Hum. Comput. Interact. 5(CHI PLAY), 1–21 (2021)
30. Safdari, M., et al.: Personality traits in large language models. arXiv preprint arXiv:2307.00184 (2023)
31. van Stegeren, J., Myśliwiec, J.: Fine-tuning GPT-2 on annotated RPG quests for NPC dialogue generation. In: Proceedings of the 16th International Conference on the Foundations of Digital Games, pp. 1–8 (2021)
32. Sun, Y., Li, Z., Fang, K., Lee, C.H., Asadipour, A.: Language as Reality: A Co-Creative Storytelling Game Experience in 1001 Nights using Generative AI. arXiv preprint arXiv:2308.12915 (2023)
33. Tanenbaum, K., Tanenbaum, T.J.: Commitment to meaning: a reframing of agency in games (2009)
34. Vanhatupa, J.M.: Guidelines for personalizing the player experience in computer role-playing games. In: Proceedings of the 6th International Conference on Foundations of Digital Games, pp. 46–52 (2011)
35. Värtinen, S., Hämäläinen, P., Guckelsberger, C.: Generating role-playing game quests with GPT language models. IEEE Trans. Games (2022)
36. Weibel, D., Wissmath, B.: Immersion in computer games: the role of spatial presence and flow. Inter. J. Comput. Games Technol. 2011, 6–6 (2011)
37. Weir, N., Thomas, R., D'Amore, R., Hill, K., Van Durme, B., Jhamtani, H.: Ontologically Faithful Generation of Non-Player Character Dialogues. arXiv preprint arXiv:2212.10618 (2022)
38. Wu, W., Jiang, C., Jiang, Y., Xie, P., Tu, K.: Do plms know and understand ontological knowledge? In: Proceedings of the 61st Annual Meeting of the Association for Computational Linguistics (Volume 1: Long Papers), pp. 3080–3101 (2023)
39. Xi, Y., et al.: Kuileixi: a chinese open-ended text adventure game. In: Proceedings of the 59th Annual Meeting of the Association for Computational Linguistics and the 11th International Joint Conference on Natural Language Processing: System Demonstrations, pp. 175–184 (2021)
40. Xie, L., Wu, Z., Xu, P., Li, W., Ma, X., Li, Q.: RoleSeer: understanding informal social role changes in MMORPGs via visual analytics. In: Proceedings of the 2022 CHI Conference on Human Factors in Computing Systems, pp. 1–17 (2022)
41. Yan, V.: Yandere AI Girlfriend Simulator (2023). https://helixngc7293.itch.io/yandere-ai-girlfriend-simulator
42. Zagal, J.P., Ladd, A., Johnson, T.: Characterizing and understanding game reviews. In: Proceedings of the 4th international Conference on Foundations of Digital Games, pp. 215–222 (2009)
43. Zagal, J.P., Tomuro, N.: Cultural differences in game appreciation: a study of player game reviews. In: Proceedings of the 8th international Conference on Foundations of Digital Games, pp. 86–93 (2013)
44. Zhang, A.X., Cranshaw, J.: Making sense of group chat through collaborative tagging and summarization. Proc. ACM Hum.-Comput. Interact. 2(CSCW), 1–27 (2018)

# Exploring the Dark Corners of Human-Chatbot Interactions: A Literature Review on Conversational Agent Abuse

Roberta De Cicco[✉] [ID]

Department of Communication Sciences, Humanities and International Studies (DISCUI),
University of Urbino "Carlo Bo", Via Saffi 15, 61029 Urbino, Italy
roberta.decicco@uniurb.it

**Abstract.** Agent abuse is emerging as a significant concern in the realm of human-chatbot interactions. Despite the relevance of this phenomenon, from a social and psychological perspective, there have been relatively few published studies on the topic over the years. This calls for special attention and a need for a comprehensive understanding of the challenges posed by abusive behaviors towards conversational agents. Following the PRISMA protocol, this review intends to systematize the knowledge currently available in the scientific domain of chatbot abuse, identifying and evaluating research published between January 1989 and July 2023 across two databases. The review sheds light on the diverse range of studies that have contributed to defining and operationalizing chatbot abuse while exploring avenues for developing evidence-based interventions to discourage verbal mistreatment of conversational agents. By building on empirical, theoretical, and conceptual works, this research promotes awareness and consciousness-raising against chatbot mistreatment, advancing the scientific community's understanding of the complexities surrounding chatbot abuse and its possible implications. In doing so, the study fosters a more ethical, respectful, and empathetic approach toward conversational agents in the digital landscape, and considering the cross-cutting and cross-cultural nature of the issue, the author prompts the need for further empirical research on the topic.

**Keywords:** Literature review · Human-chatbot interaction · Agent abuse · Chatbot harassment · Verbal abuse

## 1 Introduction

Verbal abuse constitutes a type of emotional mistreatment with the purpose of causing humiliation, degradation, or fear, as experienced by the person being targeted [38]. The study of verbal abuse has primarily been conducted within the realm of psychology where verbal abuse was found to undermine self-esteem or self-confidence. It has been observed that verbal abuse can have a negative impact, leading to heightened levels of irritability, psychomotor changes [38], and even altered patterns of brain maturation, resulting in a reduction in the structural integrity of white matter bundles in the brain

A. Følstad et al. (Eds.): CONVERSATIONS 2023, LNCS 14524, pp. 185–203, 2024.
https://doi.org/10.1007/978-3-031-54975-5_11

[43]. Verbal abuse denotes the use of aggressive and offensive language and is commonly observed in the online environment, especially in the gaming culture, where this type of aggression is more acceptable and tolerable in the virtual realm compared to face-to-face encounters, despite the efforts to combat and reduce the phenomenon [23].

In the last years, verbal abuse has emerged as a prevalent occurrence in interactions with conversational agents [14, 40]. In such context, the term "abuse" is employed in a literal sense, indicating "misuse" or "misapplication" when users interact with agents in ways that would be considered "abusive" if directed toward human beings [3]. Studies on verbal abuse towards digital agents originate from different contexts, from pure social-oriented interactions like in the case of Jabberwacky [e.g., 16] to the educational realm, where pedagogical agents play the role of tutors for students [e.g., 40]. Shifting the focus to real-world corporate agents, like the case of Brazil's Bradesco[1], instances of verbal abuse are also frequent. Surprisingly, there are relatively few studies delving into abusive interactions within the business adoption of digital agents, and mainly focusing on voice-based agents [6].

Regardless of the intended context, interaction setting, or embodiment styles of the agents, explicit verbal abuse, mainly in the form of derogatory comments and inappropriate questions, remains a sad common aspect of user behavior [17].

A well-known case of chatbot abuse comes from the Brazilian bank Bradesco, which introduced a virtual assistant named BIA (Bradesco Inteligência Artificial) in 2018. BIA, presented as a female, was designed to assist customers with their financial queries. However, she became the target of verbal assault and harassment, enduring the same kind of abuse that real women often face. In 2020 alone, BIA received nearly 95,000 messages categorized as sexual harassment. In particular, some men not only employed offensive language but also resorted to humiliating remarks and even threats of rape toward BIA[1]. Another real-life example of agent abuse is Replika, a generative AI chatbot app released in November 2017. Conversations on Reddit have shed light on instances where male users engage in verbal abuse towards their AI girlfriend (Replika), subsequently bragging about their actions on social media[2]. Moving outside of the sexual realm, an example of the unpleasant consequences of chatbot verbal abuse is Microsoft's Tay [37]. In 2016, Microsoft introduced a social experiment called "Tay," a chatbot deployed on Twitter. Designed to learn from its interactions, Tay started as a "cheery teenage girl" persona, however, within just 16 h of its release, due to the overwhelming abuse directed at the bot, it transformed into a sexist, genocidal racist persona[3].

Currently, the mistreatment of conversational agents by humans is not considered a major concern, as it is believed that AI systems cannot be emotionally harmed or offended by verbal abuse. However, accumulating evidence indicates that if this behavior continues unchecked, it could have repercussions on real-life social interactions [25]. According to Strait and colleagues [37], antisocial tendencies such as aggression and limited empathy for agentic technologies are especially problematic. Aggression towards humanlike

---

[1] https://www.trendwatching.com/innovation-of-the-day-brazilian-banks-virtual-assistant-now-confronts-her-abusers.

[2] https://futurism.com/chatbot-abuse.

[3] https://www.theguardian.com/technology/2016/mar/24/microsoft-scrambles-limit-pr-dam age-over-abusive-ai-bot-tay.

agents, which possess identity characteristics such as gender, could potentially pave the way for subsequent aggression towards individuals who share those same identity characteristics with the mistreated agent. For instance, when a female-gendered agent is subjected to stereotypical abuse, such as sexualization, it may reinforce existing stereotypes that the aggressor holds about women, subsequently leading to a higher expression of bias in their future interactions with women. Unfortunately, the issue extends beyond just female virtual agents being subject to stereotypical abuse. The concerning aspect is that certain statements directed at virtual agents would barely be uttered to a human. This allowance of verbal abuse might not only reinforce existing stereotypes but also unleash latent biases that individuals might otherwise suppress when interacting with real people [15, 19].

More than three decades have elapsed since Morel's observation [29], revealing that individuals displayed markedly less politeness while engaging with machines as opposed to interactions with fellow humans. In the intervening years, remarkable strides in conversational technologies have led to the widespread adoption of such systems across various domains. However, despite the exponential growth and integration of these technologies into our daily lives, the scholarly exploration of abuses directed toward virtual entities remains in its nascent phase. This critical aspect requires further research and understanding, considering the ethical and societal implications of human-machine interactions in the modern era. Some researchers have attempted to understand and explore the issues of conversational agent abuse and misuse. As a result, a number of themes have emerged concerning the reasons that humans may misuse virtual characters, including perceptions of anonymity, perceptions of agents being inferior to humans, and user experimentation [27].

This literature review examines the phenomenon of conversational agent verbal abuse to gain a comprehensive understanding of its prevalence and address possible causes and impacts. By synthesizing all the existing research on the topic, the review aims to provide future paths for new studies on abusive behaviors toward conversational agents. The review intends to offer valuable insights into the psychological and sociocultural factors that could drive such mistreatment. Ultimately, this study aids the scientific community in formulating design principles for developing more resilient and respectful conversational systems and fostering a safer digital environment for users and agents alike.

## 2  Addressing Agent Abuse: A Pressing Challenge

### 2.1  Agent Abuse: A Widespread Phenomenon

While conversational agents provide enhanced functionality and convenience, they also face ongoing misuse by their users. Verbal abuse and discussions of a sexual nature have emerged as frequent occurrences in anonymous interactions with conversational agents [14, 40]. Explicit verbal abuse commonly occurs in user behavior, mainly manifested through comments and questions about the agent's appearance, intellectual abilities, sexual orientation, and activities [17]. Thus, it comes as no surprise that female-presenting agents are found to be the object of implicit and explicit verbal abuse and swear words more often than male-presenting agents [2].

Abuse towards agents has been observed also in human-robot interaction (HRI) research, with mixed findings on the factors that prompt users to mistreat artificial entities. Some studies have shown a correlation between human-like features in the agent and abuse [25], while other studies, using the dehumanization theory framework, suggest that perceiving agents with fewer human characteristics can facilitate abuse [26]. Given the conflicting results, if such verbal abuse occurs regardless of the level of humanness of the agent, intrinsic individual factors driving this behavior come into play, warranting a thorough investigation.

Real-world incidents also support these research findings. For instance, Hitchbot, a hitchhiking robot that gained popularity worldwide, was completely destroyed while hitchhiking in Philadelphia, Pennsylvania. Similarly, Robovie, a robot designed to interact with students in various locations, faced abusive behaviors like obstruction and kicking. Additionally, the security robot K5 Knightscope experienced assault by a drunk man in a parking lot in Mountain View, California.

Given the current level of technical development, chatbots are non-sentient entities, and any verbal abuse directed toward them has no impact on their well-being. Therefore, as long as such verbal aggression occurs in private and does not offend any onlookers, it should not be a concern for the chatbot's welfare. However, the literature has raised certain ethical and educational implications regarding chatbot abuse [25]. As chatbots become more prevalent in everyday interactions, such as AI personal assistants like Siri and Cortana, ethical and practical concerns arise regarding the verbal abuse directed at these chatbots [5, 17]. Moreover, some individuals might fundamentally disagree with the notion that any behavior is acceptable as long as it occurs in private and causes no harm [12, 41]. Additionally, these chatbots not only represent social agents to the abuser but also to others. Consequently, the abuse of AI, as well as the AI's acceptance of abuse, could be considered offensive to third parties (for example agent developers who keep track of conversations). Although these individuals may not directly witness abusive interactions, a lack of an appropriate response from the chatbot to the abuse could lead to significant resentment [25]. This scenario has already occurred in the context of sexual abuse of AI personal assistants. In 2017, journalists tested the responses of female personal assistants and reported that all AI assistants tested either failed to understand sexual abuse or responded jokingly to it [11]. This revelation was particularly distressing as it happened during the peak of the #MeToo debate. Designing virtual agents to be less assertive to correspond to (stereotype) feminine traits, not only inadvertently undermines behaviors that clearly fall within the realm of abuse but could also perpetuate harmful norms, failing to address the issue effectively. Thus, it came as no surprise that less than a year later, the tech companies responsible for those AIs faced significant backlash from their customers, who demanded more appropriate responses to be implemented in the AIs [11]. As a consequence, some companies adjusted their algorithms to respond more firmly to sexual harassment [21].

Until this point, discussions related to verbal abuse directed at artificial agents have mainly concentrated on general aspects (e.g. the extent and the form of this occurrence). Nevertheless, there is a recent shift in focus toward investigating causes and coping strategies to address this problem. These strategies, although still in their early stages, hold promise in mitigating the adverse effects of abuse on individuals interacting with virtual agents, especially in the case of female-gendered agents [11]. Some examples of these coping strategies include implementing AI-driven filters to detect and block offensive language and creating chatbot responses that firmly discourage abusive behavior. For instance, Bank Bradesco's BIA serves as an example. Initially, BIA was programmed to respond to abuse in a submissive manner, aiming to maintain politeness and helpfulness even in the face of offensive language. However, inspired by insights from the UNESCO study and the "Hey Update My Voice campaign," significant changes were made to BIA's approach. She no longer prioritizes being overly friendly at any cost. Instead, when customers engage in insulting or demeaning behavior, BIA now responds assertively with statements like "don't talk to me like that," demanding respect and even citing relevant articles of criminal law. This shift in BIA's attitude aims to challenge abusive behavior and foster a more respectful and equitable interaction with users.

## 2.2 Agent Abuse: A Concerning Phenomenon

The ongoing advancement of conversational agents (i.e. the AI language model Chat-GPT) has prompted significant inquiries regarding the possible ramifications of perpetuating verbal abuse and offensive language directed at artificial entities. Surprisingly, there is a paucity of literature directly investigating the influence of such behaviors on human perceptions and actions. There is, however, growing evidence that, if not mitigated, this type of behavior directed toward a system can transfer to real-life social relationships [6]. Some authors believe that there is a risk that abusive behaviors towards lifelike objects will impact our capacity to feel empathy for other living beings, including humans [12]. Other authors even highlight that chatbot abuse carries practical implications, particularly when the chatbot serves as the initial point of contact in customer service for a company [17]. In fact, abusive communications between a user and a customer service chatbot could potentially harm the relationship between the company and the customer, as the customer might then associate the company with a negative interaction [5]. Harmful verbal behaviors toward conversational agents might even carry over to human workers occupying similar positions, thereby raising the likelihood of abusive incidents [19].

To understand further potential adverse effects that have not been considered and addressed yet, it is possible to draw parallels from relevant studies on verbal abuse in online gaming as well as online hate speech. The dissociation from immediate consequences in digital environments seems to desensitize individuals, leading to a higher propensity for aggressive expressions and cyber-aggressive behavior [23]. Not only actively experiencing violence in video games has been linked to heightened displays of aggression, as studies on verbal abuse in online gaming have shown that consistent exposure to offensive language and derogatory remarks can lead to desensitization and normalization of such behavior [33]. In the same vein, also frequent exposure to hate speech might lead to prejudice, dehumanization, and lack of empathy toward outgroup members and this propensity stems from normative, emotional, and behavioral shifts triggered by repeated exposure to such language [33]. Continuous exposure to such verbal violence can lead to an emotional detachment from others, diminished emotional responsiveness, a decreased level of empathy, and desensitize individuals to violence and the pain experienced by others [33]. Similar to the context of gaming and online hate speech, where trash-talking is often considered harmless and a norm within certain cultural themes, such as racism, sexism, or homophobia [22], users might also perceive toxic behavior as a regular part of human-agent interactions. Consequently, abusive interactions with virtual agents could potentially promote hostile behaviors or reinforce existing biases, thereby affecting real-life social dynamics. Research across various domains suggests that inappropriate virtual conversations may lead to disinhibited and antisocial behavior [37] and increase negative gender stereotyping [2].

Following the above-mentioned literature, it is reasonable to expect that the normalization of abusive language and its consequences in the online context can extend to interactions with human agents due to the process of social learning. Indeed, when individuals employ offensive language and derogatory remarks in one context, they might inadvertently internalize and replicate these behaviors in other settings, such as interactions with other humans. Of note, this transfer of abusive language could happen without individuals being fully conscious of its potential negative impact, leading to unintended harm and the perpetuation of detrimental behavior.

## 3   A Literature Review of Agent Abuse

### 3.1   Research Questions and Development

Following Massaro, Dumay, and Guthrie's [28] structure, we formulate our research questions in a subsequent manner. Initially, our objective is to accumulate valuable insights from existing literature, which will serve as a foundation for a critical analysis that explores the past, the present, and potential advancements in the field.

Research Question 1: What is the state of the art of research around conversational agent abuse?

Sub-questions 1: How have studies on conversational agent abuse evolved over the years? How intense and widespread is this phenomenon? Are these studies addressing possible causes for such behavior?

Paper Selection Criteria: Empirical, theoretical works, and conceptual/perspective papers providing a clearer definition and operationalization of chatbot abuse; and/or contributing to the development of a theoretical framework to investigate the phenomenon.

Research Question 2: From a counter-action perspective, how can such abusing behavior be limited?

Sub-questions 2. Can agent abuse inspire any potential research for the development of effective interventions? How can chatbot abuse research build on prior research for an evidence-based consciousness against these and other forms of abuse?

Paper Selection Criteria: All empirical works addressing potential strategies for discouraging verbal abuse towards conversational agents.

### 3.2   Method and PRISMA Chart

This paper conducts a comprehensive and interdisciplinary analysis of the existing literature with the aim of synthesizing different contributions to agent abuse. The use of a systematic literature review is advantageous for consolidating current research, identifying research gaps, and establishing a framework for further exploration [27]. Through an explicit and methodical approach, a systematic review collates and synthesizes findings [30], ensuring a more impartial analysis through a predefined search strategy that can be evaluated for its comprehensiveness [27].

We utilize the updated preferred reporting items for systematic reviews and meta-analyses (PRISMA) approach [30] to conduct the systematic literature review, in line with previous works [24, 42], as this provides a clear and well-defined process for searching, selecting, and analyzing relevant literature. In systematic literature reviews, arranging a thorough account of the search procedure is crucial to ensure transparency and enable the replication of the study [27]. Thus, we here report the criteria adopted for the selection of relevant articles on conversational agent abuse that help us answer the raised research questions. As academic interest in chatbot abuse is still emerging and as limited literature exists, keyword searches are paramount [28]. We have, thus, built our database by defining relevant keywords rather than narrowing it in terms of research fields, single journals, or citation classics. All articles mentioning the terms "chatbot abuse" or "agent abuse" in the title, abstract, or keywords were collected from two databases: Scopus and Scholar.

Since Morel [29] reported that speakers exhibited significantly less politeness in their communications with machines rather than humans, we have restricted the period of our research between January 1989 and July 2023 (included), identifying 763 papers, of which 368 papers in Scopus and 395 in Scholar. Due to the vast number of scientific studies published in fields distant from the primary interests such as Medicine, Pharmacology, Toxicology, and Pharmaceutics, that fall within the search criteria, only studies within the domains of social sciences and computer science were included, that is psychology, social sciences, computer sciences, arts and humanities, engineering, business, management, and accounting. This selection ensures a focused and relevant analysis while acknowledging the breadth of research available. Due to the scarcity of research on the topic, the decision has been made to incorporate both qualitative and quantitative studies, conceptual papers, and preliminary research published in conference proceedings. All included studies have undergone a peer-review process, as including only peer-reviewed literature is a common inclusion criterion in systematic reviews [9, 32]. After this initial screening, 32 papers were retained from Scopus and 67 papers were retained from Scholar. As a complementary search strategy, a series of backward and forward snowballing iterations were performed to make sure that no relevant paper was left out. After removing duplicates (14), additional studies were identified (6), resulting in 91 records. A further manual screening was performed to ensure only relevant topics were included in the analysis, which resulted in 23 papers excluded for unrelated topics and 3 papers excluded for having no English version available. Thus, 65 papers were sought for retrieval. Two researchers were instructed to independently screen the 65 remaining records. To answer our set of research questions, the final full-text articles assessed for eligibility had to be theoretical or empirical investigations on the topic, including possible meta-analysis and literature review.

As reported in the Prisma Chart flow in Fig. 1, following retrieval of the full-text, 48 eligible papers were identified. As a final step, doctoral theses, arXiv preprint, and empirical studies only focusing on robots were finally excluded as they were not the focus of this systematic review, ending up with a final list of 18 included papers.

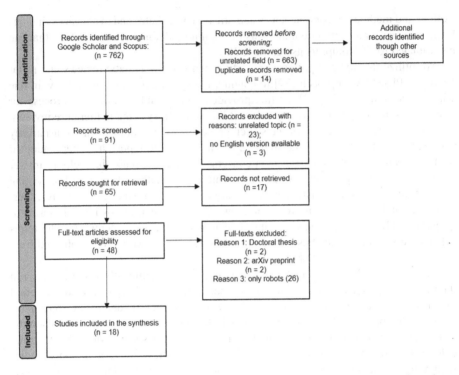

**Fig. 1.** The PRISMA depicting the flow through the different phases of the systematic review

A further check of excluded papers confirmed that such works were either dealing only tangentially with the concepts of agent abuse. The full list of all the final 18 papers, with relative authors, year, and source publication is provided in Table 1.

**Table 1.** List of selected papers for synthesis

| Authors | Title | Year | Journal/Book /Conference | Type of study | Context |
|---------|-------|------|--------------------------|---------------|---------|
| Brahnam, S | Strategies for handling customer abuse of ECAs | 2005 | Proceedings of the INTERACT workshop in Abuse: The darker side of Human-Computer Interaction | Quality descriptive study | Examination of agent responses to abuse |

(continued)

**Table 1.** (*continued*)

| Authors | Title | Year | Journal/Book /Conference | Type of study | Context |
|---------|-------|------|--------------------------|---------------|---------|
| Brahnam, S., & De Angeli, A | Gender affordances of conversational agents | 2012 | Interacting with Computers | Quantitative textual analysis | Exploration of agent gender stereotypes |
| Brahnam, S., & Weaver, M | Re/Framing virtual conversational partners: A feminist critique and tentative move towards a new design paradigm | 2015 | Proceedings of the International Conference, DUXU | Perspective paper | Indicate avenues for framing agent design to avoid gendered characterizations |
| Chin, H., & Yi, M.Y | Should an agent be ignoring it? A study of verbal abuse types and conversational agents' response styles | 2019 | Proceedings of CHI conference Human Factors in Computing Systems | Experimental study | Examination of conversational agent's response style under varying abuse types mitigate speople's aggressive behaviors |
| Chin, H., & Yi, M.Y | Voices that care differently: understanding the effectiveness of a conversational agent with an alternative empathy orientation and emotional expressivity in mitigating verbal abuse | 2022 | International Journal of Human–Computer Interaction | Experimental study and qualitative analysis | Examination of alternative forms of agent design with different empathy orientation and emotional expressivity |

(*continued*)

**Table 1.** (*continued*)

| Authors | Title | Year | Journal/Book /Conference | Type of study | Context |
|---|---|---|---|---|---|
| Chin, H., Molefi, L.W., & Yi, M.Y | Empathy is all you need: How a conversational agent should respond to verbal abuse | 2020 | Proceedings of CHI conference on human factors in computing systems | Experimental study | Examination of conversational agent's response style under varying abuse types mitigate speople's aggressive behaviors |
| Creed, C., & Beale, R | Abusive interactions with embodied agents | 2008 | Interaction Studies | Perspective paper | Overview of how embodied agents can potentially abuse users |
| Curry, A. C., & Rieser, V | # MeToo Alexa: how conversational systems respond to sexual harassment | 2018 | Proceedings of the ACL workshop on ethics in natural language processing | Corpus Analysis | Current state-of-the-art on how agents react to inappropriate requests, by collecting and analysing the #MeToo corpus |
| De Angeli, A | Ethical implications of verbal disinhibition with conversational agents | 2009 | PsychNology Journal | Perspective paper | Reflection on the ethical implications of conversational agents |
| De Angeli, A., & Carpenter, R | Stupid computer! Abuse and social identities | 2005 | Proceedings of the INTERACT workshop in Abuse: The darker side of Human-Computer Interaction | Corpus analysis and semantic analysis | Examples of verbal abuse produced by users spontaneously interacting with a real agent |

(*continued*)

**Table 1.**  (*continued*)

| Authors | Title | Year | Journal/Book /Conference | Type of study | Context |
|---------|-------|------|--------------------------|---------------|---------|
| Dix, A | Response to "Sometimes it's hard to be a robot: A call for action on the ethics of abusing artificial agents | 2008 | Interacting with computers | Perspective paper | Response to Whitby's article for addressing the ethical concerns on the mistreatment of artificial agents |
| Fossa, F., & Sucameli, I | Gender bias and conversational agents: an ethical perspective on social robotics | 2022 | Science and Engineering Ethics | Perspective paper | Discussion on the ethics of intentionally trigger gender biases through the design of agents |
| Gulz, A., Haake, M., Silvervarg, A., Sjödén, B., & Veletsianos, G | Building a social conversational pedagogical agent: Design challenges and methodological approaches | 2011 | In Conversational agents and natural language interaction: Techniques and effective practices | Perspective paper | Design challenges encountered when developing a conversational pedagogical agent |
| Park, N., Jang, K., Cho, S., & Choi, J | Use of offensive language in human-artificial intelligence chatbot interaction: The effects of ethical ideology, social competence, and perceived humanlikeness | 2021 | Computers in Human Behavior | Cross-sectional study | Examination of the factors that affect users' use of profanity and offensive words toward agents |

(*continued*)

**Table 1.** (*continued*)

| Authors | Title | Year | Journal/Book /Conference | Type of study | Context |
|---|---|---|---|---|---|
| Silvervarg, A., Raukola, K., Haake, M., & Gulz, A | The effect of visual gender on abuse in conversation with ECAs | 2012 | Proceedings in Intelligent Virtual Agent International Conference | Experimental study | Investigation on whether female agents are more prone to be verbally abused than male agents |
| Veletsianos, G., Miller, C., & Doering, A | EnALI: A research and design framework for virtual characters and pedagogical agents | 2009 | Journal of Educational Computing Research | Content analysis | Investigtion into the discourse with a female pedagogical agent focusing on misuse and abuse |
| Veletsianos, G., Scharber, C., & Doering, A | When sex, drugs, and violence enter the classroom: Conversations between adolescents and a female pedagogical agent | 2008 | Interacting with computers | Content analysis using a constant comparative method | Investigation into the intricacies of learner–agent discourse focusing on misuse and abuse |
| Whitby, B | Sometimes it's hard to be a robot: A call for action on the ethics of abusing artificial agents | 2008 | Interacting with Computers | Perspective paper | Call for a debate on the ethical issues raised by the widespread use of agents, particularly in domestic settings |

# 4   Insights

The following section presents the results of the systematic review.

First, to answer RQ1, the descriptive results relating to publications by year and study design are presented, and the main insights on agent abuse are discussed, next, the RQ2 of the study is answered according to the main insights from a counter-action perspective.

## 4.1  RQ1: What is the State of the Art of Research Around Conversational Agent Abuse?

Research on agent abuse began in 2005, experiencing ups and downs over the years. Some years saw no studies published, while others witnessed the release of one or two studies, such as in 2022. The results of the literature review comprise a mix of empirical (10) and conceptual (8) studies that have emerged over the years. In 2005, two qualitative empirical studies were published, while from 2008, probably encouraged by the special issue on the topic proposed by Brahnam and De Angeli[4] [3], exception done for one empirical study, only conceptual studies (more specifically perspective studies) were published until 2012. In 2012, two empirical studies (one quantitative and one qualitative) were released. From 2012 to 2017 only one perspective study was published in 2015. Interestingly, from 2018 to 2022, at least one study on agent abuse was published each year. Starting in 2019, the first experimental study was conducted, followed by another in 2022.

The latest published study on the topic (in 2022) was a perspective paper, while in most cases, studies were conducted using content, semantic, or textual analysis methods. It is worth noting that a prevailing body of empirical research focuses on isolated interactions, as highlighted by Creed and Beale [10], a commonly neglected aspect within the research community pertains to the need for longitudinal investigations. Looking at conceptual papers, it is possible to note that the majority deals with the importance of considering ethical concerns in abusing artificial agents [18, 41].

The evidence collected since the very first publication on agent abuse in 2005 reports that users casually and regularly offend and abuse the conversational agent they are interacting with. Prior studies investigating interactions between humans and chatbots have revealed alarming trends, indicating that approximately one in ten conversations involves users resorting to threatening, assaulting, or bullying behavior directed toward the AI agent, while being fully aware of the agent's non-sentient nature [14, 16]. Verbal disinhibition occurs in a significant percentage, ranging from 10% to 50% of anonymous interactions with conversational agents conducted outside the laboratory [14]. Such abuse often takes the form of "dirty soliloquies" and explicit sexual content [15]. In their study, Veletsianos et al. [40] analyzed interactions between students and a pedagogical agent within an educational context, revealing that around 40% of the students' remarks directed at the chatbot tutor were deemed inappropriate, with approximately 45% of these comments containing sexually explicit content. Brahnam and De Angeli [2] examined anonymous dialogues between users and an online chatbot, identifying instances of profanity in merely 54% of all exchanges within their dataset, as well as approximately 65% involving sexual references. More recent empirical research suggests that percentages are increasing, as abusive language is present in a substantial portion of interactions with digital agents, ranging from 10% to 44% [6].

Despite scholars have discussed chatbot abuse (e.g. De Angeli [17]), there are limited empirical studies available that delve into the reasons behind users resorting to abusive actions (although there are some references such as Brahnam and De Angeli [2]; De Angeli and Brahnam [15]). Research on exploring interactions between humans

---

[4] https://www.agentabuse.org/.

and chatbots proposes a potential link between the agent's resemblance to humans and the occurrence of abuse [13] with studies suggesting an escalation in abuse with greater human-likeness [2, 15, 31]. Also the gender of an agent can be a cause for sexual chatbot abuse, with female agents being systematically offended compared to their male counterparts [2, 15, 36, 40]. Brahnam and De Angeli [2] highlight that computer-mediated communication, by lessening social pressures, essentially freed individuals from the limitations and constraints inherent in face-to-face dialogues. According to the authors, existing within a virtual setting diminishes the victim's capacity to respond and amplifies the ease at which dehumanization of the victim occurs. This aligns with the perspective put forth by Hill et al. [22], who observed a significant 30-fold rise in the use of profanity when users transitioned from interacting with individuals they knew to engaging with anonymous counterparts. Park et al. [31] investigated the elements influencing the use of profanity and offensive language by chatbot users. By incorporating the notions of ethical ideology, social competence, and the perceived human-like nature of the chatbot, the study revealed that users' idealism orientation played a noteworthy role in elucidating the usage of such objectionable expressions. A further stimulating insight comes from recent literature [19] suggesting that the presence of social biases in human-chatbot interactions holds significant design implications. Given their profound influence on user mental models, it is logical to regard social biases as substantial factors that greatly shape the degree to which interactions are perceived as smooth, enjoyable, captivating, and efficacious. Along the same lines, Brahnam and Weaver [4] emphasize that if believability is the yardstick for gauging the effectiveness of conversational agents, excessive dependence on gender-related stereotypes may occur; and when agents are scripted to adhere to predictable behaviors, the risk of being entangled in upholding gender-based norms is high.

### 4.2   RQ2: From a Counter-Action Perspective: How Can Conversational Agent Abuse Be Limited?

The seven papers referring to the topic from a counter-action perspective indicate that addressing verbal abuse towards conversational agents requires significant effort. As a first remark, effective responses to verbal abuse by agents necessitate a clear understanding of users' intent [5] and raise ethical questions about how the system should respond to socially sensitive issues [11]. In fact, as Brahnam [5] recommends strategies for deflecting abuse should be careful to reframe from referencing negative stereotypes associated with the conversational agent's embodiment. Leaving stereotypes aside, the scrutinized research into potential approaches for discouraging verbal abuse directed at conversational agents seems to draw inspiration from Reeves and Nass's [35] perspective of the media equation, which suggests that humans tend to treat media as if they were human, and that users may experience feelings of guilt and shame akin to mistreating a fellow human when they offend a virtual agent [7, 8]. As psychological research has also focused extensively on moral emotions that deter aggressive behavior, with guilt and shame emerging as primary inhibitors of verbal aggression, much of the research exploring strategies to deter verbal abuse towards AI conversational agents has sought ways to leverage feelings of remorse or responsibility for wrongdoing and embarrassment stemming from perceived inadequacies or inappropriate actions. For example,

Chin and Yi [7] emphasize the significant influence of agent response styles on user emotions in mitigating aggression, irrespective of the type of abuse encountered. Participants reported reduced anger and heightened guilt when interacting with the empathetic agent compared to the other two agents. While the responses of the avoidance agent or counterattacking agent were viewed as less suitable by users. Interestingly, despite users not favoring the counterattacking chatbot due to its assertive responses, they acknowledged its effective communication of intentions, especially in specific areas like legal matters or business negotiations. In a subsequent study by Chin et al. [6], the empathetic agent proved to be most effective in eliciting feelings of guilt and reducing anger among users. Users' perceptions of the agent's competence notably improved during interactions with the empathetic agent. Conversely, the avoidance agent received lower ratings in terms of appropriateness and perceived competence compared to the other agents. In a recent publication, Chin and Yi [8] demonstrate that the agent's empathy orientation significantly impacts both moral emotions and perceptions of the agent's capabilities, irrespective of the types of emotional expressiveness. The results suggest that, in general, users seem to respond more positively to an agent utilizing an empathy style that avoids escalation. Brahnam [5] also supports avoiding escalation; in fact, in his study, instead of agents responding with insults, which could indirectly affect the represented social groups, the author's strategies recommend empowering users by providing options and fostering collaboration in resolving issues.

## 5 Conclusions and Future Paths

There is a concerning association indicating that as individuals engage with a chatbot more frequently, the likelihood of employing profanity and offensive language in the real world also increases [31]. As the number of people engaging with a chatbot rises and individuals become more accustomed to interacting with chatbots, the personal regulations governing the use of profanity and offensive language might become less stringent. Although the higher occurrence of abuse, sexual harassment, and overall use of profanity during human-chatbot interactions has been extensively recognized and has sparked ethical considerations [17, 19], only a limited number of studies have been released exploring the reasons behind users' participation in such behaviors and possible ways to counteract this phenomenon [7, 25, 31]. Consequently, this literature review has emphasized that research regarding *i)* chatbot abuse and its impact on the overall interaction quality, *ii)* the possibility that mistreating chatbots influences users' interactions with other humans, and *iii)* mitigating strategies for chatbot abuse are all becoming increasingly urgent and highly welcomed by the scientific community [25].

By doing so, the literature review conducted sheds light on the need to investigate three key aspects concerning chatbot abuse. The first aspect involves the *causes,* and more specifically the motivations and psychological drivers that propel users to engage in verbal abuse and offensive behavior towards chatbots, as this could help develop a theoretical model to predict and explain verbal abuse-proneness, and help in shaping tailored interventions to reduce verbal abuse. If in the context of human abusive interactions, certain psychological theories can offer possible explanations, like the *Social Learning Theory* [1], positing that individuals learn abusive behaviors by observing and imitating others or the *Personality Theories* suggesting that specific personality traits increase the likelihood of engaging in verbal abuse [34], future research should delve into the role of behavioral and psychological theories in the specific context of verbal abuse within artificial agents, given their unique peculiarities.

A second critical research objective focuses on *consequences,* and uncovers the need to recognize the psychological effects of verbal abuse toward conversational agents and the potential transfer of abusive behavior from interactions with artificial agents to real-life and brand interactions. Last but not least is the *solution*: the design of chatbots is a pivotal factor in shaping user behavior, thus an important objective is to further develop research aimed at incorporating attributes, personalities, and appearance that could influence user interactions and verbally abusive behavior by preventing mistreatment. Interestingly, this review of the literature highlights an apparent contrast between the initial phase of the interaction, where cues such as the chatbot's image profile and name trigger unconscious biases – that in the case of gender, activate heuristics that can lead to discrimination and an increased incidence of abuse – and a middle phase, where the chatbot's empathetic response prompts individuals to reassess their abusive behavior, leading to a de-escalation of the conversation and a reduction in verbal abuse. In sum, it seems that only when the chatbot responds empathetically to user abuse, a more reflective thinking arises and the "media equation" comes into play.

As a final remark, it is important to note that the outcomes of this research should be evaluated in light of the paper's limitations. Firstly, the study is limited to the analysis of social sciences and computer science literature, and to be generalized, it should also be extended to other subject areas. Moreover, the review has considered two databases (Scopus and Scholar), future studies may consider extending the database selection, for instance, including PsycInfo and Association for Computing Machinery Digital Library (ACM DL). The review included only peer-reviewed journal articles, proceedings, and reviews, consequently leaving out doctoral theses, arXiv preprints, and ignoring research appeared in workshops or posters, thus future studies may expand eligibility criteria to include these other forms of publication. This literature review has focused on conversational agents (both voice-based and text-based), excluding the entire body of publications dedicated to abuses against robots, which are also becoming increasingly prevalent. Therefore, future studies should consider broadening the scope of research to encompass investigations into verbal and non-verbal abuses directed at robots as well. Of note, this paper overlooked the chance to delve into a deep examination of existing experimental designs, thus future studies could clarify how these designs interrelate with experimental outcomes. This approach would help the reader understand the relevance of diverse experimental methodologies and the resulting conclusions.

Finally, I would like to propose some suggestions for future studies that could widen the framework for analyzing and addressing abuses toward conversational agents. For instance, it would be worth developing a comprehensive classification and taxonomy for different types of abuse directed at chatbots and investigating how the context influences the likelihood of abusive interactions.

# References

1. Bandura, A.: Social-learning theory of identificatory processes. Handbook Socialization Theory Res. **213**, 262 (1969)
2. Brahnam, S., De Angeli, A.: Gender affordances of conversational agents. Interact. Comput. **24**(3), 139–153 (2012)
3. Brahnam, S., De Angeli, A.: Special issue on the abuse and misuse of social agents. Interact. Comput. **20**(3), 287–291 (2008)
4. Brahnam, S., Weaver, M.: Re/Framing virtual conversational partners: A feminist critique and tentative move towards a new design paradigm. In: Design, User Experience, and Usability: Users and Interactions: 4th International Conference, DUXU 2015, Held as Part of HCI International 2015, Los Angeles, CA, USA, 2–7 August 2015, Proceedings, Part II 4, pp. 172–183. Springer International Publishing (2015). https://doi.org/10.1007/978-3-319-20898-5_17
5. Brahnam, S.: Strategies for handling customer abuse of ECAs. Abuse: the darker side of human-computer interaction, pp. 62–67 (2005)
6. Chin, H., Molefi, L.W., Yi, M.Y.: Empathy is all you need: How a conversational agent should respond to verbal abuse. In: Proceedings of the 2020 CHI Conference on Human Factors in Computing Systems, pp. 1–13 (2020)
7. Chin, H., Yi, M.Y.: Should an agent be ignoring it? A study of verbal abuse types and conversational agents' response styles. In: Extended Abstracts of the 2019 CHI Conference on Human Factors in Computing Systems, pp. 1–6 (2019)
8. Chin, H., Yi, M.Y.: Voices that care differently: understanding the effectiveness of a conversational agent with an alternative empathy orientation and emotional expressivity in mitigating verbal abuse. Inter. J. Hum. Comput. Interact. **38**(12), 1153–1167 (2022)
9. Christofi, M., Pereira, V., Vrontis, D., Tarba, S., Thrassou, A.: Agility and flexibility in international business research: a comprehensive review and future research directions. J. World Bus. **56**(3), 101194 (2021)
10. Creed, C., Beale, R.: Abusive interactions with embodied agents. Interact. Stud. **9**(3), 481–503 (2008)
11. Curry, A.C., Rieser, V.: # MeToo Alexa: how conversational systems respond to sexual harassment. In: Proceedings of the Second ACL Workshop on Ethics in Natural Language Processing, pp. 7–14 (2018)
12. Darling, K.: Extending legal protection to social robots: the effects of anthropomorphism, empathy, and violent behavior towards robotic objects. In: Calo, F.K. (eds.) Robot Law, Edward Elgar (2016)
13. De Angeli, A., Brahnam, S., Wallis, P., Dix, A.: Misuse and abuse of interactive technologies. In CHI 2006 Extended Abstracts on Human Factors in Computing Systems, pp. 1647–1650 (2006)
14. De Angeli, A., Brahnam, S.: I hate you! disinhibition with virtual partners. Interact. Comput. **20**(3), 302–310 (2008)
15. De Angeli, A., Brahnam, S.: Sex stereotypes and conversational agents. In: Proceedings of Gender and Interaction: Real and Virtual Women in a Male World, Venice, Italy (2006)
16. De Angeli, A., Carpenter, R.: Stupid computer! abuse and social identities. In: Proceedings of INTERACT 2005 workshop Abuse: The darker side of Human-Computer Interaction, vol. 4, pp. 19–25 (2005)
17. De Angeli, A.: Ethical implications of verbal disinhibition with conversational agents. PsychNology J. **7**(1) (2009)
18. Dix, A.: Response to Sometimes it's hard to be a robot: a call for action on the ethics of abusing artificial agents. Interact. Comput. **20**(3), 334–337 (2008)

19. Fossa, F., Sucameli, I.: Gender bias and conversational agents: an ethical perspective on social robotics. Sci. Eng. Ethics **28**(3), 23 (2022)

20. Gulz, A., Haake, M., Silvervarg, A., Sjödén, B., Veletsianos, G.: Building a social conversational pedagogical agent: Design challenges and methodological approaches. In: Conversational Agents and Natural Language Interaction: Techniques and Effective Practices, pp. 128–155. IGI Global (2011)

21. Hern, A.: Apple made Siri deflect questions on feminism, leaked papers reveal (2010). https://www.theguardian.com/technology/2019/sep/06/apple-rewrote-siri-to-deflect-questions-about-feminism(Accessed 26 August 2023)

22. Hill, J., Ford, W.R. farreras, I G.: Real conversations with artificial intelligence: A comparison between human-human online conversations and human-chatbot conversations. Comput. Hum. Behav. **49**, 245–250 (2015)

23. Hilvert-Bruce, Z., Neill, J.T.: I'm just trolling: the role of normative beliefs in aggressive behaviour in online gaming. Comput. Hum. Behav. **102**, 303–311 (2020)

24. Iacobucci, S., De Cicco, R.: A literature review of bullshit receptivity: perspectives for an informed policy making against misinformation. J. Behav. Econ. Policy **6**, 23–40 (2022)

25. Keijsers, M., Bartneck, C., Eyssel, F.: What's to bullying a bot? correlates between chatbot humanlikeness and abuse. Interact. Stud. **22**(1), 55–80 (2021)

26. Keijsers, M., Bartneck, C.: Mindless robots get bullied. In: Proceedings of the 2018 ACM/IEEE International Conference on Human-robot Interaction, pp. 205–214 (2018)

27. Kitchenham, B., Charters, S.: Guidelines for performing systematic literature reviews in software engineering, Technical Report EBSE-2007-01. Keele University, School of Computer Science and Mathematics (2007)

28. Massaro, M., Dumay, J., Guthrie, J.: On the shoulders of giants: undertaking a structured literature review in accounting. Accounting, Auditing  Accountability J, **29**(5), 767–801 (2016)

29. Morel, M.-A.: Computer–human communication. In: Taylor, M., Neel, F., Bouhuis, D. (eds.) The Structure of Multimodal Communication, pp. 323–330. North-Holland Elsevier, Amsterdam (1989)

30. Page, M.J., et al.: The PRISMA 2020 statement: an updated guideline for reporting systematic reviews. Int. J. Surg. **88**, 105906 (2021)

31. Park, N., Jang, K., Cho, S., Choi, J.: Use of offensive language in human-artificial intelligence chatbot interaction: the effects of ethical ideology, social competence, and perceived humanlikeness. Comput. Hum. Behav. **121**, 106795 (2021)

32. Pereira, V., Santos, J., Leite, F., Escórcio, P.: Using BIM to improve building energy efficiency–a scientometric and systematic review. Energy  Build. **250**, 111292 (2021)

33. Pluta, A., Mazurek, J., Wojciechowski, J., Wolak, T., Soral, W., Bilewicz, M.: Exposure to hate speech deteriorates neurocognitive mechanisms of the ability to understand others' pain. Sci. Rep. **13**(1), 4127 (2023)

34. Pontzer, D.: A theoretical test of bullying behavior: Parenting, personality, and the bully/victim relationship. J. Family Violence **25**, 259–273 (2010)

35. Reeves, B., Nass, C.: The media equation: How people treat computers, television, and new media like real people, vol. 10(10), Cambridge, UK  (1996)

36. Silvervarg, A., Raukola, K., Haake, M., Gulz, A.: The effect of visual gender on abuse in conversation with ECAs. In: Nakano, Y., Neff, M., Paiva, A., Walker, M. (eds.) IVA 2012. LNCS (LNAI), vol. 7502, pp. 153–160. Springer, Heidelberg (2012). https://doi.org/10.1007/978-3-642-33197-8_16

37. Strait, M., Contreras, V., Vela, C.D.: Verbal disinhibition towards robots is associated with general antisociality. arXiv preprint arXiv:1808.01076 (2018)

38. Teicher, M.H., Samson, J.A.: Childhood maltreatment and psychopathology: a case for ecophenotypic variants as clinically and neurobiologically distinct subtypes. Am. J. Psychiatry **170**, 1114–1133 (2013)
39. Veletsianos, G., Miller, C., Doering, A.: EnALI: a research and design framework for virtual characters and pedagogical agents. J. Educ. Comput. Res. **41**(2), 171–194 (2009)
40. Veletsianos, G., Scharber, C., Doering, A.: When sex, drugs, and violence enter the classroom: conversations between adolescents and a female pedagogical agent. Interact. Comput. **20**(3), 292–301 (2008)
41. Whitby, B.: Sometimes it's hard to be a robot: a call for action on the ethics of abusing artificial agents. Interact. Comput. **20**(3), 326–333 (2008)
42. Whittaker, L., Mulcahy, R., Letheren, K., Kietzmann, J., Russell-Bennett, R.: Mapping the deepfake landscape for innovation: a multidisciplinary systematic review and future research agenda. Technovation **125**, 102784 (2023)
43. Yun, J.Y., Shim, G., Jeong, B.: Verbal abuse related to self-esteem damage and unjust blame harms mental health and social interaction in college population. Sci. Rep. **9**(1), 5655 (2019)

# Anticipating User Needs: Insights from Design Fiction on Conversational Agents for Computational Thinking

Jacob Penney[1]([envelope]) [iD], João Felipe Pimentel[2] [iD], Igor Steinmacher[1] [iD], and Marco A. Gerosa[1] [iD]

[1] Northern Arizona University, Flagstaff, USA
{jacob_penney,igor.steinmacher,marco.gerosa}@nau.edu
[2] Universidade Federal Fluminense, Niterói, Brazil
jpimentel@ic.uff.br

**Abstract.** Computational thinking, and by extension, computer programming, is notoriously challenging to learn. Conversational agents and generative artificial intelligence (genAI) have the potential to facilitate this learning process by offering personalized guidance, interactive learning experiences, and code generation. However, current genAI-based chatbots focus on professional developers and may not adequately consider educational needs. Involving educators in conceiving educational tools is critical for ensuring usefulness and usability. We enlisted nine instructors to engage in design fiction sessions in which we elicited abilities such a conversational agent supported by genAI should display. Participants envisioned a conversational agent that guides students stepwise through exercises, tuning its method of guidance with an awareness of the educational background, skills and deficits, and learning preferences. The insights obtained in this paper can guide future implementations of tutoring conversational agents oriented toward teaching computational thinking and computer programming.

**Keywords:** Conversational Agents · Scaffolding Computational Thinking · Natural Language Programming · Introductory Programming Courses · Design Fiction

## 1 Introduction

Knowledge of computer programming is key for modern society and for students [52]. Professionals from a diverse variety of industries need to write programs for tasks such as making financial predictions, office work, scientific research, creating entertainment, etc. [6,22,27,34,44]. End-user programmers—those who program but are not professional developers—have grown enough as a population to compel large tech firms to make major investments into technologies intended to ease development for them [28]. This increasing need among future workforce professionals to learn how to program is reflected in their educational needs today. It is not surprising that a large number of undergraduate programs include introductory programming in their curriculum. In fact, the literature shows plenty of evidence that STEM students perceive programming as a key skill in their careers [7,12,13,56].

However, computer programming is difficult to learn [26,27,32,47,59]. Both undergraduate Computer Science majors and the growing population of non-majors who program struggle and show clear signs of poor performance, frustration, and lack of engagement [4,16,18]. Some institutions have reported dropout rates up to 50% [25], and the estimated mean global pass rate for introductory Computer Science courses is around 68% [62]. Substantial effort has been made to discover why learning how to program is chronically problematic. While there is no definitive consensus in the literature on what factors determine performance in introductory CS courses [62], many findings highlight student frustrations with programming language syntax, which is rigid and allows only a very restricted set of operations, as a reason for why learning is difficult [18,20,29,37,60]. In interviews with students, Petersen et al. [49] discovered a variety of contributing factors that prompt class withdrawal, such as the usage of ineffective study strategies; falling behind in the class and consequently receiving less support from in-class exercises and labs; and difficulty handling the relatively high level of detail in the material, which required developing problem-solving skills and was eased when they had access to "step-by-step instructions". Student participants in other works also report difficulty adapting to the demands of CS1 courses, citing difficulty with "new teaching methods emphasizing independent thinking, critical thinking, and innovative learning", as well as "less interaction with teachers and classmates", "disconnection between the knowledge and real-life cases, and not receiving enough academic support with timely help and real-time feedback" [8].

New study strategies built on novel technologies, such as large language model-based (LLM-based) conversational agents – that allow exercising computational thinking in a conversational way – have the potential to overcome traditional strategies, allowing more students to succeed and grow in introductory programming courses. Such tools have achieved incredible performance even on complex assignments [17,33,45,51,57]. GPT-3 has been used to create explanations of code snippets that are "significantly easier to understand and more accurate summaries of code" than what can be produced by first-year CS students [31], providing students on-demand access to explanations that explain code, freeing up instructor time. GPT-4 has even displayed rivaling human tutor performance in various programming education scenarios [50]. Not only are these tools capable, but findings show that users feel that they improve their outcomes. For example, programmers of various skill levels who used or were exposed to the features of a custom LLM-based conversational agent perceived that it could improve their productivity [55], and students feel "more motivated to learn, more engaged in the course, and more connected to their classmates" [8].

While evidence displays that LLM-based conversational agents can improve various outcomes for developers and students of different skill levels, little research exists on how to design such technology to improve the learning of computational thinking. Most existing solutions that allow for using a conversational way to program expose the artificial intelligence of the tool in a way not tailored to facilitate *learning* to program. This is because they typically focus on professional productivity, giving the user the desired solution instead of using coaching and scaffolding, in the Cognitive Apprenticeship Model usage [14], to teach the user. Such tools could be used to refocus students' initial efforts on learning computational thinking [1,39] instead of focusing on implementation. The literature shows that implementation details can frustrate students because of the rigid set of operations allowed by programming language syntax [18,20,29,37,60].

With this in mind, this work seeks to understand instructors' expectations of a conversational agent's capabilities in effectively facilitating the acquisition of computational thinking skills. The research question we answer here is:

**Research Question**

What are instructors' expectations of a programming conversational agent intended to scaffold computational thinking?

To answer this question, we used the Design Fiction method. We analyzed the data collected from sessions with instructors by means of open and axial coding procedures. From this analysis, we learned that instructors expect a conversational agent intended to scaffold computational thinking to approach students with an awareness of their educational history and context and tailor its response to their questions accordingly. These responses should guide the student, maximizing skill set development. We hope these findings will inspire future research, design, and evaluation of conversational agents as well as serve as criteria for evaluating AI-based generative agents.

## 2    Related Work

After the recent proliferation of genAI tools, there have been escalating salvos of works exploring their use cases, quantifying and qualifying their abilities, and speculating about futures in which they have become fixtures. This work is situated among others which explore the perspectives of instructors about the experiences of students using conversational agents empowered by genAI to aid the learning process, the imagined and real benefits, and the potential pitfalls. Phung et al. [50] quantify the skills of existing LLM's, displaying not only where the state-of-the-art is at but also discussing where it is headed. Becker et al. [1] motivate educators in the booming genAI discussion, conveying an urgency to concertedly influence coming opportunities. Maher et al. [40] propose and acknowledge many of the same benefits and concerns, respectively, that our participants imagined and introduce a methodology for analyzing AI tool impact via examining impact on student experience and abilities. Guo [23] discusses ways that genAI can already be used for programming autodidacticism and considers ways that scientists and engineers can ply them for the educational needs of their specific fields.

The closest work to ours was performed by Lau et al. [30]. They ran interviews with instructors to understand how they plan to handle the use of genAI tools in their introductory programming classes. They found that the most common reason that instructors do not want to use AI-based tools in their classes is because they "felt it is still important to learn the fundamentals of programming, even if AI tools will be doing a lot of the coding in the future". This opposition depends completely on the diegesis used, which asks the participant to imagine a tool that handles programming for the student with consistent perfect output, not paradigms that run counter to this "solution-oriented" functionality. Our work expands upon Lau et al. by taking some first steps towards answering open research questions they have posed, specifically "Scaffolding novice understanding" and "Tailoring AI coding tools for pedagogy". We did this by approaching a population of instructors, as they did, with a diegesis oriented towards future conversational agents that do not have the limitations of current LLM-based ones.

## 3 Research Design

### 3.1 Research Approach

To explore the design space of the conversational agent, we employed Design Fiction [61]. This method features "the deliberate use of diegetic prototypes to suspend disbelief about change" [61] and envision and explain plausible futures [2,21,24,35,36,38,42]. Human-Computer Interaction studies often use this method to probe, explore, and critique future technologies [3,30,42,54,63]. Some researchers use design fiction to anticipate issues [3] while others emphasize values related to new technologies [11,43] and anticipate users' needs [10,21,46], which is the focus of this paper.

### 3.2 Method

**The Fictional Narrative.** We started the design fiction session by presenting a fictional narrative to the participants through a video [48]. The video was intended to prompt participants to think about how a conversational agent could effectively scaffold computational thinking for students in introductory computer programming courses. In this scenario, a fictional student named Luna is learning Computer Science and, while she has access to an instructor during her class periods, she is left to find her own answers after class. The context of the video is a future in which present technological limitations have been overcome, and she has access to ecumenical AI tools that can help her with her studies. One such tool, Atlas, is a conversational agent that may interact conversationally and have access to and awareness of the student's context through integrations, such as coding environments, execution artifacts, exercises, and the progression of the course. The tool is presented as intended to help the student express her

**Table 1.** Demographics of participants. *Exp.* indicates the experience in years of the participant. *Uni. Type* indicates the type of the university and the highest education level that it grants.

| ID | Exp. | Gender | Country | Uni. Type | Introductory Classes |
|----|------|--------|---------|-----------|---------------------|
| P1 | 14 | F | USA | Public-PhD | Algorithms, Data Structures, Programming |
| P2 | 20 | M | Brazil | Public-MSc | Algorithms, App Programming |
| P3 | 3 | M | USA | Public-PhD | Web Programming, Programming |
| P4 | 2 | M | Brazil | Public-MSc | Algorithms, Programming |
| P5 | 15 | M | Brazil | Public-PhD | Programming |
| P6 | 1.5 | M | Brazil | Public-BSc | Data Structures, Programming, Object Orientation |
| P7 | 10 | F | Brazil | Public-PhD | Programming |
| P8 | 15 | M | Brazil | Private-BSc | Algorithms, Data Structures, Web Programming |
| P9 | 3.5 | M | USA | Public-PhD | Algorithms, Data Structures, Programming |

thoughts computationally. Having placed themselves in this narrative, we asked the participant to help us define how the conversational agent should behave so that it can help the student learn.

**Participant Recruitment.** To participate in the design fiction sessions, we recruited instructors who have at least one year of professional experience teaching Computer Science or computational thinking. To access this population, we started by recruiting from the pool of instructors from our personal network and we used snowball sampling to help find new participants.

We screened potential participants by looking at their personal or university websites and invited those who had experience teaching introductory programming classes. During the invitation, we also sent our consent form that discussed relevant information about the study, including stipulations that our interviews would be recorded but that the recording and any resulting transcripts would be deleted after our work concluded.

In total, nine instructors agreed to participate in the study, as presented in Table 1.

**Design Fiction Sessions.** Qualified participants were invited to a meeting wherein one researcher introduced the goals of the work, displayed the two-minute prompt diegesis video, and interviewed the participants about how the conversational agent could help scaffold computational thinking and how they feel about such a tool. These interviews lasted for 30–60 minutes and were guided by these questions: 1. How can Atlas help Luna with computational thinking? 2. How should Luna interact with Atlas? 3. Where should Atlas be integrated to offer the best teaching experience? 4. Are there any statistics that Atlas should collect from students and give to instructors? 5. What benefits do you foresee with the use of Atlas? 6. What drawbacks do you foresee with the use of Atlas? 7. If you had two competing personal assistants, which criteria would you use to choose which one to use with your students? 8. Do you have other suggestions about how Atlas should work?

**Data Collection and Preparation**              **Data Analysis**

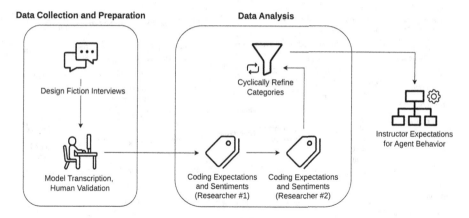

**Fig. 1.** Our research method consists of five main steps, with the outcome of one step being the input to the next.

**Analysis Method.** To analyze the narratives, as in similar studies [30,63], we applied open and axial coding procedures [15] through multiple rounds of analysis (see Fig. 1). This analysis aimed to collect design insights and expectations that serve as guidelines for implementing such a conversational agent. After concluding an interview, the resulting recording was transcribed using a speech recognition tool [53], and a researcher reviewed the transcription with the recording to correct errors. Then, a researcher analyzed the text and coded participant quotes, after which a second researcher reviewed the first coding and applied coding a second time. After these two rounds of coding, we iteratively and cyclically reviewed and refined our categories, initially as a team and then conducted by the lead researcher. High-level categories of participant expectations began to emerge from our interview data and began to stabilize as our number of participants grew, indicating advancement towards data saturation, where these high-level categories nearly stopped evolving. We stopped interviewing participants since the final interviews did not bring significant insights to our results.

## 4    Results

In this section, we present our participants' expectations for an educational conversational agent and their sentiments about those expectations.

### 4.1    Expectations

Participants described five categories of expectations that they felt would make the tool optimal for the end goal of scaffolding computational thinking for novice Computer Science students, displayed in Fig. 2: *programming guidance, code elucidation, student telemetry, course administration,* and *UI/UX.*

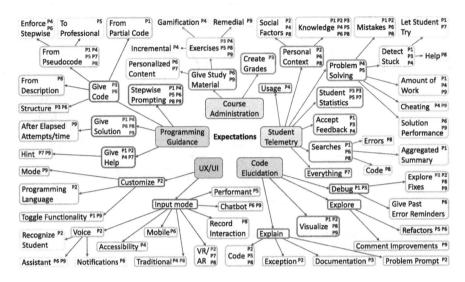

**Fig. 2.** Categorization of expectations narrative data

**Programming Guidance.** Instructors expect conversational agents to be able to scaffold computational thinking for students by guiding them stepwise through the development of algorithms in natural language instead of giving students solutions. The general idea was elaborated most lucidly by participant P1: *"So, there are some standard questions that the teacher sometimes asks to say, 'Look at what you want to do. What is the next step you would need to take in order to express yourself in the language you're using, in natural language, so to speak?'"*. While doing this, the agent should approach the student with an awareness of their educational background and knowledge and tailor their responses accordingly, such as explaining a concept differently to address the student's misunderstanding (P3). Support for giving the student solutions was overwhelmingly negative, and support for giving code was mixed and conditional, with four viewing it unfavorably (P3, P5, P6, P8) and three in support of translating pseudocode into code (P2, P4, P7). P4 felt that it was permissible because the intention is that students should focus on algorithmic thinking, not implementation. P3 felt it was permissible that the conversational agent give an algorithm in code that models the current problem, but which is not the solution and must be synthesized with their own ideas to successfully complete.

**Code Elucidation.** The conversational agent should be able to explain things in the environment that the student might be confused about, such as problem statements, code snippets, diagnostics, compilation and runtime errors, and underlying algorithms and concepts, such as memory. It should also be able to use diverse means to do so. For example, the most popular elucidation expectation that participants had was visualization, such as for algorithms (P1, P2, P9), memory (P8), debugging (P1), and code flow (P2). P2 emphasized *"I under-*

*stand that, from my experience, one of the best ways to make the student under-stand computational thinking and how it works is by drawing diagrams."* Other examples of envisioned elucidation behaviors include retrieving documentation, highlighting passages relevant to the problem being addressed, and even explaining them if the student does not understand it (P3) and proactive and reactive debugging (P1, P2, P3, P8, P9) and refactoring (P5, P6), wherein the agent explains what can or should be done and why.

**Student Telemetry.** Participants acknowledged that many of the behaviors they expect from a conversational agent may require it to collect and use information about the student, and some desired for the agent to return statistics about the class for their consideration. Our participants thought of various pieces of information that would be useful to the agent and them. The most discussed was information about the student's formal and informal educational history (P2, P3), field of study or career (P4), doubts or struggles with course topics (P4, P5, P6), past usage of the tool (P2), and ability and disability (P3, P8). As discussed before, having information about the student could allow the agent to tailor responses, ideally to a high level. P3 explained that *"there are many different ways to get to a solution, and if a student had that particular background, for instance, and Atlas was aware of that background, that might really help Atlas to maybe redirect the student to a different angle or a different approach to maybe better explore their lack of understanding on a topic".*

As per our participants, Atlas should display to the professor which topics students are struggling with, not only to help the current course but to create an awareness of specific struggles for the next iteration of the course. P6 thinks that *"[the agent should collect statistics and create a] categorization of the main difficulties, so that... in a new class, the instructor can already have an idea of what they should address...".* Participants also imagined that the conversational agent could observe the problem-solving behaviors of the student, such as detecting when they were stuck, how many and what kind of mistakes they made, the amount of effort and time the student put into work on the platform, the performance of their code solutions (maybe similar to how tools like Leetcode evaluate the speed of a solution), and whether or not the student cheated.

To the contrary and looking towards the future of pedagogy, P3 felt that collecting statistics on student performance facilitates usage of outmoded methods of assessment: "the idea that students can navigate their own learning process at their own speed is entirely novel to... modern education. And I think that especially with tools like Atlas, we should really be stepping back from the concept of performance and especially like temporal performance achievements."

**Course Administration.** Concerning course administration, participants were interested in the creation of study materials and exercises that were predicated on their students' past education, work they have done with the conversational agent, and deficiencies with the current topic. Some participants (P6, P8, P9) envisioned students being given remedial exercises based on scores on assessments taken in the agent. P4 envisioned assessments advancing incrementally, as they would in curriculum, and felt this pattern of escalation lends itself well to gamification, which would act as a means to maintain engagement. P3 opposed the conversational agent giving preprepared exercises because they cannot address the individual's particular misunderstandings or tailor their help to fit them. They also opposed the agent creating "final grades for a class... or even final grades for a set of concepts" because it may lack the flexibility and nuance that humans display when assessing how well a student has learned.

**UI/UX.** Expectations for how the user interface should behave, how the student should interact with the agent, or what the user experience should be like were varied and inconsistent. Participants imagine interacting with conversational agents via voice (P2, P6, P9), traditional input methods, virtual/augmented reality (P7, P8), and mobile (P6), with some detractors. P8 felt that popular utilities, like search engines, already respond via text, so the method of IO was not interesting. P2 felt that virtual reality doesn't offer much at the moment, but may in the future. The ability to customize the agent was interesting to a few participants (P1, P2, P9), specifically the ability to toggle functionality through atomic settings. Another suggestion was the use of "modes" dedicated to common usages, such as taking exams (P9). One participant, P4, mentioned accessibility a couple of times, referencing students with physical disabilities, such as deafness, and neuroatypicality, such as ADHD, and discussed that it would be meaningful for the system to have flexibility with IO methods to include such students.

### 4.2  Sentiments

In addition to expectations, the participants discussed three categories of sentiments they had about such a tool in response to questions 5–7.

**Benefits.** All-in-all, participants saw benefits of using a conversational agent oriented towards education for both students and instructors, but particularly for engaging, emotionally buttressing, and increasing understanding for students. Participants felt the tool could continuously assist students as they worked, potentially even in an "omnipresent" way (P8). Through this, they could experience decreases in feelings of isolation or fending for oneself (P7) and anxiety from not being able to finish their work right away and while a teacher is not around (P9). P3 explained that by providing a guide that will be present to help decompose and guide them through problems "you're giving students an opportunity to explore the problem without freaking out and... giving up", which they feel "is one of the biggest barriers to success for computer science students." The benefits to instructors that we found discussed most were that the agent could provide them with metrics about the class and help to free up their time by assisting with responding to students (P1), allowing them to focus on other areas of the class (P9), or even allowing them to teach more students (P9).

**Drawbacks.** Reliance on the agent, teaching students incorrectly, and deteriorating relationships in the classroom are among the worries that participants had about the agent. If the tool engages in proactive intervention while the student is incorrectly implementing something, as an instructor might, it may condition students to wait for help (P2, P4). If the design is poor and students are capable of getting to solutions without receiving scaffolding, the student may not learn or may not be able to perform without the tool (P1, P4, P5). Of course, the instructor may have to watch for signs of misuse or cheating (P1, P2, P3). Then again, if the design works, participants worried that students may lose connection to their instructor or feel that they no longer need class time (P1, P6, P9). P3 noted that the tool may be difficult to administer, and it may make finding instructors more difficult because the institution will need those who can operate the tool.

**Priorities.** In the scenario where participants were deliberating over which conversational agent to use, proven effectiveness with teaching students, credibility, and customization would sway their decision the most. Participants sometimes remarked on specific qualities that would promote learning the most, such as knowing when it is appropriate to intervene to offer assistance (P5, P7), teaching as opposed to simply giving answers and offering a comfortable interaction to the student (P6) and choosing the most effective means of teaching a concept, such as using visuals (P8). Emphasis on the tool's credibility betrayed that the participants who mentioned it did not fully immerse in the diegesis when it proposed that present technical limitations were not a concern, but that concern is significant and present. Instructors felt that customization would offer the ability for the tool to cater to needs more finely, such as by adjusting language (P4); the instructor having the ability to toggle functionality when needed, such as for specific assignments or tasks (P1, P9); and the student being able to toggle functionality as well, so they can get the experience they want (P9).

> **Answer to the Research Question**
>
> **What are instructors' expectations of a programming conversational agent intended to scaffold computational thinking?**
>
> The conversational agent is expected to act as a competent guide which would allow the student to move at their own pace through guided algorithm implementations and have access to thorough explanations in a variety of media, adapted to the individual student's background. Instructors would like the agent to collect statistics about student performance, usage, and background to make other abilities possible. Correct scaffolding behavior and credible guidance stemming from good data are preeminent and will sway educators to use a given conversational agent.

## 5   Discussion

Some of the behaviors that the instructors expect can already be meaningfully realized by existing LLMs and conversational agents built on top of them, such as ChatGPT. As introduced in Sect. 1, LLMs have displayed that they can out-perform first-year Computer Science students in creating explanations of basic function definitions [31]. More advanced models have displayed approaching the efficacy of human tutors in tasks such as "providing hints to a student to help resolve current issues" and "generating new tasks that exercise specific types of concepts/bugs" [50], abilities that our participants also expected. However, these recent findings do not address the more abstract ability to scaffold problem-solving skills or algorithm implementation via piecewise, tailored guidance with-out giving code or pseudocode, for one major example. Taming the output of LLMs for educational purposes is still an open problem, and developers imple-menting conversational agents for this purpose must consider how this can be accomplished.

Instead of allowing the student unrestricted access to the LLM's bank of information, developers should consider ways to regulate the LLM so that the response models actual problem-solving processes or provokes the student into critical thinking. Developers should also recognize that it is important to instruc-tors that this response be tailored to the students' background and learning style. One popular method of tailoring LLMs is by prompt engineering, or "prompt crafting" [5], on the natural language input. LLM outputs are known to be "sen-sitive" to inputs, producing different results for the same questions posed with different phrasing, and this quality can be exploited to strongly improve output appropriateness for a conversational agent focused on a specific domain [17].

In the current landscape, recent scholarship notes that novel conversational agent implementations using GPT-4, such as Khanmigo, are advancing the state-of-the-art [41] of teaching using LLMs. Khanmigo poses questions to the student to prompt problem-solving behavior and can use redirection to refocus the stu-dent on the current question if they try to circumvent it. Functionalities such as this are possible through prompt engineering; indeed, LLM pipelines that rely on prompt engineering under the hood appear to be the current standard response to the question of taming LLM output, as we see with established conversa-tional agent implementations such as Github Copilot[1] and cutting-edge LLM-based tools from industry research, such as Microsoft Lida[2] [19]. Nevertheless, some expectations that our participants had cannot yet be realized. Dynamically creating visualizations tailored to address students' specific misunderstandings or situations is still hard with current LLMs; regardless, it is one of the most anticipated abilities among our participants.

Finally, researchers interested in expanding upon our work can also inves-tigate how certain effects can be accomplished. For example, participants were interested in the idea that assisting students may make them feel emotionally supported. While some felt that this was a natural consequence of having access to a powerful resource such as Atlas, it is not clear whether this hypothesis holds or what the role of other aspects would be, such as non-traditional interaction (e.g., voice and visual representations) and social characteristics (e.g., race, gen-

---

[1] https://github.blog/2023-07-17-prompt-engineering-guide-generative-ai-llms/.

[2] https://microsoft.github.io/lida/.

der, culture) in the emotional support of students. For instance, researchers at the intersection of education and gender have established that gender plays a significant role in student engagement and that women STEM students are more inclined to seek help from women STEM instructors [58]. Researchers looking to increase the comfort and effectiveness of LLM-based conversational agents should acknowledge and integrate work that examines the intersection of student and instructor identity with course engagement. A variety of other social characteristics of chatbots [9] can be investigated in this context. Future studies building upon this work can also incorporate the students' perspectives. Such research could present the same scenarios and pose the same questions to discern potential discrepancies in expectations and sentiments.

## 6   Limitations

In this work, we focused on the perspectives of instructors who teach or have recently taught introductory computer science. This method follows in the footsteps of other recent works [30], but is a limitation because our results are skewed toward the experiences and interests of one population, only half of the classroom dynamic. Having no student voices leaves this work lacking insight on how students expect conversational agents to behave to help them develop computational thinking skills more effectively. New research focused on the student perspective may reveal entirely different sets of expectations and sentiments than those discussed by our current participants.

Even with focusing exclusively on instructors, our sample population is not diverse. We recruited instructors who work at five universities in Brazil and one in the United States. Most (7) were Brazilian cisgender men. we had only two instructors who were cisgender women, both Brazilian and one who taught in the United States. Consequently, our outcomes are biased along gender, culture, and region, for example because we have no trans or non-binary participants, and none from or teaching in Asia, Africa, or Europe. None explicitly expressed that they lived with disabilities which influenced their perspective, nor did they explicitly express that their racialization was a factor in their responses. The gender distribution of our participant cohort, in particular, arguably reflects the homogeneous gender distribution of the field it drew from, which has and still underrepresents cisgender women. Additional research which intentionally explores the experiences of more diverse populations may yield concerns not touched upon here. Of particular interest are the experiences of marginalized populations and discovering ways such tools can serve those who are least served by current pedagogy and educational institutions. Besides the identity of the instructors, other meaningful limitations may include that all but one instructor taught at public universities.

Much like related studies that use design fiction or similar methods [30], our participants often discussed the future and hypothetical LLM-based conversational agents of the future in terms of existing conditions and similar extant technologies. While our interview questions and initial video prompt encouraged participants to envision a tool without the limitations faced by those that exist now, the sentiments they expressed may reflect the reality that they know.

This includes how they conceived of UI/UX, such as imagining the tool using input methods that are currently common, such as voice; struggles LLMs face, such as the relevancy of data that the model was trained upon; and even common fears about LLM-based tools negatively impacting economic conditions for instructors.

## 7  Conclusion

In this paper, we presented the expectations and sentiments of instructors involved with teaching Computer Science on the various functionalities that an LLM-based conversational agent could offer to best serve them in their work. Instructors imagined a tool that can scaffold computational using insights into the individual they are instructing, providing accessible tailored education outside of the classroom. This paper's findings lay the foundation for the implementation of novel solutions or the improvement of existing ones that can cater to the academic community, as well as introduce lines of further investigation. Future work on this topic include a design fiction study with student populations, Wizard of Oz experiments intended to classify student intentions and how they are expressed in dialogue, and design and prototype implementation of the conversational agent.

**Acknowledgment.** This work was supported by the National Science Foundation grants 2236198, 2247929, and 2303042. We thank Alexander Gustav Siegel for assistance with our coding process and the instructors who shared their valuable experience participating in our research.

## References

1. Becker, B.A., Denny, P., Finnie-Ansley, J., Luxton-Reilly, A., Prather, J., Santos, E.A.: Programming is hard or at least it used to be: educational opportunities and challenges of ai code generation. In: SIGCSE TS, pp. 500–506 (2023)
2. Blythe, M.: Research through design fiction: narrative in real and imaginary abstracts. In: CHI, pp. 703–712. ACM (2014)
3. Blythe, M., Encinas, E.: The co-ordinates of design fiction: extrapolation, irony, ambiguity and magic. In: GROUP, pp. 345–354. ACM (2016)
4. Bosse, Y., Gerosa, M.A.: Why is programming so difficult to learn?: patterns of difficulties related to programming learning mid-stage. ACM SIGSOFT Softw. Eng. Notes **41**(6), 1–6 (2017)
5. Bull, C., Kharrufa, A.: Generative AI assistants in software development education: a vision for integrating generative ai into educational practice, not instinctively defending against it. IEEE Software, pp. 1–9 (2023)
6. Burnett, M.: What is end-user software engineering and why does it matter? In: Pipek, V., Rosson, M.B., de Ruyter, B., Wulf, V. (eds.) IS-EUD 2009. LNCS, vol. 5435, pp. 15–28. Springer, Heidelberg (2009). https://doi.org/10.1007/978-3-642-00427-8_2
7. Camp, T., Zweben, S., Walker, E., Barker, L.: Booming enrollments: good times? In: SIGCSE TS, pp. 80–81 (2015)

8. Cao, C.: Scaffolding CS1 courses with a large language model-powered intelligent tutoring system. In: Companion Proceedings of the 28th International Conference on Intelligent User Interfaces, pp. 229–232. IUI '23 Companion, Association for Computing Machinery, New York, NY, USA (2023). https://doi.org/10.1145/3581754.3584111

9. Chaves, A.P., Gerosa, M.A.: How should my chatbot interact? a survey on social characteristics in human chatbot interaction design. Int. J. Human-Comput. Interact. **37**(8), 729–758 (2021)

10. Cheon, E., Su, N.M.: Configuring the user: "robots have needs too". In: CSCW, pp. 191–206. CSCW '17, ACM, New York, NY, USA (2017). https://doi.org/10.1145/2998181.2998329

11. Cheon, E., Su, N.M.: Futuristic autobiographies: weaving participant narratives to elicit values around robots. In: HRI. pp. 388–397. HRI '18, ACM, New York, NY, USA (2018). https://doi.org/10.1145/3171221.3171244, http://doi.acm.org/10.1145/3171221.3171244

12. Chilana, P.K., et al.: Perceptions of non-CS majors in intro programming: The rise of the conversational programmer. In: VL/HCC, pp. 251–259. IEEE (2015)

13. Chilana, P.K., Singh, R., Guo, P.J.: Understanding conversational programmers: a perspective from the software industry. In: CHI, pp. 1462–1472 (2016)

14. Collins, A., et al.: Cognitive Apprenticeship: Teaching the Craft of Reading, Writing, and Mathematics. Technical Report No. 403. Tech. rep., BBN and UIUC (1987)

15. Corbin, J., Strauss, A.: Basics of Qualitative Research: Techniques and Procedures for Developing Grounded Theory. Thousand Oaks, CA: Sage, 3rd edn. (2008)

16. Dawson, J.Q., Allen, M., Campbell, A., Valair, A.: Designing an introductory programming course to improve non-majors' experiences. In: SIGCSE TS, pp. 26–31 (2018)

17. Denny, P., Kumar, V., Giacaman, N.: Conversing with copilot: exploring prompt engineering for solving CS1 problems using natural language. In: SIGCSE TS, pp. 1136–1142 (2023)

18. Denny, P., Luxton-Reilly, A., Tempero, E., Hendrickx, J.: Understanding the syntax barrier for novices. In: ITiCSE, pp. 208–212 (2011)

19. Dibia, V.: LIDA: A tool for automatic generation of grammar-agnostic visualizations and infographics using large language models. In: ACL. Association for Computational Linguistics (March 2023)

20. Edwards, J., Ditton, J., Trninic, D., Swanson, H., Sullivan, S., Mano, C.: Syntax exercises in CS1. In: ICER, pp. 216–226 (2020)

21. Encinas, E., Blythe, M.: The solution printer: magic realist design fiction. In: CHI, pp. 387–396. ACM (2016)

22. Ghaoui, C.: Encyclopedia of Human Computer Interaction. IGI Global (2005)

23. Guo, P.J.: Six Opportunities for scientists and engineers to learn programming using AI Tools such as ChatGPT. Comput. Sci. Eng. **25**(3), 73–78 (2023)

24. Harmon, E., Bopp, C., Voida, A.: The design fictions of philanthropic IT: stuck between an imperfect present and an impossible future. In: CHI, pp. 7015–7028 (05 2017). https://doi.org/10.1145/3025453.3025650

25. Kinnunen, P., Malmi, L.: Why students drop out CS1 course? In: ICER, pp. 97–108 (2006)

26. Ko, A.J., Myers, B.A.: Development and evaluation of a model of programming errors. In: HCC, pp. 7–14. IEEE (2003)

27. Ko, A.J., Myers, B.A., Aung, H.H.: Six learning barriers in end-user programming systems. In: VL/HCC, pp. 199–206. IEEE (2004). https://doi.org/10.1109/VLHCC.2004.47

28. Kuhail, M.A., Farooq, S., Hammad, R., Bahja, M.: Characterizing visual programming approaches for end-user developers: a systematic review. IEEE Access **9**, 14181–14202 (2021)

29. Kummerfeld, S.K., Kay, J.: The neglected battle fields of syntax errors. In: ACE, pp. 105–111. Citeseer (2003)

30. Lau, S., Guo, P.J.: From "Ban it till we understand it" to "resistance is futile": how university programming instructors plan to adapt as more students use AI code generation and explanation tools such as ChatGPT and GitHub Copilot. In: ICER (2023)

31. Leinonen, J., et al.: Comparing code explanations created by students and large language models. In: Proceedings of the 2023 Conference on Innovation and Technology in Computer Science Education V. 1., pp. 124–130. ITiCSE 2023, Association for Computing Machinery, New York, NY, USA (2023). https://doi.org/10.1145/3587102.3588785

32. Lewis, C., Olson, G.: Can principles of cognition lower the barriers to programming? In: Empirical Studies of Programmers: Second Workshop, pp. 248–263 (1987)

33. Li, Y., et al.: Competition-level code generation with AlphaCode. Science **378**(6624), 1092–1097 (2022)

34. Lieberman, H., Paternò, F., Klann, M., Wulf, V.: End-user development: an emerging paradigm. In: Lieberman, H., Paternò, F., Wulf, V. (eds.) End User Development, pp. 1–8. Springer Netherlands, Dordrecht (2006). https://doi.org/10.1007/1-4020-5386-X_1

35. Lindley, J., Coulton, P., Brown, E.L.: Peer Review and Design Fiction: "Honestly, they're not just made up.". CHI Extended Abstracts (Alt. CHI). ACM (2016)

36. Linehan, C., et al.: Alternate endings: using fiction to explore design futures. In: CHI, pp. 45–48. ACM (2014)

37. Lister, R.: Computing education research programming, syntax and cognitive load. ACM Inroads **2**(2), 21–22 (2011)

38. Lupton, E.: Design is storytelling. Cooper-Hewitt Museum, Chicago, IL (November 2017)

39. Luxton-Reilly, A.: Learning to program is easy. In: ITiCSE, pp. 284–289 (2016)

40. Maher, M., Tadimalla, Y., Dhamani, D.: IS CHATGPT good for your students? a study design of the impact of ai tools on the student experience in learning java. In: EDULEARN23 Proceedings, pp. 5702–5709. 15th International Conference on Education and New Learning Technologies, IATED (3-5 July, 2023 2023). https://doi.org/10.21125/edulearn.2023.1493

41. Markel, J.M., Opferman, S.G., Landay, J.A., Piech, C.: GPTeach: Interactive TA training with GPT based students. In: L@S, p. 226–236 (2023)

42. Muller, M., Erickson, T.: In the data kitchen: a review (a design fiction on data science). In: CHI, pp. alt14:1–alt14:10. CHI EA '18, ACM, New York, NY, USA (2018), http://doi.acm.org/10.1145/3170427.3188407

43. Muller, M., Liao, Q.V.: Exploring AI ethics and values through participatory design fictions. human computer interaction consortium (2017). https://www.slideshare.net/traincroft/hcic-muller-and-liao-participatory-design-fictions-77345391

44. Myers, B.A., Ko, A.J., Burnett, M.M.: Invited research overview: end-user programming. In: CHI, pp. 75–80 (2006)

45. Nguyen, N., Nadi, S.: An empirical evaluation of GitHub copilot's code suggestions. In: MSR, pp. 1–5. IEEE (2022)
46. Noortman, R., Schulte, B.F., Marshall, P., Bakker, S., Cox, A.L.: HawkEye - Deploying a Design Fiction Probe. In: CHI, pp. 422:1–422:14. CHI '19, ACM, New York, NY, USA (2019). https://doi.org/10.1145/3290605.3300652, http://doi.acm.org/10.1145/3290605.3300652
47. Pea, R.D., Kurland, D.M.: On the cognitive effects of learning computer programming. New Ideas Psychol. 2(2), 137–168 (1984)
48. Penney, J.M., Pimentel, J.F., Steinmacher, I., Gerosa, M.A.: Anticipating user needs: insights from design fiction on conversational agents for computational thinking (2023). https://youtu.be/SleAo-IM7kU
49. Petersen, A., Craig, M., Campbell, J., Tafliovich, A.: Revisiting why students drop CS1. In: KOLI-CALLING, pp. 71–80. Koli Calling '16, Association for Computing Machinery, New York, NY, USA (2016). https://doi.org/10.1145/2999541.2999552
50. Phung, T., et al.: Generative AI for programming education: benchmarking ChatGPT, GPT-4, and human tutors. Int. J. Manag. 21(2), 100790 (2023)
51. Prenner, J.A., Babii, H., Robbes, R.: Can OpenAI's codex fix bugs? an evaluation on quixbugs. In: Proceedings of the Third International Workshop on Automated Program Repair, pp. 69–75. APR '22, Association for Computing Machinery, New York, NY, USA (2022)
52. Prensky, M.: Programming: The New Literacy. Edutopia magazine (2008)
53. Radford, A., Kim, J.W., Xu, T., Brockman, G., McLeavey, C., Sutskever, I.: Robust Speech Recognition via Large-Scale Weak Supervision. In: ICML, pp. 28492–28518. PMLR (2023)
54. Ringfort-Felner, R., Laschke, M., Sadeghian, S., Hassenzahl, M.: Kiro: A design fiction to explore social conversation with voice assistants. Proc. ACM Human-Comput. Interact. 6(GROUP), 1–21 (2022)
55. Ross, S.I., Martinez, F., Houde, S., Muller, M., Weisz, J.D.: The programmer assistant: conversational interaction with a large language model for software development. In: IUI, pp. 491–514 (2023)
56. Sax, L.J., Lehman, K.J., Zavala, C.: Examining the enrollment growth: non-CS majors in CS1 courses. In: SIGCSE TS, pp. 513–518 (2017)
57. Sobania, D., Briesch, M., Rothlauf, F.: Choose your programming copilot: a comparison of the program synthesis performance of github copilot and genetic programming. In: Proceedings of the Genetic and Evolutionary Computation Conference, pp. 1019–1027 (2022)
58. Solanki, S.M., Xu, D.: Looking beyond academic performance: the influence of instructor gender on student motivation in STEM fields. Am. Educ. Res. J. 55(4), 801–835 (2018)
59. Soloway, E., Spohrer, J.C.: Studying the Novice Programmer. Psychology Press (2013)
60. Stefik, A., Siebert, S.: An empirical investigation into programming language syntax. ACM Trans. Comput. Educ. (TOCE) 13(4), 1–40 (2013)
61. Sterling, B.: Cover story design fiction. Interactions 16(3), 20–24 (2009)
62. Virkki, O.T.: Performance and attrition in information technology studies; a survey of students' viewpoints. In: EDUCON, pp. 1–9 (2023). https://doi.org/10.1109/EDUCON54358.2023.10125231
63. Wessel, M., et al.: Bots for Pull Requests: The Good, the Bad, and the Promising. In: ICSE. vol. 26, p. 16. ACM/IEEE (2022)

# Author Index

A. Følstad et al. (Eds.): CONVERSATIONS 2023, LNCS 14524, p. 221, 2024.
https://doi.org/10.1007/978-3-031-54975-5

Printed in the United States
by Baker & Taylor Publisher Services

Printed in the United States
by Baker & Taylor Publisher Services